GLOBAL MACROECONOMIC PERSPECTIVES

Jagdish N. Sheth
Brooker Professor of Research
Graduate School of Business
University of Southern California

Abdolreza Eshghi
Associate Professor of Marketing
Bentley College

GN67AA
SOUTH-WESTERN

PREFACE

It is no exaggeration to assert that today macroeconomic issues of inflation, employment, taxes, and interest rates are truly global in scope. It is virtually impossible for a nation to develop its domestic economic policy or implement its domestic economic rules and regulations without calculating their global repercussions. Today, there is global economic interdependence among nations, no matter what their political ideology, geographic location or domestic self sufficiency.

Today, no nation is able to isolate itself from globalization of its economic policy and programs for a variety of reasons. First, soon after World War II, nations began to liberalize bilateral and multilateral trade through GATT (General Agreements of Tariffs and Trade). This has resulted in greater interdependence among domestic economies as theory of comparative advantage encouraged certain nations to become dominant suppliers of goods and services to the rest of the world. In the process, mutual economic interdependence which was at one time limited among the advanced countries has been extended to all countries, including advanced and developing nations.

Second, in the early seventies, the United States decided to float the dollar and abandon the gold standard. The buying and selling of world currencies and their free movement among the advanced countries has resulted in synchronous global economic recessions and booms. Interest rates, capital markets, and investment climates have become more homogeneous with free market processes resulting in greater interdependence among the monetary systems of the world. Furthermore, this has necessitated the holding of annual economic summits among the dominant world economies in the free world.

Third, government is the biggest buyer in any nation. This is even more true in those countries where there is a preference for a large public sector such as India, France and Italy. Recently, many governments of the world have announced programs to privatize, liberalize or deregulate their public sectors. For example, the United Kingdom has privatized its airline, telecommunications, stock exchange, and airport. This is also true in Japan and in many developing and newly developed nations. Opening up the domestic government market to offshore procurement and encouraging its public enterprises to go offshore has further created greater economic interdependence among nations.

Finally, the twelve nations of the European Community, have agreed to more fully integrate their economies in the hopes of becoming more efficient in global competitiveness and in restructuring their domestic industrial base. It is inevitable that EC '92, as the Single Europe Act (SEA) is referred to, will create a domino effect among other economic regions and result in regional integrations in North America, Asia, and possibly in Latin America and Africa.

This volume is not organized around traditional macroeconomic concepts. It is, however, designed around global flows and economic interdependence among nations. We have identified four major flows: products and technology, people, money, and information. We believe that domestic macroeconomic policy and programs are likely to be influenced by patterns of global movement of these flows.

The volume is designed to supplement standard textbooks in macroeconomics for required courses in the MBA program. It is intended to fulfill the accreditation requirements for globalizing the required courses in business schools.

A number of criteria were utilized in selecting the papers for this volume:

- They must have a policy orientation.
- The authors must be well recognized for their contributions to the field.
- The authors must represent a perspective that is worldwide rather than limited to the United States.

The editors and the publisher are grateful to the authors and publishers who granted permission to reprint articles included in this volume.

Jagdish N. Sheth
Abdolreza Eshghi

CONTENTS

INTRODUCTION

Need for Global Macroeconomic Perspective

Macroeconomic policy of a nation, an economic region and, for that matter, the whole world is significantly shaped by the global implications of government policy, intervention and control. In this book, we will focus on the "global economy" of the world and how it influences the flows of products including technology, people, money, and information across national and regional sovereign borders. In our view, global macroeconomic issues directly relevant to domestic economy relate to the degree and direction for cross-border flows of products, people, money and information.

A number of forces suggest that global macroeconomic perspectives are growing in importance (see Figure 1).

FIGURE 1
Forces Shaping Global Economy

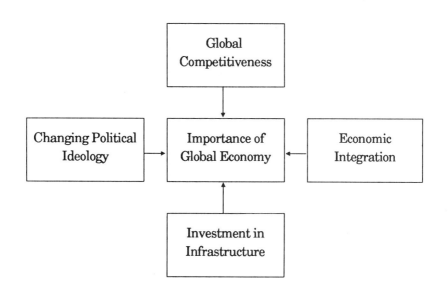

First, all nations and especially the advanced countries have come to realize that, as a consequence of liberation of trade through GATT (General Agreements on Tariffs and Trade) and bilateral trade agreements, their domestic markets have become competitive since World War II. For example, major domestic economic sectors with significant employment base have been adversely impacted by international trade in the agriculture, textile, ship building, steel, automobile and machine tools industries. Contrary to expectations, and certainly different from the colonial days, competition from nontraditional and less developed nations has proven to be powerful and often devastating. No one really expected that countries such as Japan, Korea, Taiwan, Brazil, and India would start dominating world trade by capturing a significant share of European and U.S. domestic markets. As a consequence, governments have begun to rethink their traditional domestic-oriented economic policies and procedures which are likely to impact the flow of products, money, people and information.

Second, a number of nations have agreed that economic survival is at least as important as national sovereignty. This has led to economic integrations of regions, especially those which are in close proximity to one another. For example, the ASEAN economic block of the sixties and the seventies and more recently, the Single European Act (SEA) of 1987 resulting in EC '92 are designed to break trade and tariff barriers among cooperating nations in order to make regional industries more efficient on a global basis.

We believe that EC '92 is such a major economic event that it will have a domino effect on the rest of the world. For example, it is conceivable that North America, consisting of the U.S.A., Canada and Mexico, may become a single economic region. Similarly, in the Far East, Pacific Rim Asian nations may form a single Asian economic region.

Third, most governments of the world have come to realize that, in order to achieve the national goals of productivity and growth, it is absolutely essential to develop and invest in domestic infrastructures such as electricity (energy), highways, air transport, telecommunications, and financial institutions. Since the government is the biggest buyer for most of these infrastructure products and services, they are shaping the industry structures on a global basis for telecommunications, capital markets, and transport markets through their procurement policies. Finally, there is a clear shift in the political ideology of nations. For example, most governments, including the socialist nations such as the Soviet Union and India, have begun to privatize, liberalize or deregulate public sector enterprises. The fever of market-based domestic economies with less government intervention and control is radically shifting the global aspects of business. What was inconceivable only a short time ago between nations of different and opposing political ideologies is happening today with respect to freer flows of information, capital, products and technology, and people. For example, many still have not recovered from amazement over the recent announcement by the United States to declare the Soviet Union as a Preferred Nation in its bilateral trade. This is even more radical than what was considered a radical shift in China's willingness to align with the Western economies of the world.

National Goals and Global Economics

In our opinion, there are, or ought to be, two fundamental national economic objectives: productivity and growth. Productivity ensures efficient utilization of resources: people, money, technology and natural resources. Growth ensures effective direction or channeling of those resources.

A nation's economic policy is directed toward balancing productivity and growth. In general, there is a life cycle of economic development. For example, developing nations such as India or China may be growing but they tend not to be efficient. Newly industrialized nations, such as Korea and Taiwan, however, are both efficient and growing. On the other hand, advanced nations including the United States and Japan may be efficient, but their economic problems tend to be lack of growth. Finally, stagnant nations tend to be low both on growth and productivity.

Productivity

	High	Low
High	Newly Industrialized Nations	Developing Nations
Low	Advanced Nations	Stagnant Nations

Growth

If possible, a nation should be self sufficient in resources to achieve the twin objectives of productivity and growth. Unfortunately, most nations tend not to be self sufficient and must rely on other nations to assist them in achieving their productivity or growth objectives. In general, a nation tends to import resources (technology, people, money or information) to achieve efficiency and tends to export these resources to achieve growth. For example, many developing nations need transfer of technology, capital and information to leverage their domestic natural resources. This is especially true of many large countries such as India, China, Indonesia, Brazil and Egypt. We expect that this is likely to become prevalent for many East European nations.

On the other hand, advanced countries including Japan, the United States and Western European nations need to export resources to maintain growth of their economies. This is especially true of those industrialized nations which have small domestic markets such as Denmark, Sweden, Korea and Taiwan.

Balancing import and export flows of money, people, technology and products, and information becomes critical to the nation's economic policy and procedures. However, it is highly contingent on whether the primary objective is one of productivity or one of growth.

Government policy related to each flow constitutes the global macroeconomic perspectives. For example, global capital flow is determined by interest rates and investment policy of nations. Global people flow is determined by immigration/emigration laws, and by employment policy of the nations. Global product/technology flow is determined by international trade rules and regulations, and by policy with respect to technology standards. Finally, global flow of information is shaped by bilateral and multilateral agreements as well as by infrastructure policy of nations.

In short, global macroeconomic issues including employment, capital, interest rates, and trade are shaped by national economic policies and procedures anchored to the twin objectives of productivity and growth.

Balancing Economic vs. Noneconomic National Objectives

Although both the domestic and global macroeconomic aspects are or ought to be predominantly determined by the twin economic objectives of productivity and growth, it is obvious that each nation tries to balance its economic objectives with three other objectives: social, cultural, and national sovereignty.

Most developing nations tend to have a strong social national agenda such as literacy, population control, and wealth redistribution. They try to balance their social objectives with their economic objectives and often believe that there are inherent trade-offs between these two objectives.

Similarly, countries rich in history, culture and traditions and countries with diverse cultures worry about cultural homogenization due to economic development and prosperity. Recently, this has been a major issue in many newly industrialized nations such as Korea, Taiwan and Singapore as well as more advanced countries such as Japan and Western Europe.

Finally, national sovereignty and consequent military and political sovereignty also become counter-balancing forces to macroeconomic policy. For example, Western Europe and Japan have constantly struggled with this issue since World War II. Similarly, developing countries such as China, India, Yugoslavia and Brazil have shaped their economic policy in light of military and political sovereignty considerations.

Therefore, global macroeconomic issues related to flows of products and technology, money, people and information are really determined by four national objectives: economic, cultural, social and sovereignty (see Figure 2).

FIGURE 2
Economic and Noneconomic Objectives Driving Global
Macroeconomic Perspectives

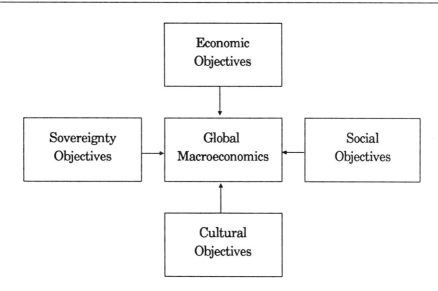

Book Summary

In this volume, we provide global macroeconomic perspectives. Part I of the book focuses on flow of goods and discusses impact of industrialization, foreign trade and protectionism. Part II is related to flow of technology. It discusses concepts related to two-way transfer of technology and impact of technology on society. Part III consists of capital flows and addresses issues of foreign investment, international debt crisis, inflation and interest rates. Part IV is focused on flow of people. It discusses labor policy, immigration laws, and a more recent phenomenon of growth with unemployment experienced in Europe. Finally, Part V relates to information flow. Although it is highly focused on information technology (computing and communications) and cross-border data flow, it is important to recognize that a broader issue related to flow of information has to do with impact of mass media on society's values and cultures.

I   THE GLOBAL TRADING SYSTEM: THE FLOW OF GOODS

Industrialization and Foreign Trade
Sarath Rajapatirana

Protectionism and Non-Tariff Barriers in World Trade
Anne O. Krueger

The Role of GATT in the International Trading System
Willy DeClercq

1. INDUSTRIALIZATION AND FOREIGN TRADE

SARATH RAJAPATIRANA

Sarath Rajapatirana from Sri Lanka, earlier was Chief, Policy Analysis Unit, in the Office of the Vice President of Economics and Research. Before joining the Bank staff he was with the Central Bank of Ceylon.

What is the relationship between industrialization, trade, and economic performance?

The World Development Report 1987 was prepared by a team led by Sarath Rajapatirana and comprising Yaw Ansu, Thorkild Juncker, Alasdair MacBean, Chong-Hyun Nam, Vikram Nehru, and Geoffrey Shepherd. The Bank's Economic Analysis and Projections Department, prepared the main projections and statistical materials. Anne O. Krueger played a principal role in the initial stages of the preparation of the Report. The work was carried out under the general direction of Benjamin B. King and Constantine Michalopoulos.

In the first decades following World War II, economists viewed industrialization as an essential stage in reaching rapid economic development. But the real question is not how fast an economy can industrialize but how its industrial sector can be structured to support sustained growth. In other words, the aim is to seek ways of achieving efficient industrialization. This quest for efficient industrialization relates directly to foreign trade. Foreign trade allows countries to realize gains by subjecting domestic production to foreign competition and by providing access to a wider market to achieve economies of scale. At the national level, trade has allowed countries to specialize between industry and other sectors, between different branches of industry, and increasingly even between different stages in production. Trade has provided access to critical industrial inputs, including technology, for countries incapable of producing them. In turn, the advent of new technologies has shaped the pattern of specialization, and hence the pattern of trade. Trade has also meant expanded demand for exports which itself can spur technological development, and thus smooth the way for industrialization.

This article, based on the World Development Report, 1987, examines three critical issues in the relationship between industrialization and foreign trade.

Reprinted from *Finance and Development*, Vol. 24, No. 3, September 1987, pp. 2-5 by permission of the publisher.

These are:
- Factors that determine the pace and efficiency of industrialization, in particular the role of the government in that process.
- The impact of different trade strategies on industrialization and economic performance in developing countries.
- Lessons from trade policy reforms.

Factors in Industrialization _____

There has been no single path to industrialization. It involves the interaction of technology, specialization, and trade, bringing about structural change within economies and leading to high investment and employment. At the heart of the process has been the role of the government in influencing both the pace and the efficiency of industrialization. A broad view of the history of industrialization reveals five factors that have shaped this process.

Initial conditions. A country with a large domestic market is in a better position to establish industrial plants that take advantage of economies of scale. Since distance between countries in many cases confers natural protection to domestic firms, everything else being equal, a country with a larger domestic market, in terms of area and population, can begin industrializing earlier than one with a smaller domestic market. But size is not the only factor necessary for industrialization, as shown by the cases of Japan and the United Kingdom. A rich endowment of natural resources may provide a country with the financial means to import foreign technology and its high income level may support a large domestic market for industrial projects.

Domestic and foreign trade policies. The transition from a primarily agricultural and trading economy to an industrial economy has required, at least in the initial stages, an increase in the skills of the labor force. More than general education is required, but high achievement at the frontiers of science is not necessary for this transition.

State support for technical education made significant contributions to French and German industrialization. The United States broadly emulated the German system, with government financial support for research in universities. Private industry also maintained research laboratories that sometimes received public support. In Japan today most industrial research is carried out within private firms, but in the early period of industrialization the government helped to promote technological change, for example by setting up demonstration factories that were later sold to the private sector.

Transport and communications. Transport and communications networks integrated domestic and foreign markets into the global economy, making it easier for exporters to compete. But transport and communications networks are very capital-intensive and therefore expensive during the early stages of industrialization. They demand direct or indirect government support.

A stable institutional and macroeconomic environment. Laws and institutions that allow markets to function efficiently—property rights, standardized weights and measures, patent laws, and so forth—have all helped to promote faster and efficient industrialization. Such laws and institutions help promote long-term investment and risk taking. Yet they should also be flexible enough to allow institutional innovation.

Industrialization, especially in its early stages, requires large investment in machines and infrastructure. Moreover, one of the most important means by which technological innovation has been incorporated in production has been investment in new machines. Macroeconomic policies in the countries that were industrializing in the nineteenth century encouraged domestic savings and foreign finance required for investment.

Role of government. Markets and governments complement each other on the path to industrialization. Markets, while effective in pricing and sifting through investments, are rarely perfect. Government must sometimes intervene to achieve an efficient outcome. First, governments have to set the "rules of the game" to define the use, ownership, and conditions of transfer of physical, financial, and intellectual assets. Irrespective of the type of economy—whether it favors private enterprise or is a command economy—these rules impinge on economic activity. The more they are certain, well defined, and well understood, the more smoothly the economy can function. When these rules are unclear, interpreted in unpredictable ways, and managed by a cumbersome bureaucracy, they raise the costs of doing business and thereby discourage the increase in the number of transactions that are essential for industrial specialization.

As experience has shown, governments must continue to be the main providers of certain services to facilitate industrialization:
- All governments play a dominant role in education, especially in providing the basic skills of literacy and numeracy that are vital to a modern industrial labor force.
- Most governments provide the physical infrastructure of industry: transport, communications, and power systems.

- Most governments provide economic information and regulate such standards as weights, measures, and safety at work.
- Governments in the industrial economies promote scientific and technological research.
- State-owned enterprises are often established to carry out some of these tasks.

Governments also intervene somewhat less directly in the running of their economies. This indirect role creates the policy environment. Trade policy, fiscal incentives, price controls, investment regulations, and financial and macroeconomic policies are the main instruments available to governments. Capital-market failures and externalities are the justifications most often cited for direct intervention. Capital market failures arise when entrepreneurs cannot borrow adequate amounts or at opportunity costs that allow them to undertake investments. Externalities arise when the beneficial effects of an investment cannot be recouped by the investor himself. Both concepts have been used, for example, to defend policies toward new, or "infant" industries.

Different forms of intervention will have different effects on the economy. Indeed, in most cases the important question often is not whether to intervene, but how. Quantitative restrictions on imports, for example, may be used to protect domestic infant industries. But these will raise social costs more than a tariff, because they encourage unproductive activities and may lead producers to avoid the controls. Tariffs, on the other hand, raise prices to consumers. Subsidies to the infant industry could give the same assistance without raising prices—but they raise public spending and add to budgetary deficits.

Trade, Industry, and Growth _____

Economists and policymakers in the developing countries have long agreed on the role of government in providing infrastructure, promoting market efficiency, and maintaining stable macroeconomic policies. But they have disagreed on trade strategies that have enabled countries to attain high growth and develop their industrial potential.

Outward- and inward-oriented policies. Trade policies can be characterized as outward oriented or inward oriented. An outward-oriented strategy provides incentives which are neutral between production for the domestic market and exports. Because international trade is not positively discouraged, this approach is often, though somewhat misleadingly, referred to as export promotion. In fact, the essence of an outward-oriented strategy is neither discrimination in favor of exports nor bias against import substitution. An inward-oriented strategy, on the other hand, is one in which trade and industrial incentives are biased in favor of domestic production and against foreign trade. This approach is often referred to as an import-substitution strategy.

An inward-oriented strategy usually involves overt and high protection. This makes exports uncompetitive by raising the costs of the foreign inputs used in their production. Moreover, an increase in the relative costs of domestic inputs may also occur through inflation—or because of an appreciation of the exchange rate—as the quantitative import restrictions are introduced. Industrial incentives are administered by an elaborate and extensive bureaucracy.

Outward-oriented policies favor tariffs over quantitative restrictions. These tariffs are usually counterbalanced by other measures, including production subsidies and the provision of inputs at free trade prices. Governments seek to keep the exchange rate at a level that maintains equal incentives to produce exports and import substitutes. Overall protection is lower under an outward-oriented strategy than under inward orientation; equally important, the spread between the highest and lowest rates of protection is narrower.

Which policy has fostered greater success? An analysis of 41 economies by Bank staff explored the relationship over 1963-85 of trade strategies to economic performance. The results of the study indicate that outward-oriented economies have performed better than inward-oriented ones (see chart).

Some economies which did not fall clearly in either the outward- or inward-oriented category showed mixed results. There was no strictly discernible relationship between trade orientation and economic and industrial performance. This is not surprising, since factors other than trade strategy influence economic performance

Lessons of Policy Reforms

If outward-oriented strategies are associated with better economic performance than inward-oriented strategies, why are policymakers in developing countries generally hesitant to undertake trade policy reforms to achieve such strategies? One reason is that there are many unresolved issues in the area of trade reform that economic research is only just beginning to answer. Another is that many

Figure 1
MACROECONOMIC PERFORMANCE OF 41 DEVELOPING ECONOMIES GROUPED BY TRADE ORIENTATION

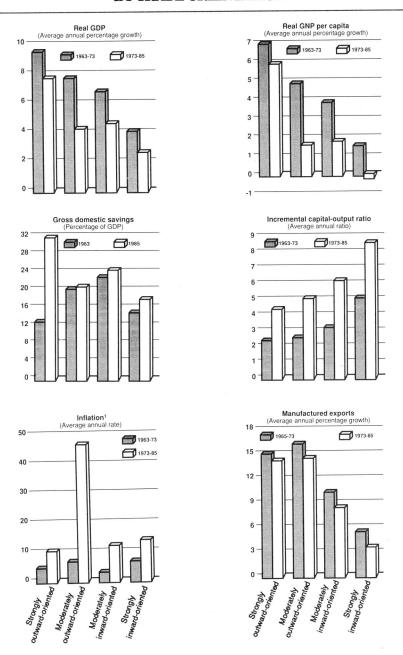

Note: Averages are weighted by each country's share in the group total for each indicator.
[1] Inflation rates are measured by the implicit GDP deflator. Values are group medians.

trade reforms have had to be reversed, leading to the perception that they entail high costs and produce limited benefits.

The shift toward outward orientation inevitably involves transitional costs. Major shifts in resources accompany trade reforms aimed at liberalizing the trade regime, as some activities contract and others expand in response to the changes in prices. If the economy is highly distorted to begin with, the changes that are likely to be necessary are very large. One visible cost is increased unemployment, though recent research on trade reform shows that this is more the result of poor macroeconomic policies than of the trade reforms themselves.

More often than not, trade liberalization comes in the wake of economic crises, usually associated with budget and balance of payments deficits and inflation. Such crises may create the political will for change—an important ingredient for undertaking trade reforms—but reforms undertaken in a crisis atmosphere may not be sustainable. So a government's long-term commitment to reform needs to be substantial and credible if economic agents are to respond to the incentives the reform creates. Moreover, a strong initial shift in policy can quickly boost exports, enough to create vested interests in support of further liberalization. Stable macroeconomic policies, to reduce inflation and prevent currency appreciation, are also crucial for the success of trade reforms. The fate of the reforms, once undertaken, often rests mainly with what happens to the balance of payments—and this is determined by macroeconomic policy.

Experience suggests that export performance is closely related to the level and stability of the exchange rate. Conversely, using the exchange rate to stabilize domestic prices hinders trade reform. In the countries of the Southern Cone of Latin America—Argentina, Chile, and Uruguay—that attempted trade reforms, capital inflows led to the appreciation of exchange rates, which offset the incentives for increasing the production of exports and import substitutes. Large capital inflows were in some cases the result of an ill-timed or uncoordinated liberalization of the financial markets in which domestic interest rates rose very sharply. This provoked heavy borrowing from abroad. Thus, poor macroeconomic policy was more to blame than the trade reforms for the crisis that followed. Trade reforms, however, fell into some disrepute because of their guilt-by-association with poor macroeconomic policies.

The design of trade policy reform. A review of the recent history of trade policy reform suggests that three elements seem to matter most in the design of such efforts. The first is the move from quantitative restrictions to tariffs. This links domestic prices to foreign prices and allows greater access to foreign inputs while increasing competition. The second is the narrowing of the variation in rates of protection even as its overall level is reduced. The third is direct promo-

Table 1

CLASSIFICATION OF FORTY-ONE DEVELOPING ECONOMIES BY TRADE ORIENTATION, 1963-73 AND 1973-85

Outward-oriented		Inward-oriented	
Strongly	Moderately	Moderately	Strongly
		1963-73	
Hong Kong	Brazil	Bolivia	Argentina
Korea,	Cameroon	El Salvador	Bangladesh
Rep. of	Colombia	Honduras	Burundi
Singapore	Costa Rica	Kenya	Chile
	Côte d'Ivoire	Madagascar	Dominican Rep.
	Guatemala	Mexico	Ethiopia
	Indonesia	Nicaragua	Ghana
	Israel	Nigeria	India
	Malaysia	Philippines	Pakistan
	Thailand	Senegal	Peru
		Tunisia	Sri Lanka
		Yugoslavia	Sudan
			Tanzania
			Turkey
			Uruguay
			Zambia
		1973-85	
Hong Kong	Brazil	Cameroon	Argentina
Korea,	Chile	Colombia	Bangladesh
Rep. of	Israel	Costa Rica	Bolivia
Singapore	Malaysia	Côte d'Ivoire	Burundi
	Thailand	El Salvador	Dominican Rep.
	Tunisia	Guatemala	Ethiopia
	Turkey	Honduras	Ghana
	Uruguay	Indonesia	India
		Kenya	Madagascar
		Mexico	Nigeria
		Nicaragua	Peru
		Pakistan	Sudan
		Philippines	Tanzania
		Senegal	Zambia
		Sri Lanka	
		Yugoslavia	

ports to offset the effects of import tariffs. Specific measures to promote exports risk acquiring a permanent status, however, and lead to the postponement of more fundamental changes relating to the exchange rate. They also contravene rules of the General Agreement on Tariffs and Trade (GATT), create domestic lobbies that will oppose their removal, and risk countervailing duties from trading partners.

Trade reforms alone cannot lead to efficient industrialization and improved economic performance without addressing a number of areas that constrain domestic supply response. Among these, four areas are particularly important.

- *Reduction of price controls.* Such controls are pervasive in developing countries and are usually aimed at protecting consumers from monopolies and helping industry by restraining increases in prices of inputs. They restrict supply and distort relative prices, however, causing inefficiency and retarding industrial growth.

- *Investment licensing regulations.* These regulations are imposed to influence the pattern of private investment in line with government priorities. If designed poorly, however, they distort patterns of prices and incentives, discourage foreign private investment, and encourage foreign investments, if any, in activities with low social returns.

- *Financial market reforms.* Interest rate and portfolio controls can discourage savings and distort investment patterns. Reforms are needed to let resources move from one activity to another in line with the incentives created by trade reforms.

- *Labor market reforms.* Some of these regulations also distort factor prices, technology choices, and lead to lower employment. Labor market flexibility is also an important ingredient in trade reform.

The combination of trade and domestic market reforms can make countries move from inward-oriented to outward-oriented trade strategies. This, of course, presupposes that the other ingredients of industrialization and growth—physical infrastructure, education, and legal and institutional factors—are adequate for the task. But benefits from trade reforms can be increased only if the international trading environment is freer than it is now and protection is both low and relies more on price measures than quantitative restrictions.

The International Trading Environment and the Developing Countries

While the lessons from trade policy reforms show that the process is manageable under certain conditions, the benefits from trade liberalization can be increased if the world trading environment is free. Such an environment will also make it politically viable for developing countries to undertake trade reforms. But in recent years there has been a resurgence of protection in the form of nontariff barriers. The proportion of North American and European Community imports affected by various nontariff restrictions has risen by more than 20 percent from 1981 to 1986. These restrictions cover large volumes of imports and particularly affect exports of developing countries. Nontariff barriers in clothing and footwear have proved porous, so some developing countries have been able to increase their exports to the industrial economies even as gaps in these barriers are being plugged.

Costs of protection to industrial countries

There are several ways of measuring the costs of protection. These methods generally underestimate the costs due to the negative effects of restraining competition on managerial efficiency, acquisition of new techniques, economies of scale, and savings and investments.

- *Costs to the consumers.* Protection of apparel in the United States is estimated to have cost US companies in 1984 between $8.5 billion and $18.0 billion; of steel, between $7.3 billion and $20 billion; and of automobiles, around $1.1 billion.

- *Welfare costs.* This concept covers the extra cost to the economy as a whole of producing more of the goods domestically rather than importing them. Normally the welfare cost is considerably less than the consumer cost—particularly for tariffs or quotas. Even so, the estimates for textiles and apparel range from $1.4 billion to $6.6 billion in the European Community and the United States and nearly $2 billion for steel in the United States.

- *The cost of preserving a job.* Each protected job often ends up costing consumers more than the worker's salary. For example, each job preserved in the automobile industry in Britain is estimated to have cost consumers between $19,000 and $48,000 a year. In the United States the cost was between $40,000 and $108,500 a year. Looked at another way, the cost to consumers of preserving one worker in automobile production in the United Kingdom was equivalent to four workers earning the average industrial wage in other industries. In the US automobile industry, the equivalent cost would be the wages of six ordinary industrial workers. The voluntary export restraints by foreign steel producers cost US consumers $114,000 per protected job each year.

Costs to Developing Countries

Developing countries bear heavy costs emerging from their own highly protective policy environments. But they also suffer costs from the protection in industrial countries.

Few studies exist of the latter. The available studies attempt to measure only the increase in export earnings for developing countries that would arise from reductions in the tariffs and nontariff barriers which face them. Studies by the World Bank, the Fund, and the Commonwealth Secretariat show that the result would be substantial export gains—worth several billion dollars a year. More detailed studies have been made for individual countries such as the Republic of Korea. Restrictions on Korean exports of carbon steel cut sales to the United States by 33 percent, or $211 million; but Korea had offsetting gains in the form of higher prices and increased sales to other markets.

The costs of protection are high for both industrial and developing countries. They bear heavily on the latter, however. Protective structures in industrial countries discriminate more against developing countries than each other.

The International Environment

Given their high unemployment, slowing growth, and the increased competition that they face from developing countries' manufacturers, there is the danger that industrial countries will increase barriers to manufacturers from developing countries. This may mean more discriminatory nontariff barriers, more effectively administered. Such steps would further undermine the integrity of the GATT system and would restrict the growth of exports from developing countries. Many developing countries are already heavily in debt, so a reduction in their export earnings would aggravate the problems of world debt. Protectionist acts will have very serious implications for resource growth and maintaining orderly foreign exchange and capital markets in the world. These developments could produce widespread disillusionment with the outward-oriented trade strategies which have proved so successful for the newly industrializing countries in recent years.

If industrial countries become more protectionist, developing countries would be forced into exploring other, second-best, options. These would include trying to expand trade with the centrally planned economies and with other developing countries on a discriminatory basis. But the prospects of greatly improved trade in either of these directions are not good. Neither could replace trade with the industrial market economies.

2. PROTECTIONISM AND NON-TARIFF BARRIERS IN WORLD TRADE

ANNE O. KRUEGER

Anne O. Krueger is the Arts and Sciences Professor of Economics at Duke University and was formerly Vice-President, Economics and Research, at the World Bank. Dr. Krueger has written extensively on international economics and development, including a recent book entitled Exchange-Rate Determination.

In recent years, a variety of non-tariff barriers (NTB's) to trade have sprung up. Ranging from "voluntary export restraints" (VER's) to "trigger-price arrangements" (for steel) and quantitative regulations governing trade in certain commodities (especially agriculture and services), these barriers have become increasingly important as a threat to the open multilateral trading system which has served the international economy so well since the end of the Second World War.

To understand the emergence of these NTB's, assess the harm that they do, and evaluate the prospects for dismantling them, it is necessary to start with a brief stylized history of international trade since the Second World War. Thereafter, the major forms of NTB's are described and assessed. Finally, prospects for adequately addressing NTB's, and rolling back their use in the Uruguay Round of trade negotiations are discussed.

The Background

The period from 1945 to 1973 will undoubtedly go down in history as an unparalleled quarter century of growth in world GNP. The expansion of economic activity was shared by almost all parts of the world—Western European growth in real terms averaged in excess of 5 percent annually, Japanese growth 9 percent, North American well over 3 percent, and the developing countries about 4 percent. The result was an increase in living standards worldwide in less than 30 years proportionately greater than that of the nineteenth century. Indeed, it is noteworthy that, despite all the concern about the growth slowdown since 1973, economic growth has nonetheless proceeded more rapidly than it did before 1945.

Economic historians will doubtless find a number of factors that contributed to the prosperity of the 1950's and 1960's. Postwar recovery, catch-up after the Great Depression, appropriate government policies in some cases, technological

Reprinted from *Harvard International Review*, Vol. IX, No. 3, Feb/March 1987, pp. 19-23 by permission of the publisher.

change, and other phenomena all created favorable conditions for growth. However, there will be no disagreement that a major driving force in the unprecedented expansion was the liberalization of world trade. Liberalization and the increased integration of the international economy contributed directly to growth. Perhaps even more importantly, rapid growth could not have been sustained had trade liberalization not taken place. A "virtuous circle" of growth generated in part by trade liberalization, and trade liberalization fostered by growth, resulted.

It will be recalled that, at the end of the Second World War, memories of the horrors of the Great Depression and the war dominated efforts to shape the post-war world. The Great Depression had been accompanied by, and intensified by, the erection of increasingly high barriers to international trade. "Beggar-thy-neighbor" protectionism, competitive devaluations, and the shrinkage of international trade were prominent features for the international economy during those years. The architects of the post-war system had vivid memories of these events, and much of their concern was to prevent a repetition of the protectionist environment which had so damaged living standards throughout the world.

Only the United States among the now-major industrial countries emerged economically strong in 1945. American economic dominance was so overwhelming that the US could and did take the lead in structuring the international economy. The vision was one of an open, multilateral trading system; the General Agreement on Tariffs and Trade (GATT) was to be the international organization charged with responsibility for assuring that signatories to the Agreement abided by the "rules of the game" and for providing a framework in which countries would simultaneously reduce their barriers, primarily tariffs, on international trade.[1]

In the early post-war years, the European and Japanese economies were devastated. With little productive capacity and a demand for goods for rehabilitating capital stock and for feeding and clothing the population, the United States was the major source of supply. "Dollar Shortage" was the predominant characteristic of the international economy, as these other countries imposed severe restrictions on imports and maintained nonconvertible currencies.

Under American leadership through the Marshall Plan, European countries were gradually able to liberalize their international trade and payments regimes, first within the European Payments Union, and later through the European Common Market and multilateral trade liberalization. Somewhat later, Japan began liberalizing, as did Australia and the Scandinavian countries. This move toward more open trade regimes was a persistent theme of the 1950's; even as late as 1959 only four currencies were fully convertible, but the restrictiveness of the trade regimes by 1960 was sharply less than it had been even five years earlier, and bore little resemblance to that of 1950.

By the early 1960's, most of the industrial countries had abandoned their quantitative restrictions on trade; the remaining trade barriers among the industrial countries were almost entirely tariffs. Thereafter, successive rounds of multilateral trade negotiations (MTN's) under the auspices of the GATT (the so-called Dillon, Kennedy and Tokyo rounds) led to sharp reductions in the industrial countries' tariff levels. For example, the US reduced tariffs by an average of 20 percent in the Dillon round and a further 44 percent in the Kennedy round.[2] The Tokyo round reductions, when fully implemented, resulted in tariff levels that were extremely low—few imports into the industrial countries were subject to tariffs in excess of 5 percent.

Given their relative importance and size, the main "bargainers" in the three tariff rounds were the United States, Canada, Japan, and the European Community. The other industrial countries also participated, reducing their own tariffs in exchange for tariff reductions on their major exports, and benefitting also from the tariff reductions negotiated among the large industrial countries. The developing countries, by contrast, insisted that their relative economic weakness should permit them to maintain tariffs for infant industry or balance of payments purposes, and that they should be subject to "special and differential" treatment within the GATT, benefitting from other countries' tariff reductions but not necessarily reciprocating.[3] This posture persisted throughout the various rounds of trade negotiations.

An important legal feature of each of these three rounds of trade negotiations was that the contracting parties undertook to "bind" the tariffs at the new, lower, levels they had negotiated. Tariff "binding" means that the country is bound, by treaty, not to raise the tariff above the negotiated level. To be sure, there are "safeguard" provisions within the GATT, but the conditions under which countries may reimpose higher tariffs are necessarily and naturally quite restrictive (and usually permit the country whose exports are subject to higher duties to take retaliatory action).

Obviously, as tariff reductions were negotiated and bound, tariffs became a less and less important instrument of protection. Some other forms of protection, NTB's, became more important and more visible simply because they were what was left. For example, many countries maintained restrictions against some agricultural imports. These restrictions had been present from 1945 onward, but they became more visible as tariffs were reduced. Further efforts to liberalize the international trading system would, for that reason alone, have to address the issue of NTB's: tariffs as an instrument of protection were becoming increasingly less significant.

Simultaneously, however, the fact that tariffs were bound meant that protectionist pressures in developed countries could be met only through the imposition of NTB's. One question, of course, is why protectionist pressures arose at all in the face of rapid economic growth and rising living standards. A thorough examination of the question is well beyond the scope of this essay.[4] But several factors contribute: (1) as economic growth proceeds, those with low levels of educational attainment and skills are disadvantaged as real wages rise and employers replace workers with machines in manual jobs, so that the process of economic growth itself puts pressure on low-wage, low-skill using activities in the economy; (2) these are precisely the sorts of economic activities in which low-income countries have their competitive advantage; (3) there are significant differences between the interests of individual groups in society, taken one at a time, and the interests of those same groups when all do the same thing.

The first two points are important because they focus on the facts that efforts to protect are also efforts to slow down economic growth and that a good deal of protectionist sentiment is misplaced in that the real hardships suffered in the course of economic growth are blamed, partly erroneously, on imports. This, of course, means that protection even when granted may not provide the relief that is expected of it.[5] And the second point became increasingly significant as developing countries adopted growth-oriented strategies and rapidly expanded their manufactured exports. The last point is also important: even in cases where workers (or owners of capital, as seems more often to be the case) might benefit from protection if theirs was the only protected industry, protection once granted to one industry induces calls for it from other activities. Moreover, once a particular country turns increasingly protectionist, its trading partners are likely to retaliate. For the United States, given its size and importance in the world economy, this last consideration is especially important: if the United States abandons its traditional adherence to an open multilateral trading system, other countries are likely to follow suit. The damage to the United States of a reversion to a world economy of protected, insular states and bilateral trading arrangements would far exceed the damage of one particular protectionist measure.

Regardless of the reasons, protectionist pressures are always present.[6] They tend to intensify in times of slow growth and overvalued real exchange rates, and to diminish in times of prosperity and exchange rate relationships that are conducive to appropriate trade and current account balances.

After 1973, growth slowed down sharply in all industrial countries. One consequence was an intensification of protectionist pressures. Since tariffs were already bound, the only way in which politicians could respond was through NTB's. To be sure, tariff rates were still being reduced according to timetables negotiated in the various tariff rounds. And many pressures for protection were resisted. Nonetheless, NTB's became much more visible on the international economic scene. The ongoing momentum toward trade liberalization of the Kennedy and Tokyo Rounds was offset, at least in part, by the opposite tendency with respect to NTB's.

It was the industries that used unskilled labor intensively that were most vociferous in their demands for protection, for reasons, already outlined. Textiles, apparel, shoes, and electronics assembly were among the sectors appealing for protection. In addition, for a variety of other reasons, steel and automobiles joined the queue seeking protection for competition abroad.

Forms of NTB's _____

To the extent politicians bent to political pressures, they could not do so through tariff increases because of binding. Instead, the response was NTBs—in different shapes and forms in different industries. The rhetoric of those seeking protection is always that protection will be "temporary"—to permit time to adjust. The reality is that protection, once granted, is hard to remove.

Nonetheless, in keeping with the myth, policy-makers sought "temporary" instruments to afford some protection. The most visible (and costly, at least for American consumers) of these measures was the Multifibre Arrangement (MFA), which is a VER. Under it, countries which are producers and exporters of particular items of textiles and apparel "voluntarily" agree to restrict their export levels of these items to negotiated levels. These agreements are, in reality, a quota imposed by importing countries and administered by exporting countries.

Although tariff levels against textile and apparel imports were high prior to that time, the first voluntary export restraint (and hence NTB) against textiles and apparel was negotiated between the United States and Japan, taking effect in 1957. Under it, the Japanese undertook "voluntarily" to limit their export of cotton textiles and apparel to prespecified quantities.[7] These quantities were sufficient to permit moderate growth in exports, but were designed to restrict (temporarily, it was stated) the rate of growth of imports into the American market. However, having limited those exports, Japanese producers naturally increased their exports of synthetic fibers and apparel made of synthetic materials (or blends), and simultaneously reduced their production and exportation of the cheaper grades of cotton. The result was that the VER restricted the volume of cotton textile and clothing imports much more than it restricted value. Meanwhile, other producers (including Hong Kong, Portugal, Taiwan, Egypt, and India) took advantage of restricted Japanese access to increase their own exports to the American market.

The US Administration wanted to avoid legislative action to restrict imports, and hence suggested that importers and exporters agree on an "orderly marketing arrangement" for textiles and apparel. Multilateral discussions, under the aegis of GATT, were therefore undertaken starting in 1961. A long-term agreement was reached in 1962, under which importers could apply restraints bilaterally in violation of GATT rules. Cotton goods remained the only items covered.

Over the next few years, imports of cotton goods into the American market were restrained; by 1967, the US had bilateral agreements with 17 exporting countries. Meanwhile, however, imports of manmade fiber textiles and apparel rose sharply, and the United States began to attempt to widen the scope of the agreement. Hence, the Multifibre Arrangement, covering cotton and manmade fibers, came into being in 1973. Since then it has been renewed periodically; each time, more suppliers and more particular items are subject to quota. By the early 1980's, exporting countries were subject to aggregate limits, limits of amounts of individual commodity groups they could export, and also limits on specific items.[8]

Each successive renegotiation of the MFA was more restrictive than the last, both in attempting to limit growth and in extending the coverage to more countries and more commodities. These restrictions were undertaken in response to more-rapid-than-anticipated growth of imports and continuing difficulties of the textile and apparel industry. The most recent MFA, begun in July 1986 and scheduled to last for three years, is the most restrictive yet.

There can be no doubt that the VER's negotiated under the aegis of the MFA are the most costly and restrictive barrier to trade in manufactured goods in industrial countries today. Other VER's have also been employed but then permitted to lapse: automobile import VER's with Japan and footwear VER's with Korea and Taiwan have been the most visible. They and others have also cost the American consumer large amounts—estimates are that in these sectors, consumers are paying more than $50,000 per job temporarily saved in the affected industries.

VER's are a new form of protection. They differ from out-and-out quantitative (quota) restrictions on imports in that it is the exporting countries, rather than the importer, who administer them. This in turn implies that it is the exporting interests, rather than the domestic importers, who receive the windfall gain resulting from their "license" to sell in the protected market.

Economists have always believed that tariffs are superior to quotas, for several reasons: (1) a tariff is "transparent", so that all observers know how much protection is being granted; (2) a tariff is regulated by the rules of GATT; (3) tariff revenue accrues to the government, rather than to the recipient of the quota rights; and (4) because of the above, there are a number of factors tending to limit the degree of protection that can be conferred through tariffs more than they would through quotas.

Because the "tariff-equivalent" of VER's goes to the foreign exporter, rather than to the domestic importer, they can be interpreted as a "bribe" to trading partners to accept the import restrictions. Whether this, or some other interpretation, is correct, it is clear that VER's, like other protectionist measures, adversely affect consumer interests in importing countries and producer interests in exporting countries. To be sure, they tend to keep established producers in industries longer than might otherwise be profitable for them, at the expense of newcomers (who may also be deterred from entering due to the threat of VER's). As producer interests in the protected industries are now largely in developing countries, it is apparent that VER's adversely affect the trade prospects of those countries.

In addition to VER's, other NTB's have been increasingly employed.[9] The steel "trigger-pricing system" was such a mechanism for protecting steel. Outside of manufacturing, restrictions on trade in agricultural products often take the form of NTB's. In the United States, domestic price support programs often result in quantitative restrictions (NTB's) on imports, as American prices are above world prices. In Europe, the Common Agricultural Policy (CAP) results not only in uneconomic domestic production of agricultural commodities, but even in subsidized exports. Japan's restrictions against imports of agricultural commodities are well known. Since developing countries tend to have a comparative advantage in a number of agricultural commodities, these NTB's discriminate especially against them.[10]

Prospects for Addressing NTB's _____

A significant breakthrough at Punta del Este, Uruguay in September 1986 was the agreement among the contracting parties of the GATT that the new round of multilateral trade negotiations would encompass not only the traditional manufacturing protection, but also trade in agriculture and services.

If the momentum toward a liberalized trading system, which has served the world so well since the Second World War, is to be maintained, it is vital that these issues be meaningfully addressed. Yet, by their very nature they are difficult ones. Negotiation for reciprocal tariff reductions was already difficult enough when there were four key negotiators and manufacturing trade was the major stake. Now numerous other important groups of countries need to participate in the negotiations, and coverage must extend to agriculture and services. Perhaps most important among these groups are the developing countries, especially the newly industrialized countries whose manufactured exports have grown so rapidly.

Agriculture and services are both politically sensitive areas. The main basis for optimism that significant progress will be made is that all countries recognize the need for an open trading system and the severe threat that failure to roll back some existing NTB's would imply. The hope must be that all parties recognize their interest in the system, and find means whereby internal political pressures can be offset in the larger interest.

For meaningful negotiations to take place with respect to NTB's, it will be essential that governments agree on the "rules of the game" with respect to agriculture, services, and manufactures. These "rules" would, at first, presumably commit signatories to using only specified types of intervention in the relevant sectors of their economies. Major progress would be made if border protection itself were outlawed, as the cost of domestic subsidies under that circumstance would become prohibitive. Less sweeping, but still possible, might be agreements as to the maximum size and/or duration of subsidy that would be permitted.

Without some agreements of this type, the trend of the past few years toward additional NTB's will undoubtedly continue, and the Punta del Este round will not achieve its purpose. While the negotiations will no doubt be difficult, and result in politically painful compromises in many countries, failure to achieve agreement would in the long run have vastly more serious implications for the international economy.

Notes

1. The original vision of the architects of the post-war world was that there would be three international organizations within the United Nations system charged respectively with maintenance of a stable international monetary system (the International Monetary Fund), assurance of an efficient allocation of capital in the international economy (the International Bank for Reconstruction and Development), and an organization to oversee the open, multilateral trading system (the International Trade Organization, ITO). The US Senate refused to ratify the treaty that would have established the ITO; without US membership, it could not meaningfully exist. The alternative was the GATT, to which the US acceded by executive agreement (hence, the General Agreement) in the absence of senatorial support.

2. Finger, Table 1, p. 425. Other detailed estimates of average tariff reductions can be found in Ernest Preeg, *Traders and Diplomats*, The Brookings Institution, Washington, DC, 1970; and in UNCTAD, *Kennedy Round Estimated Effects on Tariff Barriers*, United Nations, New York, 1968.

3. However, two things deserve note. First, most developing countries had highly restrictionist trade and payments regimes in the 1950's; as such, their share of world trade fell sharply as the international economy expanded rapidly. Secondly, in the 1960's and 1970's, many developing countries in their own self interest have liberalized their trade and payments regimes, eliminating quantitative restrictions on trade, adopting realistic exchange rates, and reducing the average height of their tariffs.

4. The interested reader could refer to Krueger 1980 for a fuller discussion of the ways in which economic growth puts pressure on the same sectors as may be vulnerable to import competition.

5. That protection has not bestowed the relief expected of it is evident in any number of ways. Perhaps the most obvious is the fact that textiles and apparel have been subject to very high and increasing levels of protection (by standards of the industrial countries) since the mid-1950's in most industrial countries, yet employment has been reduced and the industries have nonetheless contracted. (See the discussion of the MFA below.)

6. It has sometimes been argued that, within national boundaries, producer and consumer interests are both represented, but that across national boundaries producers cannot defend themselves; the absence of political pressures, e.g., from American exporters in Japan and Japanese exporters in America, makes it easier for political measures to be taken than would be the case if both producer and consumer interests were represented.

7. It is ironic that one of the factors that provided a degree of competitive edge to foreign cotton textile and apparel producers was that their American competitors could purchase cotton only at higher prices (because of the American price support program) than could their foreign counterparts (as "surplus" cotton was exported from the United States).

8. See Kessing and Wolf, and Pelzman for more detailed accounts of the evolution of the MFA.

9. A variety of measures can have protectionist effects and yet are nonborder measures. For example, health regulations on food imports (such as restrictions on meat to prevent the spread of food and mouth disease), safety regulations governing airplanes, and environmental regulations (such as auto emission standards) may all be imposed for motives entirely independent of imports, and yet may have a protective effect. And, on occasion, they may even be used to protect domestic industries, although in those circumstances the government typically invokes the other rationale for the measure imposed.

10. See the World Bank's 1986 *World Development Report* for an analysis of the impact of agricultural protection on developing countries.

For Further Reading _____

Baldwin, Robert E. 1970. *Non-tariff Distortions to International Trade*, Brookings Institution, Washington, DC.

Finger, J.M. 1979. "Trade Liberalisation: A Public Choice Perspective." Chapter Six in Amacher, Ryan O., Harverler, Gottfried, and Willett, Thomas D. (eds) *Challenges to a Liberal International Economic Order*, American Enterprise Institute, Washington, DC.

Keesing, Donald B. and Wolf, Martin, 1980. *Textile Quotas against Developing Countries*, Trade Policy Research Center, London.

Krueger, Anne O., 1980. "LDC Manufacturing Production and Implications for OECD Comparative Advantage," in Irving Leveson and Jimmy W. Wheeler, eds., *Western Economies in Transition: Structural Change and Adjustment Policies in Industrial Countries*, Westview Press, Boulder, Colorado.

Pelzman, Joseph, 1984. "The Multifiber Arrangement and Its Effects on the Profit Performance of the US Textile Industry," in Robert E. Baldwin and Anne O. Krueger, eds., *The Structure of Recent US Trade Policy*, National Bureau of Economic Research, Chicago University Press.

3. THE ROLE OF GATT IN THE INTERNATIONAL TRADING SYSTEM

WILLY DE CLERCQ

Willy De Clercq is Commissioner for External Affairs, the European Community

It is commonplace to say that the multilateral trading system is under strain. There is much comment in the media about the inadequacies of the existing trading arrangements between nations and regarding threatening trade wars, especially between the world's major trading partners—the European Community, the United States, and Japan. It is, moreover, customary to blame the General Agreement on Tariffs and Trade—that much-maligned Geneva-based institution which has acted as a kind of sentinel of open international trade since 1947—for the failure of nations to manage their trading relations in perfect harmony.

It is well to remember that the GATT (which is as much of a contract as it is an institution) was set up as a framework of rules and principles to underpin the revival of the war-torn economies of the then-industrialized world—industrialized, notwithstanding the material damage inflicted on the thirty or so original contracting parties during World War II. The founders of the GATT, many of them Western democracies with broadly comparable economic traditions, undertook to conduct their trading relations within a set of rules appropriate to them, their colonies or dependents, and a small number of co-founders from the non-industrialized world.

Today the GATT consists of over ninety contracting parties made up of a kaleidoscope of nations: developed countries with a Western democratic tradition, with an Eastern heritage (Japan), less developed countries (such as India, the ASEAN group, and most nations of Latin America), least developed countries (such as Bangladesh and a number of African countries), newly-industrialized countries (such as Korea and other, more advanced developing countries in the Far East and in South America), and a number of state-trading countries of Eastern Europe. In parallel with the expanding membership of GATT, the complexities of economic relations between nations has grown beyond all recognition. Add to this a fundamental qualitative change in the conditions underlying world trade—namely the emergence in the major world markets of conditions of over-supply in many of the traditional sectors of production—and it is clear that we are dealing in 1986 with a wholly different set of problems

Reprinted from *Harvard International Review,* Vol. IX, No. 3, Feb/March 1987, pp. 10-12 by permission of the publisher.

compared with 1947. Viewed from this standpoint, it is remarkable that the multilateral trading system has survived so well!

Despite the evident tensions (whose origins extend beyond the trade field to such unfavorable developments as abrupt and massive changes in energy prices, imbalances in economic and monetary policies between major trading partners entailing, *inter alia*, highly volatile exchange rates), trade continues to expand.

Indeed, the growth of world trade has exceeded the growth of world production in most of the last 40 years. Again, despite the admitted shortcomings of certain GATT rules (or of the countries called upon to implement them), the GATT is continuing to attract new customers: Mexico has recently joined, Morocco and Tunisia have applied to join, and China is in the wings! Most significantly of all, the trading nations ascribing to the GATT have now reached a common view on an ambitious new program of negotiations. They have thus demonstrated their faith once again that the GATT provides the best means for sustaining and developing the world's trading rules.

Before the recent GATT conference in Punta del Este, Uruguay, questions were raised about the commitment to GATT. The temptation in certain quarters, not least in Washington, to seek to regulate trade bilaterally is considerable (partly, no doubt, in frustration over the difficulty in achieving rapid results in Geneva). There is also a regrettable tendency to undermine GATT through domestic legislation or action based on a unilateral redefinition of commonly agreed rules. Nevertheless, the verdict on the GATT so far seems unmistakable: the world trading community needs a single multilateral trading system, and the GATT constitutes this system. Bilateral or even pluralistic arrangements do not provide a viable alternative. There has to be a paramount international institution which lays down the rules of the game for all. But the multilateral trading system must be broad enough to encompass the full range of economic diversity now to be found within GATT and it must take into account the great variety of economic relationships between individual countries or sets of countries. A legal straight-jacket for world trade would not do.

A Dynamic GATT? _____

The agreement reached in Punta del Este in September to launch the Uruguay Round of multilateral trade negotiations was a historic decision of far-reaching consequences. The preparatory process for that decision had been long and arduous. It left many wondering whether the GATT really was capable of renewing itself to confront the problems of tomorrow, as well as to overcome unsolved problems of yesterday and today. What is called for, and what was recognized at

Punta del Este, is a process of negotiation designed not only to give new impetus to the liberalization of world trade and to strengthen the multilateral ground rules for trade, but above all, to create an appropriate environment for trade in the 1990's and into the 21st Century. The European Economic Community sees a need for a multilateral trading system which spans the complete range of economic interchange between it and its trading partners. It has a major interest in a widening of the horizon of GATT to include non-traditional items, particularly trade in services. It is plainly absurd to rely on rules for that part of world trade which is conducted in tangible products and to leave intangible trade to the whim of each individual country.

But a dynamic GATT which services all its membership must avoid exclusive or even predominant concentration on the newer issues. The removal of traditional barriers to trade, both in the tariff and non-tariff areas, and the imaginative handling of some of the other contentious issues, such as safeguards, would contribute enormously to reinvigorating world trade. The Community intends to make its proper contribution to this work. A crucial stepping stone toward these goals is a firm commitment to the decision reached at Punta del Este not to take any new protective measures inconsistent with GATT, and to set about the process of dismantling inconsistencies in existing GATT measures—an operation due to be completed by the end of the negotiations.

The Goals of the EC in the Uruguay Round _____

There are many problems besetting international trade in the 1980's which need to be tackled in the forthcoming negotiations. Their importance, taken individually, is perceived differently by different contracting parties. For example, the urgency seen in the United States for rapid multilateral action in the field of intellectual property is matched in many developing countries by the desire for action in the area of tropical products. For these reasons, the Community has resisted the notion of priorities in the negotiations. We need to see the Uruguay Round as one single undertaking; if it transpires that early agreement can be achieved in one field or another, then it is important that such "early harvests" be taken fully into account when the overall balance of the result of the negotiations is assessed. All participants must find advantage in the negotiations.

The issues which need to be addressed in the course of the negotiating process may be broadly divided into five types. (The problem associated with trade in agriculture cuts across several of the divisions set out below. This sector of trade, which has given rise to considerable tensions between the United States and the Community, is subject to quite specific factors which require separate treatment):

- Access to market problems, *i.e.* barriers to trade
- Institutional problems, including the functioning of the GATT system
- Rule-making problems
- New Issues; and
- "Disequilibria"

It may be instructive to examine the type of question which arises under each of these five headings in a little more detail and to review the Community's overall approach to them.

The progressive removal of barriers to trade under conditions of equality and equity is clearly at the heart of the GATT and synonymous with its purpose. A great deal has been done to achieve lower levels of tariff protection in the major trading countries in previous negotiating rounds. What is at stake now is the extension of the level of commitment on tariffs more widely, and at a lower level of tariff protection, in all developed and in some of the more advanced developing countries. We must also come to grips with a host of non-tariff barriers which have sprung up over the years—partly as a reaction to the diminishing value of tariff protection and partly for other, often very genuine, reasons. It is highly desirable that universal criteria be established for assessing the legitimacy of measures which can act as non-tariff barriers. But the experience of the Tokyo Round suggests that it will be difficult to find formulas acceptable to developed and developing countries alike, and the system of Codes—adhered to by some but not all GATT members—may well prove the best approach in the new negotiations. The Community is willing to look carefully into issues such as government procurement, standards, customs valuation, and, of course, quantitative restrictions, in order to reduce progressively the impact of such measures in a balanced manner.

Is GATT capable of applying the rules it makes? That institutional question has recently reverberated through the corridors of parliaments, congresses, ministries, and national administrations responsible for trade policy. The answer, of course, depends on the rules themselves and the manner in which they are to be implemented. The issue will come to the fore again over the question of surveillance of the standstill and roll-back commitments undertaken at Punta del Este and over the improvement of the GATT dispute-settlement procedure. It will also underlie the future debate on which kind of safeguards clause the GATT should have in order to do away with the bilateral, semi-clandestine arrangements outside the system. For its part, the Community has consistently taken the view that "solutions" to trade problems which are perceived to be against the fundamental interests of a particular contracting party, for whatever economic or political reasons, are no solutions. That is why the consensus rule of

GATT is so crucially important; that is also why the GATT can never act as a court of law where the majority view is imposed on a minority party. Whether in the area of surveillance, dispute settlement, safeguards, or in any other field, the GATT will need rules which contracting parties can "live with." Therein lies the essence of consensus.

The area of rule making is clearly akin to the institutional question in the Uruguay Round. The rules made today will determine the viability of the organization tomorrow. This maxim will need to be borne in mind when (and if) the GATT sets up definitions of acceptable or objectionable subsidies, when it reviews existing GATT articles and codes and, of course, in dealing with the vexed safeguards issue.

Much has been said about the need to prepare the GATT for the 21st Century, and new issues are obviously a key component of any revamped multilateral trading system. But we would do well to dampen any enthusiasm for early results in areas as complex and diverse as trade in services, the protection of intellectual property, and trade-related investment issues. At the outset, it must be recognized that perceived interests among contracting parties in these areas tend to be divergent, or even mutually exclusive. As far as the Community is concerned, while there is now a considerable volume of knowledge in the various service sectors, it is now reasonable to steer negotiations toward a general framework of rules and principles, having regard to the particularities of individual service sectors, with the overall purpose of liberalizing trade in services. In the other "new" areas, on the other hand, it would be difficult to envisage more than examination and clarification at the present early stage.

Last but certainly not least, as far as the Community is concerned, the Uruguay Round will be an occasion to first examine and subsequently seek to redress problems of disequilibrium which have surfaced as an inevitable by-product of the expansion of GATT membership and the increased impact of multilateral trade relationships. While in no way calling into question the principle of special and more favorable treatment for developing countries, the Community wishes to ensure that the more advanced of these countries increase their contribution to the GATT—in the form of greater commitment to open their markets to world trade. Similar considerations also apply to the state-trading countries of Eastern Europe that are members of the GATT. But the main source of disequilibrium in world trade today stems from the imbalance in advantage between Japan and almost all her trading partners. If the GATT is to respond to the aspirations of all contracting parties, it is vital that Japan's advantages should be more equitably shared and that a means should be found to match obligations and benefits more evenly.

After the successful launching of the Uruguay Round in Punta del Este the real work has to begin. It will not be easy and I agree with those who expect this round of negotiations to be the most difficult in the history of the GATT. But the way in which agreement was reached in Punta del Este is an encouraging sign for the negotiations themselves. The 92 trading nations who are Contracting Parties of the GATT declared, in the firmest possible terms, that protectionism was not an appropriate basis for the nations of the world to conduct their economic relations with each other.   Instead, they unanimously announced their determination "to preserve the basic principles and to further the objectives of the GATT" and "to develop a more open, viable and durable multilateral trading system;" and with a general consensus — *i.e.* without an embittered minority forced to give way in a vote—they launched the ambitious Uruguay Round. That such an enterprise is considered possible is itself an eloquent testimony to the GATT's capabilities as an effective and durable forum for the regulation of world trade. If protectionism was the principal victim of Punta del Este, then the GATT, for its part, was undoubtedly the principal victor.

II _____ THE GLOBAL TECHNOLOGY TRANSFER: THE TECHNOLOGY FLOW _____

Technology Transfer and Applications
C. Beaumont, J. Dingle and A. Reithinger

A New Industrial Revolution?
Howard Rosenbrock et al.

4. TECHNOLOGY TRANSFER AND APPLICATIONS

C. BEAUMONT

State petrochemical enterprise CNP, Lisbon

J. DINGLE

Double L Consultants Ltd., London

A. REITHINGER

Commission of the European Communities' Directorate-General for Development

Transfer of technology is examined from three points of view:

1. The international political framework within which tendencies towards co-operation or confrontation between the "developed" and the "developing" world are largely determined;
2. The commercial framework in which the interplay of corporate motives and negotiating strategies determines the outcome of individual projects;
3. The operational framework in which the transferred technology may contribute —or may fail to contribute — to the recipient's economic and social development.

Using case histories, the conflicts inherent in these points of view are analysed in order to show the conditions which seem to be necessary to achieve success in international technology transfer, in a world where trends in techno-economic evolution are seldom in tune with trends in political aspiration.

Editor's Note. This paper was originally written in early 1980 as a contribution to a symposium organized by the Institution of Chemical Engineers on the theme "Achieving Success in International Projects". The symposium was cancelled, but the Editors of *R & D Management* think that the opinions expressed in the paper merit discussion. The authors are all engaged in various aspects of large-scale technology transfer in commercial terms. Their outlook is therefore different, and perhaps divergent, from that of workers in more "fundamental" areas of research and development. The authors point out that although their paper has not been updated, the tenor of their remarks remains unchanged. They invite comment from readers of *R & D Management* as contributions to the original theme of "Achieving Success in International Projects".

Reprinted from *R&D Management,* Vol. 11, No. 4, 1981, pp. 149-155 by permission of the publisher.

The International Political Framework _____

Although the transfer of technology has always been a factor of paramount importance for economic and industrial development, it has become the subject of broad discussion and of a whole series of international negotiations only in the last few years.

Ideas and demands for changes which would accelerate industrialization and reduce foreign influence on their economies originated in Latin American—mainly in Brazil and Mexico. Since then, similar ideas and demands have been adopted by all developing countries, and have been embodied in their hopes for a new international economic order.

But the developing countries continue to complain that the transfer of technology necessary for their economic and industrial development has become an excessively heavy financial burden, and that the existing pattern of technology transfer does not offer them the opportunity to alleviate this burden in the course of time. The basic question is whether industrialization and development are economic assets which, by being transferred under the present conditions, only benefit the developed countries, and serve to widen the gap between them and their developing contemporaries. This question is at the core of all the pressure for a different framework of technology transfer. Thus, the developing countries mention particularly their weaker bargaining position relative to the technology suppliers, which leads to unfavourable transactions characterized by unjustified restrictive practices, overpricing, supply of inappropriate technologies, insufficient guarantees against malfunctioning and the like. They therefore claim that there is a need for new instruments in this field to ensure their right of access to the technologies of developed countries, the possibility to unpackage the technologies they want to buy and the elimination of abuses practised by suppliers.

In order to protect themselves against these negative effects, many developing countries have adopted restrictive technology policies, allowing far-reaching public interference in technology transactions, such as registration and control of contracts, the regulation of their terms and conditions, the determination of their legal effects, of the applicable law and jurisdiction, of arbitration procedures, and so on. Many of them have set up special administrations for this purpose.

This proliferation and diversity of national legislation and administrative activities has created considerable concern on the side of technology suppliers, and has contributed a good deal of turbidity and unpredictability to an already opaque and complex market. If policies like these gain ground, they could seriously hamper the further promotion of technology transfer to developing countries and thus affect, in the long run, the latter's technological progress.

It is obvious that the principal reason for the developing countries' position is the insufficiency of their own technological capacity. Lack of suitable infrastructure and know-how in practically all technological fields prevents these countries, especially the least developed among them, from applying and adopting imported technology in a rational, reproducible and self-sustaining manner.

The best way to promote the transfer of technical knowledge and to improve the terms of these transactions seems therefore to be, in the long run, the development of suitable local conditions for the efficient absorption of the transferred technology. There are signs, fortunately, that more emphasis is being laid on this side of the problem in international discussion. Many recent resolutions have stressed the importance of co-operation between developed and developing countries to establish, consolidate and expand the latter's technical and scientific capacities and infrastructure.

International instruments for furthering the transfer of technology will therefore have to respond to a twofold objective: on the one hand, they should lead to liberalizing the exchange of technology, eliminating obstacles which indirectly limit international technology transfer and creating predictable and stable conditions for suppliers and buyers of technology, thus contributing to the formation of wider and more transparent technology markets and the acceleration of technological development. On the other hand, they have to be shaped in a way which makes allowance for the immense needs of developing countries in this field, as well as for their lack of technological capacities and the fragility of their institutions and infrastructure.

As western industrialized countries are the main source for the international exchange of technology, these instruments must necessarily be in line with the basic principles of the legal and economic system of those countries.

Now, it is well known that in countries with market economies, the greater part of applied technology, especially industrial technology, is invented and developed by independent individuals and firms and, although the bulk of technology is freely available, parts of it are protected by industrial property rights. Access to this technology is therefore only possible through specific agreements between those who own the various techniques and those who wish to acquire them. The public authorities of these countries can exert only a limited and indirect influence on the conclusion and content of such agreements.

However, if one considers that the transfer of technical knowledge is, in western countries, mainly the business of independent economic operators, one should be aware of the fact that encouraging the transfer of technology to the developing countries raises problems which necessitate the involvement of public authorities, both in the industrialized and in the developing countries, and of international organizations such as World Intellectual Property Organisation (WIPO) or United Nations Industrial Development Organisation (UNIDO). Despite the limits referred to, the public sector can do a great deal here, particularly in the fields of strengthening the developing countries' technological infrastructure, transferring and exploiting technologies at its disposal, providing information to make technology markets more transparent, organizing contacts between the owners and potential acquirers of technological knowledge, encouraging and facilitating the operators' initiatives, and the like.

An international framework for technology transfer suited to fulfill these functions must therefore be based on a series of principles which respond to the economic, legal and political diversity of the parties—states or enterprises—concerned. Among these principles must be, in particular:

- respect of sovereignty and political independence of states;
- respect by states for their international obligations and for the legitimate interests of parties to technology transfer, when legislating and regulating in the field of technology;
- respect for the sovereignty and the laws of the recipient country by enterprises engaged in technology transfer;
- the separate responsibility of enterprises engaged in technology transfer on the one hand, and of governments on the other;
- the basic freedom of parties to negotiate, conclude and perform technology transfer within the limits of national laws and international agreements;
- the mutual benefit of the parties to technology transfer.

These rather theoretical reflections raise inevitably the question whether technology transfer can be regulated and, if so, to what extent it should be regulated.

Technology can be transferred in an immense variety of forms, from the sale of a turnkey plant to the licensing of a patent or to the mere provision of an engineer or a skilled worker for a specific task. If the transfer of technology is defined in this broad sense, it is evident that it cannot be subject to total regulation without entering into conflict with fundamental property and other rights, and without putting it into a strait-jacket which would wreck it immediately.

Extremely difficult problems arise in this context. It may be appropriate, for example, to define those restrictive practices in technology transfer arrangements which should be prohibited, and to include, say, export restrictions. But is it reasonable in each and every case to provide for their elimination? It may be acceptable, as a general rule, that transfer of technology operations should respond to certain internationally agreed standards, but is it appropriate and feasible to extend this principle to transfers between a mother company and its affiliates abroad?

An international framework for the regulation of technology transfer must, therefore, be flexible enough to allow pragmatic solutions suitable to reconcile the different legal and economic conditions of countries with the legitimate freedom of parties to deal as effectively and profitably as possible with this extremely complex matter.

The present efforts undertaken within the U.N. to set up such a framework concern mainly three lines of action:

- the modification of the international industrial property system, and especially the Paris patent convention, within WIPO;
- the changing of the present pattern of technology transfer on the basis of the 'Vienna Programme of Action,' to be carried out by a newly created Intergovernmental Committee on Science and Technology of the General Secretariat of the U.N.;
- and the setting up of a code of conduct on international transfer of technology by a special conference under the auspices of the United Nations Conference on Trade and Development.

Whereas the negotiations on the Paris Convention are only in the early starting phase and the action referred to in the Vienna Programme will possibly need a very long time before getting off the ground, the code of conduct elaborated within UNCTAD is in its final stage and may soon be adopted.

This code, which is meant to be universally applicable by all parties to transfer of technology transactions, and by all countries, contains a set of standards aimed at guiding government policies and regulations, as well as the conclusion of transfer arrangements by private enterprises. It is thus another element in a series of agreements concluded over the years within the U.N. system to enforce international standards for various social and economic areas.

Following the concept of developed countries which, for legal reasons and with a view to the necessary flexibility of such rules, could only agree to a set of voluntary guidelines, the code will be adopted, at least in an initial phase, in this form, probably by means of a General Assembly resolution of the U.N.

In order to meet the developing countries' concern to set up an effective instrument for the shaping of international technology transfer, the code provides for a monitoring and revision mechanism, aimed at controlling its practical implementation, which opens the possibility to revise its provisions as well as its legal status after a five-year period.

The future will show if this code proves to be efficient. It will most probably need more than five years to become the generally accepted yardstick for international technology transfer. As pointed out earlier, it seems advisable to western industry to adopt progressively these guidelines and to respect provisions designed to protect developing countries' interests. This may help to create conditions of stability and mutual confidence which, as many developing countries' governments claim, are lacking in their present relationship with developed countries' technology suppliers. If this code succeeds in reaching its objective, it would considerably contribute to calming the discussion about technology, and, thus, to promoting new and promising perspectives for the future.

The Commercial Framework

We now move out of the political arena to where—as we rather grandly put it in the synopsis—the interplay of corporate motives and negotiating strategies determines the outcome of individual projects. To where, in a phrase, business is done.

Technology transfer is a commercial activity. One might not think so, however, from some of the proposals made for the international code of conduct to regulate technology transfer. In one draft (U.N., 1979), for instance, the word 'commercial' appears but once outside the footnotes, and then only as part of a disputed text.

We suppose that some kind of regulation of business activities has to be accepted, if only to avoid the presumption of anarchy, but we suggest that the appropriate basic discipline should be that of the market. The discipline of the law court should be invoked only in a case of dispute which cannot be resolved elsewhere.

Despite the high hopes of international legislators, what seems to bedevil the regulation of technology transfer is a legalistic approach which is at best inappropriate, at worst fat-headed. It does nothing to make technology transfer more effective. It does much to inhibit transfer of technology to the people in most need.

Paradoxically, it is the less developed countries (ldc's) who seem most to favour legalistic regulation of technology transfer. Perhaps they feel outmatched by the negotiating skills of the technology suppliers, and imagine that business would be better balanced if the rules of the game were somehow rigged in their favour.

We believe that this view—if indeed it were the view of the ldc's—would be misconceived. Worse than this, however, is that it *is* the view implicit in many of the actions of policy makers in the developed countries, whose ideas for the regulation of technology transfer are thereby distorted. It is accepted that clear guidelines are needed, but they should be of the nature of road markings, not tramlines, as is understood by anyone with experience of multi-disciplinary traffic.

Here is an illustration of a not untypical situation which could be held to justify the need for 'legalistic' regulation. It refers to a 'turnkey' contract, but one in which the transfer of a range of technologies was recognized by both parties as essential for the success of the project. For obvious reasons, the identity of the parties will not be disclosed: the buyer, a government agency in a 'lower middle income' country, we will call B; the seller, an engineering contractor leading a group of sub-contractors and process licensors, we will call S.

B's government, following conversations with promoters, became convinced that the nation needed its own oil refinery. The installation would secure supplies of refined products for the home market, increase export potential and contribute to the balance of payments. DCF calculations showed a favourable rate of return. The government appointed B to manage the refinery project.

B made a deal with a nearby government for supplies of crude oil. It put the refinery project out for competitive bidding, and received three offers. B understood very well that it needed help to get the project under way. To be precise, it needed know-how in developing designs, in choosing process technology, in negotiating with contractors and licensors, in construction management, in training operational personnel, in marketing exportable products.

So, very sensibly, B entered into agreements with companies expert in these areas: with Company X as technical and commercial advisers; with Company Y to provide operating supervision and training services, and with Company Z to sell products not needed for the home market.

In the ensuing negotiations B aimed at getting a turnkey supply with one hundred percent credit, at lowest cost. Two bidders dropped out. The remaining bid, for a refinery tightly designed for the crude previously chosen, was accepted and the contract duly signed with S.

Before engineering was complete, changes in oil and refined products markets world-wide put a premium on refinery flexibility. Moreover, political problems between B's government and the crude supplier led the latter to withdraw its undertaking. The maneuvering of B and S led to pressure building up against X (B's adviser) whose opinion was thought too often to favour S, while Y (operational training) was increasingly regarded as technical adviser. Well before construction was complete, X's contract was terminated.

By then Y's position—between B and S — came to be seen as ambiguous. Training was discontinued and already-trained personnel dispersed. The agreement with Y was terminated, the marketing contract with Z declared invalid.

The stage now cleared of the supporting cast, B and S launched into an increasingly bitter dispute over acceptance of the now completed plant.

In such a situation, it would be tempting for B — or, indeed, any other ldc buyer facing a like situation—to feel hard done by.

- If the transfer of technology (X's, Y's, Z's know-how, as well as the contractor's and the sub-contracted process licensor's) had been governed by an international legally binding instrument . . .
- if the technology suppliers had been obliged to guarantee pre-determined results by the use of their know-how, and . . .
- if failure to fulfill these obligations had been subject to the appropriate applicable law, namely that of the technology acquiring country, and any disputes settled by 'neutral' arbitrators applying that law in the technology acquiring country . . .

they might well feel that the dispute would not have broken out in the first place, or, if it did, then it would have been quickly and favourably resolved.

These points are, of course, among the ldc's recommendations for inclusion in the proposed industrialization code of conduct for technology transfer.

But let us consider what actually happened.

1. B decided to award the refinery contract to the bidder with the *cheapest* financial package. That was sure to motivate S towards the strictest interpretation of his contractual design and supply obligations.
2. B's government made a *political* deal for crude oil. Politics is notorious for short-term switches in motivations. Crude oil supply needs long-term stability.
3. B chose X (a promoter of the original scheme) as technical and commercial adviser. X was therefore likely to be subject to conflicting motives regarding development of the project.
4. B chose a multinational refiner Y—which already supplied under a favourable contract nearly the whole of B's home demand for refined products—as operational training adviser, and later chose to use Y in a more general advisory role.
5. Finally, *the world oil market changed*. B was not prepared to face the consequences of this change, and neither X nor Y seemed prepared to help. Their strongest motives were, not surprisingly, aimed at perpetuating their individual view of the *status quo*. Z, who understood world-wide marketing, was not consulted.

After that cautionary tale, it may be useful to take a fresh look at the objectives of technology transfer, but from the different, conflicting points of view commanding the process.

Recipient organizations often have nationalist objectives (e.g. industrialization, balance of payments, etc.) in view, as well as 'corporate' (e.g. profit) objectives. The transferrer— at any rate, the vehicle for transfer—is often an engineering company acting, even if it is a public sector enterprise, in an entrepreneurial way. In a commercial sense, the transferrer's motive is to make profitable *immediate business* by exploiting the markets for technology wherever these markets may lie. The recipient's motives are to do with improving his chances of making profitable *future business* through gaining a technological advantage over the perceived competition.

In the overwhelming majority of cases, the real objective of case-to-case technology transfer seems to have little directly to do with considerations of development. Instead, it has been aimed at what were thought to be profitable business operations. On the international scene, the pressures generated by this aim have to be accommodated within the existing sources of adequate technology and the political relations between countries. Sometimes the establishment of strong and numerous technological ties drags the recipient country excessively deep within the sphere of unwanted economic influences.

Understandably, in global terms, the recipient country seeks to become as independent (technologically and economically) as possible, and consequently governments put political constraints on corporate freedom in international technology negotiations.

Strategically, the recipient needs the most up-to-date, most economical technology which currently gives good operational results in at least one or two industrial applications. Here is a dilemma: these 'model' applications are almost certain to be operational in a socio-economic environment much different from his own.

Meanwhile, the transferrer tries to sell either current 'off-the-shelf' technology, or new, unproven technology for which he needs a working example. Both parties seek to minimize their risks. For the recipient, this means putting as much responsibility as possible in the hands of the transferrer. Here is another dilemma, for doing so runs counter to the recipient's 'national' aims of increasing local participation and promoting domestic technology.

Sometimes, these dilemmas can be resolved by means of a joint venture. We have discussed the hazards of joint-venturing elsewhere (Dingle and Beaumont, 1978). It is, however, specially attractive when (a) the local market is too small to absorb the full production of a well-sized, economically feasible plant, and (b) the foreign partner has captive markets abroad. Joint ventures can also be attractive if the technology is evolving rapidly, and if the foreign partner who controls its evolution is willing to transfer improvements to the local partner.

But joint-venturing should not be regarded as a way to finance a sizable part of the cost of the project. The foreign partner is not in business to act as a financial institution. On the other hand, financial participation which is merely symbolic will not motivate the transferrer's real involvement and drive towards achieving success for the joint venture.

We should mention a relatively unfamiliar operation which sometimes makes sound economic and commercial sense: the 'reverse' joint venture. In this case, the recipient country has an intermediate product (say, ethylene) in quantities sufficient to feed a good sized processing facility (say, producing styrene) but lacks a market large enough to justify local production of styrene. The 'reverse' joint venture puts the transferee's capital for the new installation in the technology transferrer's country, supplies it under contract with feedstock, and receives back a proportion of the product adequate for the local market. Regrettably, the 'nationalistic' motives of some recipient governments, together with their ambitions to expand locally the importance of the domestic partner, often hinder consideration of this approach.

The Operational Framework _____

We have mentioned that neither the objectives nor the negotiating strategies of the parties to a technology transfer are likely to be directly complementary. This mis-match of basic concepts sounded off the great debate about what is 'advanced' and what is 'appropriate' technology transfer. In our opinion, the real problem is not whether a particular technology is too 'advanced' or is 'inappropriate,' but whether the productive entity in which it is embodied will become part of a viable system.

It has been said of the Recursive System Theorem that 'in a recursive organisational structure any viable system contains and is contained in a viable system' (Beer, 1979).

This means that almost all technologies may prove appropriate if nested in a viable system—that is, if the variety generated by the system can be fully absorbed by, its immediate environment. Thus a new plant embodying a technology for producing a high quality material which needs very stringent conditions for further application and processing will be successful only if the (downstream) processing industry responds to new demands on its skills, and if the marketing network takes full advantage of the improvement to effect increased sales (in both volume and price terms). It will succeed only if it is 'nested' in a larger system which is not in decline relative to international competition. Not only has the sub-system (technology) to be viable, it has to be contained in a viable larger system (infrastructure + market).

At the other extreme, modern efficient technology requires that systems 'nested' into it be viable themselves. Many new ventures eagerly expected to contribute to developing economies have failed, not because of the 'advanced' technology being transferred, but because locally manufactured equipment has proved defective, or operators have been found to be insufficiently qualified, or maintenance proved to be inadequate.

This question of system viability obliges us to look at the theory and practice of technological project feasibility assessment. We note that international development financing institutions demand elaborate analyses of the potential profitability of a new venture in order to decide whether or not to make available funds with which to put it in hand, including—as a key feature—the acquisition of technology. These analyses always rely on market and price forecasts. Yet a comparison of forecasts with eventual reality shows the uselessness of excessive dependence on the micrometric and circumstantial calculations for project feasibility assessment (to the second decimal) derived from these forecasts. Should we therefore abandon profitability calculations? No, but their use ought to be much less revered, except in the field where they are indeed useful: for comparing competitive processes or propositions, where a large error in input data derived from forecasts has only a small effect on the comparison.

The feasibility and desirability of new projects, especially in developing countries, would be better assessed if more weight were given to macroeconomic considerations: their contribution to strengthening the matrix of inter- and intra-industrial relationships, to fostering general technological development, to improving the balance of payments, and to regional and social considerations.

Pattern of Evolution in International Transfer of Technology _____

Broadly, we might envisage the transfer of technology as taking place in three sequential stages:

1. Transfer of products (development of the technology of marketing and utilization in the recipient country);
2. Transfer of production facilities (development of operating and maintenance technology in the recipient country);

3. Transfer of innovating capability (development of creative, locally applicable research and development).

The transition from the first to the second stage is accelerating, mainly because (a) importing countries face balance of payments difficulties, and need to maximize locally added value, (b) competition lures exporters into seeking to sell complete installations rather than a share of the total product consumed. (The last, however, might be held to be the most influential cause of the recent overcapacity problem affecting the developed, industrialized world.)

The installation of production facilities in the recipient countries (transfer of operating and maintenance technology) is not in fact a transfer of production know-how. It is only a time-limited possibility of remaining in the front line of competition. The recipient country does not, by this process, acquire the capability of continuing to modernize the process and upgrade equipment. This is generally what happens when the facility is the only one in the recipient country, because of the limited size of the home market. When, maybe ten or fifteen years later, a replacement is needed, new technology has again to be acquired. At that point, the recipient has no choice but to abandon the field, or buy a new ticket to remain in competition.

The solution is to go a step further and develop locally a technology-generating capacity through applied research and development. There is a strong trend now in some ldc's to adopt this attitude. It is interesting, however, to note the reaction within industrialized countries. Michel Delefortrie (1978) says:

> Indeed, it does sometimes happen, though only infrequently, that developing countries seek from the West the transfer of a considerable part of its high-technology industrial capacity and its scientific research. This is politically unacceptable and economically unjustifiable. The growth of the West depends on certain relative advantages that it possesses. Moreover, such a policy could prove detrimental to the developing countries in various ways, including having harmful consequences on their exports.

Consequences _____

It is important that we think about the likely after-effects of technology transfer, as well as studying its processes. Without seeking to be exhaustive, we can identify the following areas in the argument over whether technology transfer is the seed of permanent industrial development, or is a mere *quasi*-benefit which the passage of time will extinguish.

1. *Change and the acceptance of risk*

   We mentioned that it often happens that the recipient country buys a new technology and adapts well to its use, without being able to keep pace with the never-ending changes taking place elsewhere. We also said that the way out of such a situation is the creation of local capability for innovation and its subsequent useful application. There are preconditions, however: namely, the propensity and drive to change, and the will to accept risks. The latter are of such a magnitude that they seem only acceptable if covered by some sort of insurance. A joint institution of developing countries to insure against industrial innovation risks could perhaps be an interesting proposition.

2. *Bottlenecks*

   A probable consequence of change is that bottlenecks occur upstream and downstream of the technology transfer project. It is one link of a chain, the other links of which may be technical, financial, economic, commercial, social, political. Because a chain is only as strong as its weakest link, we are obliged to return to the concept of systemic viability.

3. *Market preparation and development*

   In the home market, transferred technology contributes to vertical integration, with the growth of synergies in upstream and downstream relationships. The recipient who competes in export markets is forced to respect the pace and the stringent conditions of international competition. The experience of firms which are successful in international markets proves how beneficial this is.

   While it would be understandable that recipients of technologies new to them should view with some apprehension the prospect of immediate entry into international competition for markets, it is normal to see ldc's launch themselves head first at sizable export targets in order to justify the huge capacities of the so-called minimum economically sized project. It is our contention that ldc recipients often give too little attention to the possibilities of increasing and developing their local markets beyond the historical trend of expansion. In many cases, huge potential is at hand for the adaptation of products and of processes for product substitution, and for preparing the public-at-large to accept—indeed, prefer—the use of end-products far away in the vertical chain of manufacture, but having nonetheless a big impact on consumption of upstream intermediates which are locally produced. In these cases, the technology recipient will benefit from going against the rules of non-interference with the market of his own customers, and deciding to promote the growth of markets for intermediates, or to assist the appearance of more aggressive customers.

Future Trends

So what of the future? The global evolution from transfer of products, to transfer of production technologies, to transfer of technological creative capability, has caused severe imbalances evident nowadays in surplus capacity in steel, ship-building, textiles, synthetic fibres, some plastics. The resulting strains should be solved by participative planning (UNECE, 1979). Hence, the ground for *co-operation*. But the biggest surpluses are found in powerful developed countries where, sometimes, voluntary reduction of national production to restore a global market balance appears to be unacceptable. Hence, the ground for *confrontation*.

The expansion of the developed world's traditional markets through technology transfer can yield only short-lived advantage, once the pace of global competition is quickened. No doubt, in the meanwhile, the benefits for individual firms can be, for limited periods of time, very substantial; but, in general, the tendency will be towards a more homogeneous distribution of knowledge—as well as of know-how—making recipients more critical and more demanding. Development in the future is therefore likely to be guided along two lines of force: (1) a north-to-south displacement of production technology, and (2) an increasing awareness in the south of the decisive role played by the innovative process and its practical application.

Are these lines of force amenable to regulation? Only slightly: for regulation can be enforced only by a reliance on a recognized position of power. Even if the less developed countries are, as a whole, increasing their potential for exerting political pressure, this collective strength can have little effect on each particular negotiation for the transfer of a specific technology. Each such negotiation will continue to be predominantly shaped by market, not political, pressures.

And the market for technology is no different from the market for any other commodity. Its existence stimulates the growth of the total supply of the commodity available to all the parties in the market: it cannot guarantee that any individual party will benefit.

References

Beer, Stafford (1979) *The Heart of the Enterprise (The Managerial Cybernetics Organisation)*. New York: John Wiley.

Delefortrie, M. (1978) 'Transfer de technologie,' *Etudes et Expansion*, No. 278. (Authors' translation of passage quoted.)

Dingle, J. & Beaumont, C. (1978) 'The management framework for effective technology transfer,' ChemPor 78 *International Chemical Engineering Conference*, University of Braga, Portugal, Sept. 1978.

Draft international code of conduct on the transfer of technology, U.N. document TD/Code TOT/14, 1979.

E.g., as proposed at the UNECE Seminar on Forecasting, Programming and Planning in the Chemical Industry, Warsaw, 10-14 Sept. 1979.

(The opinions expressed in this paper are those of the authors, and should not be taken to represent the views of the organizations with which the authors are associated.)

5. A NEW INDUSTRIAL REVOLUTION?

HOWARD ROSENBROCK ET AL.

Rosenbrock is Professor of Control Engineering at the University of Manchester Institute of Science and Technology, Manchester, England.

In contrast to the euphoria of Masuda, the authors of this piece delve into history with a look at the British Industrial Revolution of 1780-1830. They conclude firmly that we are not witnessing a social revolution of equivalent magnitude, because the new information technology is not yet bringing about a new way of living.

This is a contribution to what is now a widespread discussion on the future development of technology and its interaction with society: on the ways in which society will influence the development of technology, and technology in turn will influence society. It is a discussion generally marked by uncertainties and hesitation. Great changes are predicted, but there are wide differences of view about what they will be, the rate at which they will occur, and the extent to which they will be beneficial.

The mood of this debate can be contrasted with a similar debate in England in early Victorian times. Then, in some quarters, there was an equally strong conviction of rapid future change. There was also great criticism of some of the aspects of early industrialization: loss of independence of the workers, bad working conditions, truck shops, child labor, etc; and the threat to Christian decencies, to deference, and to order. But these were seen predominantly as defects which could be eliminated, and the underlying change was generally seen as beneficial. Men believed in "progress," which would alleviate human toil, eliminate poverty, improve communications and transport, and make available to many what had been available only to a few. The steam engine, gas-lighting, the achromatic microscope, the railway, the electric telegraph, steamships, photography, new production machinery: all of these were seen as contributing to a future in which increasing knowledge would give increasing power over nature, and increasing wealth.

The mood today seems to be different. We have unparalleled knowledge and power over nature, yet this faces us with moral dilemmas and responsibilities for which we are ill-prepared. We can if we choose keep alive the victims of brain

Reprinted from *The Information Technology Revolution,* MIT Press, 1985 by permission of the publisher.

damage, or cruelly deformed children who once would have died: reason and humanity are both confused by such choices, and the exercise of the power we have attained, in either direction, leaves us tainted. Our technology has made it easy for us to burn up in a few decades the oil produced in many millions of years, or to destroy the last forests, or drive to extinction an increasing range of living creatures. We are uneasily aware of the judgment that later generations will pass on our response to these tempting opportunities. Buried in our minds are the pictures of Dachau and Auschwitz and Hiroshima and Gulag, which make a simple belief in progress no longer possible, while the doctrine of "Mutually Assured Destruction" has accustomed us to the sober rational calculus of the unthinkable.

In many ways we have the feeling of living at the end of an era, rather than the beginning of a new one. Both those who are optimistic about the future and those who are pessimistic agree in predicting rapid change. Few believe that the world in 20 years' time will be very similar to the world as it is today, yet the feeling is of moving away from what we have, rather than moving toward a welcoming future.

The Victorian situation led toward the danger of complacency. Our own offers a choice of two: on the one hand, despondency, and on the other, a millennial optimism, both of which can be seen at the present time.

Industrial Revolutions

The future, it is widely believed, is going to see a period of very rapid change in technology, to such an extent that there is much talk of another industrial revolution. It is therefore useful to look at the first industrial revolution, say from 1780 to 1830, to see what it was about that period that led it to be regarded as revolutionary. It was not just the change in technology, but the fact that the new technology brought into being a new way of living. In this it was comparable to the transition in Stone Age times from hunting to agriculture.

The Industrial Revolution was chiefly an English phenomenon, partly Scottish and Welsh, and hardly touched other countries until a later period. It is therefore convenient to speak only of England. In 1780 England was still an agricultural country, with nearly 80 percent of the population living in the countryside. Outside London, the largest towns were Birmingham, Bristol, and Liverpool, each with about 50,000 inhabitants. Relative to earlier times, the eighteenth century was prosperous, and agriculture had been greatly improved. The enclosures of land were accelerating, driving people into the towns. Yet, for the majority, life went on in a way that can be traced back with only the slowest changes for many centuries. Country beliefs and traditions often had at their heart the rituals of pre-christian Stone Age farmers, from whom there was a continuous descent.

By 1830, though much of this still existed, it no longer seemed the way of the future. The great manufacturing towns had sprung up—Manchester based upon cotton with 182,000 people at the 1831 census, Leeds based upon wool with 123,000, and Birmingham upon engineering with 144,000, while the port of Liverpool had 202,000. There were in all 14 English towns in 1831 with a population of 50,000 or more. Life in these rapidly growing towns is largely hidden from us, but in them the old links with the countryside and its traditions were broken, and the village community was replaced by something much looser. The push from the land and from the decaying handicrafts was matched by a pull toward the towns and the new mills. An intelligent and ambitious young man could leave the countryside and live in relative prosperity as a mill-hand. A young woman would go to the mill in preference to "service" because of the greater freedom.

Conversely, those who became ill and unfit for work could no longer rely on the same care by the community. Orphans could be sent from their parishes to a kind of slavery as apprentices in the mills, while in the workhouses that were soon to be set up, husband and wife and children were separated. Above all, a new spirit of inhumanity arose, based upon a calculation of "economic necessity."

The Industrial Revolution had its heroic craftsmen in the millwrights and steam engine makers and their like. But traditional craftsmanship declined, and with it the design of manufactured articles. Around 1820 there was a sharp drop in the standard of book production. The quality of furniture and of household goods of many kinds deteriorated, and the old, easy, natural sense of seemliness and fitness in design was lost.

The worst of these developments produced in time their remedies. Factory legislation regulated safety and hours of work. Trade unions grew slowly to equalize in some degree the bargaining power of employer and employed. Much later, there began a slow and faltering attempt toward better design.

Toward the end of the nineteenth century, England was unrecognizably different from its condition in 1780: no longer based upon the countryside, but centered on the towns and on manufacturing, and past the peak of its international pre-eminence as a manufacturing country. Heavy physical labor was no longer the almost universal lot, though some perhaps in factory conditions worked more unremittingly than in the past. Food was plentiful and varied, and not yet as debased as it was later to become. Education to a certain level had become universal. A new sense of community, born in adversity, was felt in many working-class districts: later often to be destroyed by rebuilding or increased mobility. There was a feeling that life had become easier; almost a feeling of having climbed out of a pit: though, indeed, one can ask whether this was not the same pit that had opened in 1780.

How one assesses the gains and losses is not very significant. It is rather as if one were to compare the hunter with the farmer, and to assess the loss of freedom and satisfaction in the chase against the labor, but also the settled community life, of agriculture. In both cases one culture replaced the other, and to all appearances irreversibly. Not the least of the reasons for the irreversibility, in both cases, is that the new organization could support a much larger population than the old. Once the population had increased to the extent that the change permitted, a return to the earlier conditions was impossible.

Such a diversion into the past may not seem relevant to the next 20 years but it is intended to make this point: if the next 20 years are to produce something that we are justified in calling an "industrial revolution," it will have to be something as all-pervasive and far-reaching as we have described. It will have to be not just a change in our technology, but a change in the whole manner of our life. Judged by this criterion, none of the other "industrial revolutions" that have been suggested at various times qualifies for the title—whether based on the coming of railways, or electricity, or the automobile or atomic energy.

The coming changes will be based on the computer, on telecommunications, and on the power that they will give us over the manipulation of information. Will these changes be as profound as those that began around 1780? If so, the hunting and pastoral phases of man's development will have lasted some millions of years; the agricultural phase will have lasted some thousands; and the industrial phase will have lasted just about two hundred.

Among many opinions that have been expressed, it is possible to distinguish three major kinds of reply, or, rather, three extremes between which most others lie. The first answers no: the magnitude of the changes and their speed have been exaggerated, and what we shall see is just one more stage in the development of industry, comparable to other developments that have gone before. This line of thought can find support from the widespread expectation in the 1950s that automation would bring about rapid and fundamental changes in society: expectations that have not, so far, been fulfilled.

The second school of thought answers yes: we are moving out of the stage of industrial society into the stage of post-industrial society. We shall in the future need no more people to produce the goods we use than we need at present to grow the food we eat—say, 5 percent of the population for each. The remaining 90 percent will work in service industries, many of them concerned with the storage, manipulation, and dissemination of knowledge; though much that is referred to as "knowledge" is merely facts. In such a society we shall probably divorce the two functions of work, producing and earning. Leisure will become widespread, and work will be a minor and occasional diversion. This theme gives an infinite scope for imaginative elaboration, which can easily incorporate much of William Morris's "News from Nowhere."

The third school also answers yes, but predicts a total breakdown of society. There will be 5 million unemployed in Britain, and the resulting unrest will lead to the breakdown of the government and some form of dictatorship, either of the right or the left. Out of this, through a revolutionary development, will arise the kind of society described in the preceding paragraph. Russia and the East European countries are usually assumed, on no apparent evidence, to be immune from these difficulties, being able to move smoothly from their present shortage, or at least apparent shortage, of labor to the leisure of the highly automated and computerized society.

Types of Industry _____

Any detailed consideration of the effects of new developments in technology has to accept that these may be very different in different areas of industry. We have made a threefold division in the following way.

First there are the processes industries, such as oil, chemicals, glass, paper, cement, iron and steel making (but not finishing), some parts of food production, etc. It is difficult to define these precisely, but they are most often continuously operating, and deal with flows of material. They are highly automated, and often already use computers in their control systems. The operating labor force is usually very small, to the extent that its further reduction is often not a serious economic consideration, and may not be possible for safety reasons: a certain minimum staff is needed to deal with accidents to men or machines. Maintenance, planning and office work connected with their operation may, on the other hand, employ large numbers. Utilities such as gas, electricity, and water can also be put in this category.

In the operation of such plants we do not expect the new developments in microcomputers and communications to make a rapid qualitative change. The industries will probably make early and extensive use of the new technology, but chiefly to do rather better what is already being done. There will probably be greater integration of their operation, and a great deal of automatic data-gathering. In the longer term, some new processes might become feasible through better control, but this is not an imminent or a widespread possibility. Other developments, such as new processes based on biotechnology, will probably have greater effect.

At the other extreme is office work of various kinds—correspondence, ordering, invoicing, etc. Here the capital investment has in the past been relatively low, so that new equipment does not have to bear the cost of making older equipment obsolete. A relatively small investment can bring great increases in productivity. The equipment can be developed and installed rapidly, so it can use the latest developments in technology. In this area, which includes word processors and, later, the electronic office and electronic mail, we expect changes to be more rapid and extensive.

In between is the area of engineering production, where numerically controlled (NC) machine tools are beginning to spread fairly rapidly, and robots are beginning to be used in small numbers. Computer-aided design and manufacture are at an early stage, with great scope for development. In this area we expect an intermediate rate of change.

Technology and Society _____

Although, looking backward, we can select a date around 1780 as the beginning of a rapid change which is almost a discontinuity, contemporaries did not have our acute awareness of a break with the past. Even in 1830, the new was still embedded in a matrix of the old. Moreover, all the developments that we associate with the industrial revolution can be traced backwards in the eighteenth and seventeenth centuries, and in some respects at least as far as the monasteries of the Middle Ages. Newcomen's steam engine was in use from 1705, iron was made with coke by Abraham Darby in 1709, and throughout the eighteenth century there was a series of inventions and improvements in cotton spinning and weaving.

In the same way, if we are about to see a great acceleration in our ability to handle information, to control and automate machinery, and to eliminate human intervention, then the roots of this change lie far back in the past. The period around 1830 was one of special awareness, and Charles Babbage had already grasped in principle the path that was to be followed. Machinery would be made "self-acting" so that human skill and effort were no longer needed. Or if human aid was still needed, the work would be made as simple as possible. More and more, work would be broken down into its elements, which could be done by unskilled workers under supervision, and later by machine. This applied not only to manual tasks, but also to such apparently intellectual work as the calculation of mathematical tables. Babbage's "analytical engine" was an attempt to carry this process a full century forward, and to produce in the mid-nineteenth century what was achieved only in the mid-twentieth.

The later developments of this theme, by F. W. Taylor, the Gilbreths, Henry Ford, and many others, are well-known. Throughout, the development of more automatic machinery has been accompanied by fragmentation of the jobs associated with them, removal of initiative and skill from the workers, and pacing of work by the machine.

The skills removed from the workplace have been concentrated in planning and supervisory organizations and have undergone a process of development and change. New occupations and new skills have arisen, which are less widespread than those they replaced. Some of these new skills and new occupations are of a professional type and status, and they have swelled the professional class, which has also grown in other ways.

The computer now appears to be offering the power to continue this process of deskilling at the lower levels, and to extend it also to higher levels. The spray-painting of a car can be taught to a robot, which then indefinitely replicates the movements of the man whose job it was. The diagnostic skills of a physician can be incorporated, in a few weeks, into a computer, which can then match his accuracy closely. By incorporating the skills of several physicians, the computer may perform better than any one of them; and it may in time be able to learn from its own experience. Not all of this can be done at present, but none of it seems impossible in the near future. In the same way, skilled engineering designers may be largely replaced by computer systems.

If we look at past experience, it seems likely that possibilities of this kind, if they can be realized profitably with the computer, will be implemented despite any protests by those concerned. A hard-pressed hospital administration will believe that only by using computers can it offer a satisfactory service to its patients. An engineering company will see itself becoming uncompetitive unless it incorporates its design procedures in a computer.

To follow such a path of increasing automation usually requires an additional expenditure on capital equipment. Profitability then depends upon a reduction of employment for a given output, or at least the substitution of less-skilled, and so cheaper labor for more highly skilled. Both courses reduce the demands that are made on human ability, and a classical economic argument sees this as the creation of new opportunity. The human resources set free are available for other needs of society, or to increase the production of goods. Moreover, an economic mechanism will automatically ensure that this opportunity is fully used.

Yet the experience of the last 50 years does little to establish confidence in this self-regulating mechanism. The demoralizing unemployment of the 1930s ended only with the beginning of World War II, and it is not clear that the depression would have ended without the war. The 1970s, against expectations, saw a renewed increase of unemployment. During the whole period, a large proportion of those employed have done work below their capability. What is striking is that very great effort is expended upon the creation of the opportunity that unemployment or under-employment represents, and, in comparison, almost none upon using that opportunity.

A New Industrial Revolution?

We do not see microelectronics and computers and communication systems as bringing a new departure comparable to that which occurred in England between 1780 and 1830. Then, a stable society based upon agriculture and the countryside gave way to economic expansion, to great cities, and to a new expectation of continual "progress." Rather than a break with the past of that kind, we should see the effect of new technology in the next 20 years as an intensification of existing tendencies, and their extension to new areas.

To say that the next 20 years will see not a new beginning, but an intensification of old tendencies, is not to diminish the importance of the changes that will occur. These are likely to be faster and more extensive than anything in recent experience. They will for the first time impinge severely on white-collar and some professional work, as well as intensifying the pressure upon blue-collar jobs.

We also suggest that we are not likely to enter upon an era when work becomes largely unnecessary, a mere diversion from leisure. Our prosperity is based upon 200 years and more of increasingly rapacious exploitation of the earth, and it is not likely that we can continue on this path much longer. Energy and raw materials will become scarcer and more expensive under the pressure of a rapidly increasing world population and an increasing demand from poorer countries, while our impact upon the environment will have to be curbed. The new technology may serve rather to alleviate increasing difficulties than to lead us to an age of plenty.

If these judgments are correct, they go some way to explain the public mood on which we commented above. The problems we shall face will be not wholly new ones, but those with which we are familiar, though perhaps intensified and extended. There is likely, for example, to be a progression away from blue-collar jobs to white-collar or service occupations, but these could well take on more of the character that factory work has had in the past, if the tendency is not resisted.

Coming to Terms with the Past_____

We have emphasized the inhumanity and injustice that accompanied the early stages of the Industrial Revolution. These were not new things in England, but they had not previously been justified and defended by the prevailing philosophy. So powerful were the effects of this philosophy that to those who looked down from a higher level in society, the suffering became invisible, or, if not invisible, then transparent; and their view was not arrested by it but looked through it at what they took to be economic verities beyond.

Even so sympathetic an observer as Mrs. Gaskell could not trust the clear evidence of her eyes. She describes, in a time of economic hardship, the suffering of the weavers in Manchester, and the contrasting prosperity of the mill-owners:

> It is a bewildering thing to the poor weaver to see his employer removing from house to house, each grander than the last . . . while all the time the weaver . . . is struggling on for bread. . . . Large houses are occupied, while spinners' and weavers' cottages stand empty. . . . Carriages still roll along the streets, concerts are still crowded . . . while the workman loiters away all his un-employed time in watching these things, and thinking of the pale uncomplaining wife at home, and the wailing children asking for enough food. . . . The contrast is too great. Why should he alone suffer from bad times?

Yet, she continues immediately, "I know that this is not really the case; and I know what is the truth in such matters. . . ."

We have not yet as a nation fully acknowledged the wrong that was done at that time, and we have not fully rejected it. Until we do so, we are unlikely to recover our energy and self-confidence. And until we do so, fresh shoots of the same philosophy will continually arise from its underground roots.

Productivity _____

If there is one aim that is common to all industrial nations, it must be to increase labor productivity. This is held out as the cure for inflation and for an adverse balance of payments. It is regarded as a promise of increased employment following from increased competitiveness, and as the only way toward an increase in material prosperity.

We suggest that these conclusions are less firm than they seem, and will bear a deeper analysis than they have received. To begin with, at least three different ideas are confused under the one name, "productivity." First, there is the idea of benefit to mankind. There is certain essential work that has to be accomplished for survival and convenience; a reduction in the effort needed for this work frees time and energy for other desirable activities. It is the appeal of this idea that underlies the other two, though they do not necessarily offer the same rewards.

Second, there is the idea of productivity of a company or commercial enterprise, which allows it to reduce its costs and improve its competitive position. This idea is not the same as the first, because an increase in output obtained by a proportional increase in effort still seems like an increase in productivity to the enterprise. So does a subdivision of jobs, which reduces the wage bill without reducing the total effort demanded.

Third, there is the idea of productivity of a nation, in which men and women are either employed or unemployed. An increase in productivity that leads to an increase in unemployment can be thought of as an opportunity; the unemployed effort is available for other desirable purposes. But it becomes a benefit only when it is used for those purposes, and though great effort is devoted to creating the opportunity, much less is devoted to using it.

Because of the differences between the interpretations of productivity, the efforts of an enterprise can fail to bring benefits to society, and may instead bring disadvantages. They can result in one part of the population working long hours under high pressure at uninteresting jobs, while another part is unemployed. An improved competitive situation of the enterprise may also fail to be reflected in an equivalent improvement of national competitiveness. If it is achieved by an increase in unemployment, it throws a burden upon the nation which largely cancels the benefit.

The chief agent in pursuing an increase of productivity is the individual enterprise. What is actually pursuing is not the simple benefit contained in the first of the three interpretations, nor the direct improvement of national competitiveness. If the aims of the enterprise could be more closely aligned with the other two objectives, its activity and initiative could more directly contribute to the aims of society.

Economic Determinism _____

A number of economic arguments are often deployed to show that things which would otherwise be desirable cannot be achieved. For example, it would be desirable to develop a different kind of technology from the one that we have: a technology that would set out not to eliminate skill and initiative, but rather to collaborate with them in increasing productivity. But then it is said that the technology that we have has evolved by competition in the marketplace, and is therefore economically superior to any alternative. To develop an alternative would impose a cost, reduce our competitive advantage, and lead to a reduction in wealth.

This conclusion follows only if a particular set of assumptions is made. By means of an elementary example, it has been shown how an equally plausible set of assumptions leads to an exactly opposite conclusion. That is, the pursuit of a short-term advantage, enforced by market action, can lead to a technology that is economically inferior to its alternatives.

More generally, it is suggested that the development of economic theory suffers from a number of difficulties. Controlled experiments are usually impossible, and the effect of one variable cannot be studied in isolation from others. The economic system is continually changing, and there is a question whether we can learn about it more quickly than it changes. Moreover, within an economic system there are many groups pursuing their own interests, so that a deterministic model is not appropriate. Something like the theory of games is needed, which so far has not developed to the necessary degree.

For these reasons, and also because of the historical experience, it is suggested that undue reliance on economic theory is not justified. A more direct, and probably safer, course is suggested instead: that is, that so far as possible, the conditions in which the major interest groups operate should be changed, in such a way that their perceived advantage aligns itself more closely with the aims of society.

Technological Determinism _____

A related but different kind of determinism is often suggested in technology, and it is easy to see how it arises. The historical development — of steam engines, spinning and weaving machinery, machine tools, electrical power, computers, factory organization, and the rest—has led to a quite astonishing increase in productivity and material wealth. We have no experience of any alternative way in which technology could have been developed. We therefore are easily led to believe that the historical path was the only one that could have been pursued.

In particular, we may be led to believe that the development of technology must inevitably lead to the elimination of skill in the jobs that it directly affects. The conclusion that we suggest is a different one. The new technologies of microelectronics and computers and communications can be used to reinforce and extend the historical process of subordinating men and women to machines, and of eliminating the initiative and control in their work. They can also be used to reverse this process, to develop a technology that is subordinate to human skill and cooperates with it. Which of these outcomes will ensue depends upon the struggles of those concerned. What is important is to believe in the possibility of the second outcome, and to believe that the full use of human abilities is a higher and more productive goal than the perfection of machines.

Specific areas in which it appears clearly possible to develop a technology that preserves and collaborates with human skill include:

1. computer-aided design, where the process of deskilling is under way, but probably not irreversible;
2. NC machine tools and FMS systems, where for many industrial products the reintegration of the machinist's job would most likely offer economic benefits;
3. many applications of "expert systems," where development is still at an early age.

There are probably many more, but because the effort devoted to this possibility is so much less than that given to the alternative, they are difficult to identify.

On the other hand, where fragmentation of jobs has been carried to a very high degree over a very long period, the problem of developing a valid alternative may be much greater. The Volvo plant at Kalmar, and some of the work in the German "Humanisation of Work" program, show at least the beginnings of a path heading in the desired direction.

Changing the Economic Structure _____

If great effort is applied persistently by many people toward some not wholly impossible goal, there is likely to be a degree of success. Such effort has been applied toward increasing the productivity of labor according to one special definition, and it has succeeded astonishingly. No such persistent and tenacious effort has been devoted to making full use of human abilities. It has been assumed that full employment will follow from the working of the economy, either unaided or with some government control. The provision of jobs that use to the full the human abilities of those who fill them has not been a major objective: rather the reverse, since effort has been applied to reducing the skill and control of the worker.

We suggest that this order of priorities is wrong; that consistent effort toward the full use of human ability would embrace the subordinate aim of increasing productivity. It would also strive toward full employment and toward engaging the initiative and increasing the skill of workers.

To make these aims the intense and active concern of those engaged in the economic life of the country requires a change in their perceived incentives, which could arise through changes in public opinion, through trade union action, or through changes in the law. Without suggesting that they offer a complete solution, we propose that the following would repay study in this connection:

1. the operation of large Japanese companies, in which a commitment to continued employment for a large part of the workforce appears to give the company an incentive to use the ability and initiative of these workers to the full. It also removes from workers much of the fear that new technology will lead to their unemployment. We recognize that the Japanese system has its own difficulties, though lower economic efficiency is not among them;

2. the Scandinavian experience, in which trade unions have highly trained members who participate in the planning and introduction of new technology—for example the data processing shop stewards in some Norwegian plants;

3. the successful and self-sustaining development of workers' cooperatives at Mondragon in Spain, which in principle should ensure that aims similar to those we have mentioned are pursued;

4. the Lucas Aerospace Shop Stewards' "Alternative Corporate Plan," which clearly demonstrates the reserves of untapped initiative that were latent in the company.

Interdisciplinary Research _____

The central complex of questions that have been considered in this report, relating to technology and work and society, is approached from different directions by different disciplines. These include engineering, computer science, industrial psychology and sociology, ergonomics, technology assessment, management science, economics, system science, social and economic history, political science, and probably others.

What hardly exists is a study of this complex in which the different disciplines, with their different assumptions and methods, are brought into contact with one another. Until this is done, the results obtained within a single discipline are likely to be highly misleading. If it could be done, the benefit to the disciplines themselves, and to the value of their results, should be considerable.

We suggest that this is a task that might be particularly appropriate for the recently formed Technical Change Center.

A similar point arises, on a somewhat narrower front, in the development of new technology. Decisions are made, during the research stage of new technologies and of new equipment, that will later constrain all efforts to design the jobs in connection with them. This research phase should therefore attract the interest of social scientists and of trade unions. Yet this involvement hardly exists except in a few small and recent examples.

Education

If the changes that have been suggested above could be brought about, they would have profound implications for all levels of education. If skills were valued and preserved in work, education could link in a much more fruitful way with later experience. As at present, a range of skills, both physical and mental, would be acquired in the process of education. What would be more important would be to develop an ability to acquire further skills. Just as the scientific and technical knowledge learned in one's youth needs to be constantly updated, so one should regard skill as something that will continually need to change and develop.

In a similar way, the interdisciplinary work suggested in the previous section, if it were successful, could lead to deep changes in the education of technologists. At present, when elements of social sciences are introduced into technological courses, they are usually taught on the basis of an outlook and assumptions that are very different from those of technology. Any integration has usually to be provided by the student himself. A true integration of ideas around the theme of technology and society would find a much more ready acceptance.

III ____THE GLOBAL TRADING SYSTEM: THE CAPITAL FLOWS_____

6. THE STAGES OF DEVELOPING COUNTRY POLICY TOWARD FOREIGN INVESTMENT

WILLIAM A. STOEVER

*William A. Stoever has spent six years teaching, studying and traveling in
developing countries in Africa, Asia and Latin America. In 1985, while a
Visiting Fellow in the Research Program in Development Studies at the
Woodrow Wilson School of Princeton University, he spent four months in
India on an Indo-American Fellowship doing research for a book on*
Developing Country Policy toward Foreign Investment. *The author
wishes to thank Mr. Rajiv Maluste for his assistance with the background
research for this article.*

When and how much can a less-developed country change its policies to
obtain more benefits without driving foreign investment away? This article proposes a series of economic growth stages which a developing
country's policy might typically experience as its desirability as an investment site increases.

Many developing countries seek foreign private investment in order to obtain
capital, technology, managerial know-how and other benefits to further their
economic development. Multinational corporations (MNCs) are able to provide a
package of resources and abilities on a scale that recipient countries are unable to
obtain elsewhere.

However, host governments in developing countries have often driven away
potential investors by demanding too many benefits in relation to what the
countries can offer in return. The countries' demands have not been appropriate
to their endowments. In addition, host countries have on occasion changed their
terms towards investment projects after the projects were already in place.
Taken to the extreme, this could entail expropriation or nationalization, but there
are many more situations in which host governments have unilaterally changed
investment agreements or insisted that the terms be renegotiated.

On the other hand, there are many instances in which LDCs have successfully increased their demands on foreign companies as time has gone by. A country
whose industrial base is increasing, whose level of technological capability is
rising, and whose per capita GNP is growing is able to obtain more favorable

Reprinted from *Columbia Journal of World Business,* Vol. XX, No. 3, Fall, 1985, pp. 3-11 by
permission of the publisher.

terms than one whose economy is stagnating or even deteriorating. Some host governments, by accident or design, have tended to raise their demands at a pace roughly corresponding to the increase in their ability to attract investors. Thus the question arises: when and how much can an LDC change its policies to obtain more benefits without driving investors away?[1] This paper proposes a framework for analyzing this question.

Methodology

The research for this paper consists primarily of a series of case studies of different countries' experiences and dealings with foreign investment over the past two decades or so. The studies are based on statistics of investment inflows in various countries (to the extent these are available), scholarly and news articles, and country reports by services such as *Business International* and *Price Waterhouse* that report on and evaluate economic conditions and policies. In some cases these sources have been supplemented by interviews of LDC government representatives and/or businessmen in the US and in the host countries.

Benefits Sought

Among the benefits LDCs frequently seek from foreign investors are:

- technology transfer and technological training (a very important motivator for seeking foreign investment);
- the upgrading of technology in investments already in place;
- an increase in the local productive capacity and industrial base;
- industrial diversification;
- increased local value added, i.e., more inputs locally produced;
- opportunities for local suppliers and contractors;
- local ownership (full or part) of invested facilities;
- investment in remote or primitive geographic regions;
- increased employment;
- the training and advancement of host citizens;
- facilities to establish industries or produce products which the local economy is not yet able to provide (often to substitute for imports);
- exports and foreign exchange earnings;
- and government revenues.

Policy Tools _____

Host governments may use a variety of policy tools to shape and regulate foreign investment and to try to prevent abuses by such investors. It is not always possible to differentiate these from each other in practice. For example, the question of whether and how much tariff protection to offer a foreign company's local manufacturing subsidiary has a bearing on the country's incentives, investment climate, technology transfer, balance of payments and many other concerns. It is also not always possible to distinguish a "policy" from a benefit or objective sought from an investment. Thus, an LDC may view local ownership as an objective in itself or as a means to obtain other ends such as a more rapid advancement of its citizens. In a sense, every objective becomes a tool to obtain yet a further objective.

With these caveats in mind, a list follows of some of the more commonly identified policy tools:

- pre-investment screening;
- incentives:
    tax holidays,
    import privileges and tariff exemptions;
- subsidies:
    assistance in plant construction or the training of employees,
    low-interest loans;
- guarantees by the host government:
    loan guarantees,
    investment insurance,
    guarantees of currency convertibility or repatriation of dividends and capital;
- tariff protection and/or local monopolies;
- promotion (advertisements, overseas investment centers, etc.);
- regulations, licensing requirements, laws, etc. to achieve various objectives;
- tying of licenses, permits, privileges, etc. to desirable actions by an investor;
- persuasion, personal contacts, on-site visits, etc.

The appropriate mix of these and other policy tools will vary from country to country and, within a given country, over time. It will also depend on the country's economic philosophy, for example, the extent to which it will intervene in companies' decision-making processes versus the extent to which it will allow market forces to determine the nature of investment. As a generalization, the more socialist and state-directed a country's economy, the more its policy-makers will try to use policy instruments to obtain its objectives.[2]

Contrast: Rostow's Stages of Economic Growth _____

The use of the word "stages" to characterize anything related to economic development has been suspect ever since W. W. Rostow used it in his "stages of economic growth" schema. Hence it is useful to distinguish briefly the present schema from his. Rostow, an economic historian, suggested that societies could be divided into five stages according to the economics of their industrial production functions. Societies in the traditional stage were characterized by "limited production functions, based on pre-Newtonian science and technology, and on pre-Newtonian attitudes towards the physical world." Then there followed three stages in the growth process: the pre-conditions for take-off, the take-off itself, and the drive to maturity. The final stage, seemingly a sort of culmination, was "the age of mass consumption." Rostow described the characteristics of each stage; these were mostly qualitative, although he had some statistical data from a few countries. He also discussed the factors tending to move a society from one stage to the next, particularly the moves initiating the take-off: increased savings and investment, entrepreneurial activity, and the emergence of "leading sectors" in the economy.[3]

This model has been criticized on several grounds. Some criticisms relate to the weakness of all "stage" theories, while others relate to Rostow's particular theory or to his use of facts and historical data. Some criticisms in the first category no doubt would apply to the present schema, too—the stages are not clearly distinguishable from one another in practice; they do not display empirically testable characteristics; and the dynamic characteristics tending to cause movement from one stage to the next are not identifiable. In addition, the concepts of the schema are jumbled and nonspecific, and many of the phenomena he describes do not fit easily into any one stage of his model. For example, he is confused about whether agricultural improvements must take place before a society can enter the pre-conditions for take-off or whether they are achieved as part of the take-off, or are even an outcome of the take-off. He omits some important parameters, such as the growth of foreign trade. The time periods he suggests (in particular, "a decade or two" or "two or three decades" for the take-off) apply to only a few industrialized countries and cannot be generalized across many of today's less-developed countries. As a result, his model applies better to some countries than others. Rostow has also been criticized on some historical facts, such as the dating and significance of growth spurts in various industrialized countries. However, these criticisms do not make the schema useless as a concept or a framework for analysis. Even some of Rostow's critics have called his description "evocative" and have said "his terminology is here to stay."[4]

The present schema is much more limited in scope than Rostow's. Unlike his, it makes no pretense of setting specific time intervals for the progression from one stage to the next, and indeed it suggests that the pace of such movements varies depending on both internal policy actions and external, uncontrollable factors. The schema is based on a set of variables that have been identified as important in determining the amount, characteristics and economic returns of investments as observed from case studies of a fairly wide range of less-developed countries. These variables are organized into a set of categories relating to a specific and rather narrow problem, namely, how attractive a less-developed country is to foreign investors in manufacturing at a given time and what range of benefits the host country could reasonably hope to receive from those investors at that time. The scheme is not intended to suggest any sort of dynamic or analytic connection "causing" movement from one stage to another. It has no sense of historical determinism or inevitability. Rather, it is policy-oriented (more so than Rostow's schema) in that it suggests that government leaders can learn from the experiences of other countries in more-or-less similar circumstances.

Framework for Analysis: The Stages of Evolution in Foreign Investment Policy

This paper postulates a series of stages or an evolution that a developing country's policy might typically experience as its desirability as an investment site increases. Chart 1 shows a schema for characterizing the changes in an LDC's policy as its relationships to foreign companies change. The schema is useful because it facilitates comparisons among different countries with varying endowments and different levels of economic development. It is most applicable to investments in manufacturing facilities, although it has some applicability to downstream processing of agricultural or extractive products. It is less applicable to foreign investments in the extractive or service sectors.

The horizontal axis on the graph shows the host country's "attractiveness," which is a composite of many factors, primarily economic but also non-economic. Among the factors most easily susceptible to an economic analysis are:

- the country's level of development;
- the existing industrial structure;
- the present size of the country's market;

- projected future market growth;
- the availability of a skilled and motivated work force;
- low wages relative to other possible investment sites;
- the country's balance of payments position: can the foreign company get its dividends and capital out?;
- the "economic distance" from the investor's home country;
- the availability of adequate infrastructure;
- the availability of local suppliers and support systems;
- and the availability of local financing.

Another set of factors can be loosely gathered together under the heading of "governmental" or "political" considerations. These include:

Chart 1
EVOLUTION OR "STAGES" OF DEVELOPING COUNTRY POLICY TOWARD FOREIGN INVESTMENT

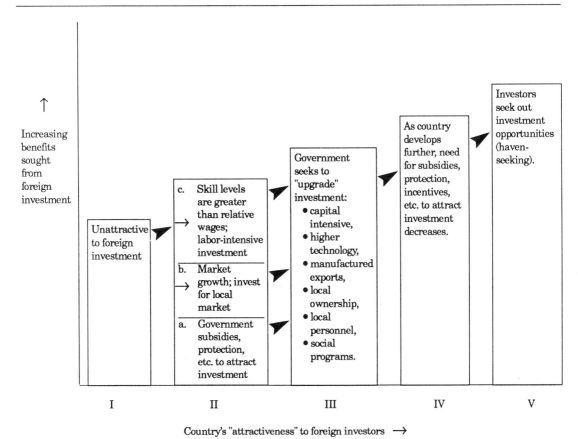

- the host government's receptivity to foreign investment (the "investment climate");
- whether the host economy is relatively market-driven or statist/socialist;
- the amount of red tape or bureaucratic hurdles to get approvals for new investment, expansion, dividend repatriation, etc.;
- the relative freedom from corruption in the government's regulatory mechanisms;
- political stability;
- and the rationality and predictability of the host country's regulatory environment.

These factors would have different relative magnitudes and would be ranked in a different order of importance for different companies. The composite "attractiveness" is indicated on the horizontal axis because it is analogous to the dependent variable of an algebraic equation; it is relatively exogenously determined.

The vertical axis shows the increasing benefits a host LDC characteristically expects or seeks from foreign investors as the country's attractiveness increases. The benefits accrue to a large extent as the natural result of market forces. But if the host government believes that the country is not receiving as many benefits as it should, it may intervene and demand a greater amount or a different kind of benefits. The increasing demands are often sought by means of policy tools such as those described above, and therefore the policies appropriate to different levels of attractiveness may be referred to as "Stage II policy," "Stage III policy," and so on. There are certainly many overlaps in policy stages, and probably some missing steps for some kind of investments. Nonetheless, the categorization into different stages is useful as a conceptualization and even as a guideline to aid decision-makers in determining whether a given policy proposal may be inappropriate to their country's net attractiveness at a particular time.

It is hazardous to cite individual countries as being at a particular level of attractiveness because critics can usually point out specific features of a country's politico-economic situation and industrialization program that do not fit easily at that level. Likewise, it may be difficult to characterize a selected country's policy as "Stage I," "Stage II," etc., for several reasons: some LDCs have not treated foreign investment as a policy matter at all and have not worked out screening devices, laws and regulations, incentives, and similar policy tools to apply to it; many LDCs' policies and programs are inconsistent, unpredictable, rapidly changeable over time, or *ad hoc* in application and thus hard to characterize, a country's economic and political attributes may seem to place it at a given level of attractiveness, while the policies it is attempting to implement seem more appropriate to a different stage; or a country's policies towards investment in one manufacturing sector may be quite different from those in another sector.

Another problem is that countries' circumstances and policies change over time. The value of a country's exports may decline, leaving it poorer and less attractive than before. A change of government may make the country more hostile (or more hospitable) to foreign investment than before. And of course critics can always claim that the generalizations and categorizations are overly broad. Nevertheless, it is still instructive to select a few countries that seem to fit fairly well into each category at the time of this writing and to use those countries as illustrations.

Stage I, in the extreme lower left, represents countries that are too poor, too small, too distant or too under-developed to attract any foreign investment in manufacturing (aside, possibly, from a few uneconomic "show" factories that might be attracted by government subsidies or protection. These are discussed in Stage II). Countries characterized by Stage I at the present writing would probably include a number of the least-developed lands in tropical Africa, Central America, Guyana, Surinam, and various island nations in the Pacific and Caribbean.[5]

There are three primary ways that LDCs can begin to attract foreign investment in manufacturing (shown by Stages IIa, IIb, and IIc on the chart). Frequently the first manufacturing investments to go into a country are plants to assemble household goods and sometimes motor vehicles from imported components to sell in the local market (IIa). Low-technology pharmaceutical and chemical factories are also common. This type of investment generally would not be competitive on the world market because of its small scale or outdated production methods, and it frequently fails to produce a net economic (or even political) benefit for the host country. It is able to survive because of subsidies or protected markets guaranteed by the host government.

Justification for this type of policy is sometimes claimed on grounds such as: the plants will eventually grow to large enough scale and efficiency to become economically viable and profitable (an "infant industry" argument); they will create a "seed core" or foundation that will attract other investors; or they will create employment opportunities and provide training to host-country citizens and thus add to the country's human capital.

Many LDCs have pursued policies that more-or-less fit into the IIa categorization. Some of the import substitution programs for economic development and industrialization attempted by many countries in the 1960s and early 1970s would fit here; examples could include the Central American Common Market (before it more-or-less disintegrated), Ecuador, Uruguay, Morocco, Senegal, Ghana (in the early years after independence), Angola, Kenya and Zambia (in the 1960s, before copper prices fell).[6] A few oil-rich, low-population countries, such as Saudi Arabia, Kuwait, the United Arab Emirates, Brunei, and probably Gabon, are also best characterized as Stage IIa. These countries' oil wealth enables them to offer subsidies without which they would probably not attract many multinational ventures. Sometimes the main differences between Stages I and IIa lies in the willingness and ability of the country's government to provide enough support to bring in investors (Stage IIa) who would otherwise consider the country unattractive (Stage I).

Another way a move toward Stage II can occur is as the country's domestic market grows, making it more attractive to foreign producers of certain consumer and industrial goods who see an opportunity to begin assembly or full production for the local market (IIb). Countries whose primary attraction to foreign manufacturing investment rests (or rested) on their existing or potential future market size might include Chile and a few other middle-sized South American countries, Nigeria (also mentioned below), India in the 1950s, and the Philippines into the 1970s (before the rising opposition to President Marcos caused increasing political upheaval).[7]

A number of countries have large populations, some indigenous industrialization activity, and in some cases substantial agricultural or mineral wealth. These countries could be well-advanced into Stage IIb (or even Stage III) if they were not hampered by political instability, civil strife, counterproductive economic policies, overly restrictive or centralized development philosophies, corrupt and inefficient administrative mechanisms, or similar woes. Examples of such countries might include Colombia, Argentina, Turkey, Egypt, Pakistan, Thailand, Indonesia, and the Peoples Republic of China.[8]

Another rather different Stage II type of investment is labor-intensive production or assembly work on materials and components brought in for re-export (Stage IIc). Foreign companies are attracted to these countries because of their low wages and willing workers. Among the most frequently attracted industries are textile and clothing factories and assembly plants for electrical appliances and electronics equipment. Many of the newly industrializing countries (NICs), including Taiwan, South Korea, Singapore and Malaysia, pursued industrialization drives by seeking this type of investment in the 1960s and 1970s. Countries consciously trying to pursue a Stage IIc type of policy in the early 1980s could include Sri Lanka and Mexico (with the "border factories" just below the Rio Grande River).[9]

An LDC government's policy may have a mixture of IIa, IIb, and IIc elements. For example, it may offer incentives, subsidies and guarantees to a potential investor (Stage IIa) in order to compete against other countries bidding for the investment, but expecting the plant eventually to be able to produce goods profitably for sale in the domestic market (Stage IIb). It may offer similar incentives to attract a textile or assembly plant, hoping that the value of the plant's exports (Stage IIc) will exceed the costs of the incentives (Stage IIa). The governments of developing countries and of individual American states often compete against each other in this same way, trying to bring in plants that create jobs and add to their jurisdiction's prosperity. This kind of competition is not inconsistent with an investment policy fitting into Stage IIb or IIc, provided that the government is realistic, hard-headed and not self-deluded in its assessment of whether or not the proposed plant will make a net positive economic contribution to the host economy. The danger is that LDC governments may offer a lot of subsidies and protection to a variety of investment projects in the hope they will become profitable. However, many projects never become viable on their own, and the country ends up with a lot of costly, deficit-ridden, inefficient plants. Turkey is a notable example here.[10] Others include many countries in South America, a few of the larger African nations, and some in Southeast Asia that brought in automobile assembly plants, factories to produce household appliances, and other "white elephants" in the 1960s and 1970s.

Countries can regress from Stage II to Stage I, due possibly to economic setbacks such as a decline in the value of their primary exports, to political disintegration and civil strife, or to severe economic mismanagement. Countries that could be characterized as having done this might include the Central American Common Market, Ghana, Zambia, possibly the Katanga region of Zaire, Iran and Burma.[11]

The transition from Stage II to Stage III is a gradual process characterized by a shift in emphasis by host government policy-makers. They begin to be more selective in the types of investments they allow in, attempting to channel investments into desired industries or geographic areas, to seek a greater ratio of benefits from existing installations, and frequently to take over part or full ownership of the foreign-owned facilities. The Ivory Coast is an example of a country beginning a cautious transition from a Stage II to a Stage III policy. Puerto Rico actively pursues "foreign" investors (mainly from the US, with a smattering from other countries), but it tries to concentrate on high-wage, high-technology industries and to obtain a "quid pro quo" such as increased employment in exchange for the incentives it grants. Iran before the fall of the Shah was toughening its stance and driving increasingly hard bargains with foreign investors.[12]

A number of countries are pursuing policies that clearly fit within the Stage III category. Singapore has been consciously trying to phase out labor-intensive assembly plants for some years and to upgrade the level of technology in all of its foreign-owned plants. Malaysia's New Economic Policy (often called the "bumiputra policy"), announced in 1971, has transferred part ownership in many foreign-owned companies to Malaysian citizens and has increased the amount of training, job opportunities and high-level managerial positions available to those citizens. Beginning in 1975, South Korea has tried to redirect foreign companies into heavy industry and industrial chemicals. India has not yet been very hospitable to foreign investment, but recently the government has been loosening its restrictions somewhat while setting up an elaborate set of regulations, allowable foreign ownership percentages, and incentives and disincentives designed to channel investment into exports, high-technology products, and poverty-ridden geographical regions. Mexico has been making efforts to "Mexicanize" foreign-owned companies for years; the 1973 "Law to Promote Mexican Investment and Regulate Foreign Investment" restated and intensified this basic policy thrust. Brazil actively seeks foreign investment but tries to channel it into priority sectors and geographic regions. It requires most investments to come in as joint ventures, bring in new technology, and limit dividend remittances.[13]

A number of countries or groupings have attempted to implement Stage III-type policies but have not been able to make them stick. Their economies have not been strong enough, or the countries' political instability has reduced their attractiveness to foreign investors. The Andean Pact countries (presently Peru, Colombia, Ecuador, Bolivia and Venezuela) have backed off considerably from a rigorous enforcement of their Decision 24, which in theory was supposed to require all foreign investors to phase down their degree of ownership to a minority 49 percent position after fifteen years. Nigeria, with the Nigerian Enterprises Promotion Decree of 1972 (amended in 1977), tried to increase local ownership and promotion opportunities for its citizens in foreign-owned enterprises, although that country seems to have slipped back to a Stage II situation since oil prices declined in the early 1980s. In addition, the country has had a hard time absorbing all the new technology and production facilities it imported in the 1970s. Independently of the Andean Pact, Peru and Venezuela each tried to pursue rather nationalistic, anti foreign policies but have liberalized their treatment of foreign investors since the late 1970s.[14]

Stage III is important to study because, like the subsidized/protected infant industries of Stage II, it is an area in which a host government's policies can have a great influence on how successfully the country harnesses foreign investments to its own development needs. The government can make errors such as inappropriate incentives that steer investors into non-competitive endeavors, burdensome regulations that drive away foreign-owned businesses, or politically-motivated social goals that reduce productivity. Programs designed to encourage capital-intensive investments, higher-technology production processes or an increase in manufactured exports may push beyond what the economy can produce at competitive prices. The government may pressure foreign investors into hiring and promoting underqualified local citizens or into accepting local part ownership for political reasons in spite of the lack of sound economic justification. Foreign enterprises may perceive government efforts to achieve some of these goals as a shift in the regulatory philosophy or investment climate and thus as an increased political risk. Stage III is thus an area in which host governments may want to consider very carefully whether the benefits of their proposed policy initiatives may be outweighed by the costs.

An LDC may evolve towards Stage IV as its economy strengthens and diversifies to the point where it is able to rely more on market mechanisms and "correct" price signals to steer investments into the most socially productive areas. In this stage the need for incentives, subsidies, protection and so on to attract foreign capital and steer it into desired areas decreases. Multinationals now seek to come in because of the inherent attractions of the market and the productive capabilities of the economy. Paradoxically, the country may no longer need foreign investment as much as it did before because of its own self-reinforcing industrial growth. Foreign businesses now operate more at the margin, upgrading employment opportunities, supplying more advanced technologies and relying on their own competitive strengths to help them compete in the host environment. The diversity of foreign-participated projects multiplies, and the scale and technological sophistication expands in response to competitive forces.

The United States was a fairly good example of a "developing country" moving into Stage IV in the late 19th century. Japan in the 1920s and 1930s and Spain, Greece and Portugal in the 1960s would be other examples. Among the countries still generally considered underdeveloped today, Brazil has the natural and human resources and the record of growth to become a Stage IV possibility within this century. Argentina would be a good candidate if it could solve its foreign debt and political stability problems. Taiwan is too small to reach a high degree of self-sufficiency, but her record of political stability, effective policies and economic growth brings her perhaps closer than any other Third World country today to Stage IV. But for many other LDCs, Stage IV may represent an ideal unattainable for many years to come.

Stage V, in which investors from other countries come to the host country seeking conditions better than in their own home markets, would seldom apply to any underdeveloped nation. The conditions investors might seek, such as large and prosperous markets, leading-edge technology, and a safe haven for nervous capital, are most easily found in the US, Western Europe and Japan.

Some LDCs do not fit well into the schema at any stage, for a variety of reasons. A few countries have not been especially eager to admit foreign manufacturing or assembly plants on *any* terms, often from a distaste left over from their colonial histories, a fear of "economic imperialism," or a belief that such plants could seldom yield net positive benefits to their country. Burma, Guinea, and to a certain extent India have fit this description in the recent past.

Some countries follow different policies depending on the source of the investment. The Andean Pact members place stricter conditions on investments from the US than from other countries, while Korea has at times discriminated against Japanese multinationals. Some countries such as Cuba, Vietnam and Ethiopia have converted from a non-aligned political status to a close affiliation with the socialist bloc, and have been leery of foreign companies from the Western nations. At the opposite extreme Hong Kong has more-or-less thrown its doors wide open to the world economy and not pursued a very interventionist policy of any sort toward foreign investment.

Another problem with the schema is that the policy choices may be swamped or "dominated" by events beyond the control of the host government. The huge foreign debts facing Brazil, Mexico and numerous other LDCs in the early 1980s forced the governments of those countries to concentrate their efforts on paring back domestic expenditures, raising stopgap funding, renegotiating their debts and pursuing other measures for handling their financial crises. Political upheavals — coups, civil wars, occasionally even external wars—can play havoc with a country's efforts to attract investors and maximize its benefits from an investment inflow. Economic swings—a decline in the value of a country's commodity exports or a general recession— can damage a host country's prospects and lower its attractiveness to foreign companies. In cases like these a government may not be able to pursue an identifiable "policy" toward foreign investment at all; its efforts to correlate its policies to its level of attractiveness may be an exercise in futility and frustration.

Conclusions _____

The schema described here has some clear policy implications. For one thing, it suggests that a developing country cannot rely too heavily on foreign investors to speed up its rate of industrialization. If a country tries to extract "too much development" from incoming investment, the result will be the discouragement of many potential investors and perhaps an actual decrease in its rate of modernization. If an LDC tries to bring in more foreign businesses than its level of development is intrinsically capable of attracting, it will only be able to do so by providing elaborate incentives and subsidies. These incentives and subsidies will be costly to the country in one way or another: either through direct drains on the government treasury and/or foregone tax revenues, or through disguised subsidies such as inflated prices for protected local manufacturing outputs. In either case, the total true costs of the investments are likely to exceed whatever benefits they bring.

The schema also suggests, however, that countries having already made substantial progress toward building an industrial base and generating significant growth internally may actually plan a strategy of gradually increasing the demands they make on foreign investors. A number of LDCs do in fact seem to be pursuing such a strategy, among them Mexico, the wealthier Andean Pact countries, India, Nigeria (attempted, at least), and some of the newly industrializing countries of Southeast Asia. A government pursuing this type of development strategy would be acting on the implicit assumption that its planners and policymakers could obtain more benefits for their countries by active intervention than by allowing free market forces to operate. Most of the countries listed here do in fact have mixed economies, with a greater or lesser extent of government involvement in their economic processes. For these countries and others following similar strategies, the problem is to assess their level of attractiveness accurately and to be sure that their increasing demands do not outstrip their bargaining power.

Notes _____

Note: Starting with footnote 5, one to three references have been selected as illustrations for some of the countries mentioned in the text.

"IL&T" refers to *Investment, Licensing and Trading Conditions Abroad*, a series of country reports published by Business International Corp., New York.

1. For a discussion of the process and outcome of renegotiations and demands for changes in terms of investments in Zambia, Chile and Indonesia, see Stoever, William A., *Renegotiations in International Business Transactions* (Lexington, Mass.: Lexington Books, 1981).

2. For a further discussion of the benefits developing countries typically seek from foreign investors and of the policies they may employ towards such investors, see Stoever, William A., "Endowments, Priorities, and Policies: An Analytical Scheme for the Formulation of Developing

Country Policy toward Foreign Investment," *Columbia Journal of World Business*, Vol. 17, no. 3 (Fall 1982), pp. 3-15.

3. Rostow, W. W., "The Take-off into Self-Sustained Growth," *Economic Journal,* vol. 66 (March 1956), pp. 25-48; _____, *The Stages of Economic Growth* (Cambridge: Cambridge University Press, 1960); _____, ed., *The Economics of Take-off into Sustained Growth* (London: Macmillan, 1964).

4. For a lengthy critique of Rostow's schema and a discussion of some of his critics, see Higgins, Benjamin, *Economic Development: Problems, Principles and Policies* (New York: W. W. Norton, 1959 (revised edition), pp. 174-187.

5. A few selected references on Stage I countries could include: MacBean, Alasdair I., "Identifying the Least-Developed in the International Line-Up," *The World Economy*, Vol. 2, No. 1 (Jan. 1979), pp. 99-123; Pine, Art, "Africa's Poorest: Sub-Saharan Countries Take First Steps to End Economic Nightmare," *Wall Street Journal,* Sept. 16, 1982, p. 1; Grynspan, Devora, "Technology Licensing Patterns and Industrialization in LDCs: A Study of Licensing in Costa Rica," *International Organization,* Vol. 36, No. 4 (Autumn 1982), pp. 795-806; *IL&T:* CACM (Central American Common Market), July 1983; "Some Investment Opportunities within the Caribbean," by Michael Griffin, *Multinational Business* (*Economist* Intelligence Unit, London: 1983), No. 2, pp. 17-28.

6. General: Shapiro, Harvey D., "LDCs: Courting the Private Investor," *Institutional Investor*, Vol. 17 (Nov. 1983), pp. 81-83; Central American Common Market: Grynspan, *op. cit.;* Ecuador: Price Waterhouse, "Doing Business in Ecuador" (Feb. 1981); *IL&T: Ecuador* (Nov. 1983); Uruguay: *IL&T: Uruguay* (Nov. 1983); Morocco: Price Waterhouse, "Doing Business in Morocco" (Sept. 1980, with Supplement April 1983); Senegal: Price Waterhouse, "Doing Business in Senegal" (June 1982): Ghana (early years after independence): Killick, Tony, *Development Economics in Action: A Study of Economic Policies in Ghana* (New York: St. Martin's Press, 1978), especially Chapter 3: Angola: Neigus, David, "Angola: The Government Haig calls a 'Soviet Surrogate' is Signing Sweet Deals with Gulf, Boeing, Texaco and More," *Multinational Monitor*, Vol. 2 (Aug. 1981), pp. 12-15; *Africa Guide* (1982): "Angola," pp. 88-92; Kenya: *Africa Guide* (1982): "Kenya," pp. 177-194; Zambia (1960s): Stoever, William A., *Renegotiations . . . op. cit.,* Chapter 2 on Zambia.

7. Chile: Lahera, Eugenio, "The Transitional Corporations in the Chilean Economy," *CEPAL Review*, Aug. 1981 (United Nations Economic Com-

mission for Latin America); *IL&T*: Chile (May 1983); Nigeria (1970s): "Foreign Private Investment in Nigeria in 1975," *Central Bank of Nigeria Economic and Financial Review*, Vol. 17 (June 1979), pp. 14-25; India (1950s): Negandhi, Anant R., *Private Foreign Investment Climate in India* (East Lansing, Mich.: Michigan State University Press, 1965), esp. pp. 2-3, 91-92; Philippines: Infante, Jaime T., *The Political, Economic and Labor Climate in the Philippines* (Philadelphia: Industrial Research Unit, Wharton School, Univ. of Penn., 1980), esp. pp. 69-82, "Foreign Investment in the Philippines"; *IL&T*: Philippines (Feb. 1984).

8. Colombia: Lombard, Francois J., *The Foreign Investment Screening Process in LDCs: The Case of Colombia* (Boulder, Colo.: Westview Press, 1979): Argentina: Alschuler, Lawrence R., " The Struggle of Argentina within the New International Division of Labor," *Canadian Journal of Development Studies*, Vol. 1, No. 2 (1980), pp. 219-41; Turkey: Erdilek, Asim, *Direct Foreign Investment in Turkish Manufacturing* (Tubingen, Germany: J.C.B. Mohr (Paul Siebeck, 1982) (Kieler Studien No. 169); *IL&T*: Turkey (August 1983); Egypt: Gillespie, Kate, *The Tripartite Relationship: Government, Foreign Investors and Local Investors During Egypt's Economic Opening* (New York: Praeger, 1984); Elsaid, Hussein H., and El-Hennawi, M.S., "Foreign Investment in LDCs: Egypt," *Cal. Mgt. Rev.*, Vol. 24 (Summer 1982), pp. 85-91; Ignatius, David, "Curse of Cairo: Egyptian Bureaucracy Galls Both the Public and Foreign Investors," *Wall Street Journal*, March 24, 1983, p. 1+; Pakistan: Amjad, Rashid, *Private Industrial Investment In Pakistan, 1960-1970* (Cambridge, England: Cambridge Univ. Press, 1982); Awan, Muhammed Mahmood, *Foreign Capital and Development Process: The Pakistani Experience* (Washington, DC: University Press of America, 1977); *IL&T*: Pakistan (Dec. 1983); Thailand: *IL&T* : Thailand (Dec. 1983); Indonesia: Astbury, Sid, "Indonesia: Investors Beware!" (3 articles) *Asian Business*, Vol. 18 (Feb. 1982), pp. 18-22; *IL&T*: Indonesia (Aug. 1983); China (PRC): Sonoko, Nishitateno, "China's Special Economic Zones: Experimental Units for Economic Reform," *International and Comparative Law Quarterly* (4th series), Vol. 32 (Jan. 1983), pp. 175-185; Stepanek, James B., "Joint Ventures: Why US Firms Are Cautious [about investments in China]" *China Business Review*, Vol. 7 (July-Aug. 1980), pp. 32-33; Wu, F. W., "The Political Risk of Foreign Direct Investment in China: A Preliminary Assessment," *Management International Review*, Vol. 22, No. 1 (1982), pp. 13-25.

9. Taiwan (1960-70s): Ho, Samuel P.S., *Economic Development of Taiwan, 1860-1970* (New Haven and London: Economic Growth Center, Yale University Press, 1978); Schreiber, Jordan C., *US Corporate Investment in Taiwan* (New York: Dunellen, 1970); Korea: Westphal, Larry E.; Rhee, Yung W.; and Pursell, Gary, "Foreign Influences on Korean Industrial Development," *Oxford Bulletin of Economics and Statistics,* Vol. 44, No. 4 (Nov. 1979), pp. 359-388; Kim, Seung H., *Foreign Capital for Economic Development: A Korean Case Study* (New York: Praeger, 1970); Singapore: Hughes, Helen; and Seng, You Poh, eds., *Foreign Investment and Industrialization in Singapore,* (Madison, Wisc.: Univ. of Wisconsin Press, 1969); Malaysia: Young, Kevin; Bussink, Willem C.; and Hasan, Parvez, *Malaysia: Growth and Equity in a Multiracial Society* (Baltimore: published for the World Bank by Johns Hopkins University Press, 1980), especially Chapter 7, "Policies to Promote Industrial Development"; Sri Lanka: "Sri Lanka Will Need Help to Sustain Economic Growth," *Asian Business,* Vol. 17, No. 8 (August 1981), pp. 20-21+; Wijesekera, Nalin, "Sri Lanka Makes Headway Despite Difficulties," *Asian Business,* Vol. 19, No. 8 (Aug. 1983), pp. 16-21 +.

10. Erdilek, *op. cit.;* Hic, Mükerrem, "The Question of Foreign Private Capital in Turkey," *Orient* (Deutsches Orient-Institut), Vol. 21 (Sept. 1980), pp. 371-384.

11. Central American Common Market: Grynspan, *op. cit.*; Ghana: Kronholz, June, "Dark Continent: Ghana's Economic Skid Illustrates Bleak Spiral of Poverty in Africa," *Wall Street Journal,* Jan. 4, 1982, p. 1 +; Mufson, Steve, "End of a Dream: Once the Showpiece of Black Africa, Ghana Now Is Near Collapse," *Wall Street Journal*, Vol. 201 (March 28, 1983), p. 1 +; Iran: *IL&T:* Iran (Jan. 1982).

12. Ivory Coast: Masini, Jean, et al., *Multinationals and Development in Black Africa: A Case Study in the Ivory Coast* (Westmead, England: Saxon House, Teakfield, Ltd., 1979); den Tuinder, Bastiaan A., *Ivory Cost: The Challenge of Success* (Baltimore: published for the International Bank for Reconstruction and Development by Johns Hopkins University Press, 1978); Puerto Rico: Baver, Sherrie L., "Transnational Corporations, Public Policy, and Copper-Mining in Puerto Rico," *Interamerican Economic Affairs,* Vol. 36 (Winter 1982), pp. 53-77; *IL&T:* Puerto Rico (July 1983); Iran: *Business International*, "Operating in Iran: An Economy Coming of Age," (1978); Price Waterhouse, "Doing Business in Iran" (1975).

13. Singapore: "Singapore: Trying for a 'Second Industrial Revolution,'"
Business Week, May 25, 1981, pp. 75, 78; *IL&T: Singapore (May 1983);*
Rafferty, Kevin, "Is Singapore Pushing Too Hard?," Institutional Investor,
Vol. 16, No. 4 (April 1982), pp. 259-260, 266-267; Malaysia: Chopra,
Pran, "Malaysia Bids for Economic Growth Plus Social Change," *Asian*
Finance, Vol. 3, No. 4 (April 13, 1977), pp. 57-76; Klitgaard, Robert; and
Katz, Ruth, "Overcoming Ethnic Inequalities: Lessons from Malaysia,"
J. Policy Anal. and Mgt., Vol. 2, No. 3 (1983), pp. 333-349; Mahathir bin
Mohamad, "Economic Development in Malaysia and Policy towards
Foreign Investment," *UMBC* (United Malayan Banking Corp.) *Economic*
Review, Vol. 15, No. 1 (1979), pp. 2-7; "Malaysia: An Investors Chronicle
Survey," *Investors Chronicle and Financial World,* Vol. 58 (Oct. 16, 1980),
pp. i-xvi; Korea: Coolidge, T. Jefferson, Jr., "The Realities of Korean
Foreign Investment Policy," *Asian Affairs* (New York), Vol. 7 (July-Aug.
1980), pp. 370-385; Jeong, Gil-Sak, "Direct Foreign Investment in Korea,"
Korea Exchange Bank Monthly Review, Vol. 17 (Oct. 1983), pp. 1-12; Leh-
ner, Urban C., and Thrope, Norman, "Economic Enigma: South Korea
Provokes Both Hope and Gloom in Its Foreign Investors," *Wall Street*
Journal, Vol. 196 (Aug. 20, 1980), p. 1; India: Lall, Sanjaya, and Moham-
mad, Sharif, "Multinationals in Indian Big Business: Industrial
Characteristics of Foreign Investments in Heavily Regulated
Economies," *J. Development Economics,* Vol. 13, Nos. 1-2 (Aug.-Oct.
1983), pp. 143-155; Singh, Tarlok, *India's Development Experience* (New
York: St. Martin's Press, 1974), pp. 328-329; Mexico: Aviel, D., and Aviel,
J.B., "American Investments in Mexico," *Management International*
Review, Vol. 22, No. 1 (1982), pp. 83-96; Jacobsen, Mark P., "Mexico's
Computer Decree: The Problem of Performance Requirements and a US
Response," *Law and Policy in International Business,* Vol. 14, No. 4
(1983), pp. 1159-1195; *IL&T:* Mexico (April 1983); Looney, Robert E.,
Mexico's Economy: A Policy Analysis with Forecasts to 1990 (Boulder,
Colo.: Westview, 1978); Brazil: French, Jan Hoffman, "Brazil's Profit
Remittance Law: Reconciling Goals in Foreign Investments," *Law and*
Policy in International Business, Vol. 14, No. 2 (1982), pp. 399-451;
Robock, Stefan H., "Controlling Multinational Enterprises: The
Brazilian Experience," *Journal of Contemporary Business,* Vol. 6, No. 4
(Autumn 1977), pp. 53-71; Rowland, Walter S., "Foreign Investment in
Brazil: A Reconciliation of Perspectives," *Journal of International Law*
and Economics, Vol. 14, No. 1 (1979), pp. 39-63; See also LaPalombara,
Joseph, and Blank, Stephen, *Multinational Corporations and Developing*

Countries (New York: The Conference Board; Research Report No. 767, 1979) [a comparative study of foreign investment in Brazil, Malaysia and Nigeria].

14. Andean Pact: Grosse, Robert, "The Andean Foreign Investment Code's Impact on Multinational Enterprises," *Journal of International Business Studies*, Vol. 14, No. 3 (Winter 1983), pp. 121-134; Cherol, Rachelle L., and Del Arco, Jose Nunez, "Andean Multinational Enterprises: A New Approach to Multinational Investment in the Andean Group," *Journal of Common Market Studies,* Vol. 21, No. 4 (June 1983), pp. 409-428; Moxon, Richard W., "Harmonization of Foreign Investment Laws among Developing Countries: An Interpretation of the Andean Experience," *Journal of Common Market Studies*, Vol. 16, No. 1 (Sept. 1977), pp. 22-54; Nigeria: *Nigeria: A Country Study* (Washington: US Government Printing Office, 1982), pp. 139-186; "Exploring Opportunities in Nigeria," *Business America*, Vol. 4, No. 9 (May 4, 1981), pp. 2-5; Peru: Price Waterhouse, "Doing Business in Peru" (1979), pp. 11-20; *IL&T:* Peru (March 1983); "Foreign Economic Trends and their Implications for the United States: Peru," (pp. 10-12) (prepared by American Embassy, Lima) (Washington: US Dept. of Commerce, International Trade Administration, Jan. 1984); Venezuela: Truitt, Nancy, and Blake, David H., "Opinion Leaders and Private Investment" [a comparative study of Venezuelan and Chilean attitudes toward foreign investment], in Fayerweather, John, ed. *Host National Attitudes toward Multinational Corporations* (New York: Praeger, 1982); Radway, Robert J., and Hoet-Linares, Franklin T., "Venezuela Revisited: Foreign Investment, Technology and Related Issues," *Vanderbilt Journal of Transnational Law,* Vol. 15 (Winter 1982), pp. 1-45.

7. THE INTERNATIONAL DEBT CRISIS[*]
DEBT, CAPITAL FLOWS, AND LDC GROWTH

ANNE O. KRUEGER

World Bank and Duke University, Durham, NC 27706

Since 1982, newspaper headlines have called attention to the "debt crisis," or debt problem of the developing countries (LDCs). Initially, most analysts believed that debt-servicing problems would be temporary and that creditworthiness and more normal growth of most countries would be restored in a period of at most several years. However, events have demonstrated that this initial assessment was optimistic. This paper focuses on the debt problem and the reasons for its persistence. That in turn permits an analysis of the policy challenges that must be met for a resumption of LDC growth and a return to more normal capital flows.

Until the 1980's, virtually all analysts viewed capital flows the LDCs and the apparent shift from official to private flows as a healthy development. Capital flowing from rich countries with relatively low rates of return in investment and high savings rates to poor ones with higher rates of return on investment and lower savings rates was seen as an efficient allocation of world resources. These flows were thought to benefit all: certainly labor in poor countries would benefit and per capita incomes would rise more rapidly with capital inflows to poor countries than if investment were constrained by domestic savings rates.

Moreover, it was thought that with high real rates of return, capital flows would be self-financing: returns on investment would cover servicing obligations. An important question for policy is whether this basic view remains correct. While a full discussion of capital flows would consider their breakdown between debt and equity financing, that issue is secondary to analysis of the current situation and is ignored here.

Evolution of Capital Flows to LDCs

After World War II, the conscious push for development began when there were virtually no long-term private capital flows. Although the private international capital market revived in the late 1950's, for LDCs capital flows remained almost entirely official. This remained the rule in the 1960's with the notable exceptions

[*]*Discussants*: Manuel Guitian, International Monetary Fund; Armeane Choksi, World Bank.

Reprinted from *American Economic Review*, Vol. 77, No. 2, May, 1987, pp. 159-164 by permission of the publisher.

of a few dramatically successful countries. They sharply increased their rates of growth, and returns on investment, by moving to integrate their economies with the world economy, borrowing to supplement domestic savings and, in some cases, encouraging larger flows of direct foreign investment.

Observers of the progress of the LDCs regarded this development as a hopeful sign: it appeared that at low levels of income, there was an initial period during which infrastructure investments in transport, communication, education, and the like could not be financed on the private market but that, with continuing growth, development could readily proceed with reliance on private international capital markets.

After the oil price increase of 1973, most oil-importing LDCs had large current account deficits. Simultaneously, oil exporters had large current account surpluses, which were used at first to accumulate short-term liquid claims in large commercial banks in developed countries. Given the banks' favorable experience with their lending to the rapidly growing outer-oriented LDCs, it is not surprising that many LDCs could finance their current account deficits through the private banks.

While most LDCs borrowed, the underlying economic rationale differed widely among countries. In some instances, LDC current account deficits financed newly profitable high-return investments which were undertaken because the countries had increased incentives for production of tradables. Those countries quickly reduced current account deficits and resumed "normal" borrowing. Other countries borrowed primarily to maintain their preexisting patterns of consumption, investment, and government expenditures. Some of them even maintained pre-1973 energy prices while incurring large current account deficits. Some countries' failure to adjust was so extreme that they met debt-servicing problems in the latter half of the 1970's. There were debt crises and debt reschedulings, although normally not for more than a few in any year.

For many oil-importing LDCs, however, adjustment to the deterioration in their terms of trade was partial, and borrowing to sustain the rate of investment while consumption had increased was frequent. The world economic environment obscured any underlying problems. It will be recalled that the 1976-79 period was characterized by largely unanticipated worldwide inflation; until at least 1978, most lending was at fixed interest rates, and the resultant *ex post* real rate of interest was negative. Developing countries' nominal export earnings grew at average annual rates in excess of 15 percent, while the real value of outstanding debt was diminished by inflation. The result was that, despite significant new borrowing, the real value of debt outstanding in 1977 was below the level of 1972. As a percent of GNP, LDCs' debt did not start rising significantly until after 1977.

Thus, although oil-importing LDCs were borrowing large sums in the 1970's, many were borrowing to permit continuation of policies that could not have been sustained had real interest rates been realistic. The external environment in effect validated their policies. While some investments probably had relatively low rates of return, that was not a concern in an environment of negative real interest rates, except for countries where excesses were too great. Although it can be argued that a shift in worldwide conditions might have been anticipated, there was little in the aggregate statistics to suggest that the capital flows of 1973-78 were unsustainable, given worldwide inflation.

The Debt Problems of the Early 1980's

The shift in worldwide conditions in 1979-80 was as dramatic as that of 1973-74. Although the proportionate increase in the oil price was much smaller than in 1973, oil and energy were a much larger share of imports and expenditures. The initial response to the second oil price increase seemed to mirror the first. In the first year, worldwide inflation accelerated, oil-importing countries' current accounts swung sharply negative (or more negative), and recession set in.

But the similarity ended in 1980. First, whereas most countries at the time of the first oil price increase had sustainable current account positions and moderate levels of debt, this was not true at the time of the second. Moreover, economic activity in the industrial countries did not revive. Instead of adopting traditional Keynesian policies, the developed countries adopted anti-inflationary policy stances which resulted in a prolonged recession, reduced growth (shrinkage, by 1982) of world trade, declining commodity prices, and sharply higher nominal and real interest rates. The result was that developing countries' current account deficits rose from the $30-35 billion range of 1978-79 to $59 billion in 1980 and over $100 billion in 1981 and 1982. Oil-importing LDCs' current account deficits rose from 2.2 percent of GNP in 1978 to over 5 percent in 1981 and 1982.

The consequent increase in debt was staggering. Although many countries financed part of their deficits by reducing reserves and borrowing short term, long-term debt rose from $359 billion in 1979 to $552 billion in 1982. The increase in real debt was even more pronounced as export unit values were virtually stationary from 1980 to 1981 and fell by 6 percent in 1982. Thus, the ratio of debt to exports, which had stood at 1.51 in 1978 and 1.31 in 1980, rose to 1.88 by 1983.

Simultaneously, the real interest rate relative to export prices had risen from a negative 3-6 percent in the late 1970's to a positive 16-20 percent by 1982! With inflation, too, the fraction of debt subject to variable rates rose sharply. The result was an increase in interest payments from 4.6 percent of exports in 1978 to 8.1 percent in 1982 and 8.3 percent in 1983. Stated in another way: of the 1982 current account deficit of developing countries of $85.7 billion, $49.5 billion were in interest payments. These payments were a significant cause of new debt just at a time when high real interest rates meant that the debt level was too high and should probably be cut back.

By 1982-83, many developing countries found themselves unable voluntarily to continue servicing their debt. Everything contributed: exports were shrinking because of the worldwide recession; even for countries that shifted incentives strongly toward the production of tradables, there were lags in supply; it proved difficult to achieve deep enough cuts in imports simply because of time lags and the fact that adverse shifts in the terms of trade and shrinking world markets impelled such sharp reductions; higher interest rates on a greatly enlarged debt outstanding further intensified the problem.

Although worldwide conditions affected all countries, their policy history in the 1970's significantly affected their positions. It is ironic and instructive that Mexico, an oil exporter, was the first large and highly publicized country with a "debt crisis." In Mexico's case, highly expansionary macroeconomic policy had been financed through capital inflows that seemed warranted based on her rapidly rising oil exports. Nonetheless, that macroeconomic policy was unsustainable; there could be no reasonable doubt that Mexico's debt crisis was the result of domestic economic policies.

By contrast, Brazil had in 1981 undertaken a series of measures designed to increase incentives for the production of tradables, reduce excess demand in the domestic economy, and hence improve the current account balance. In Brazil's case, the worldwide recession meant that policy changes which would likely have been adequate for at least a few years under normal circumstances failed. For Brazil, inability to continue normal debt-servicing came in 1983.

There were many other combinations. Argentina, for example, entered the 1980's with a strong external position, little external debt, but with macroeconomic imbalances and a highly distorted trade regime. Highly expansionary macroeconomic policies in the early 1980's exacerbated these difficulties and Argentina would probably have confronted a debt-servicing crisis sometime in the first half of the 1980's even had worldwide conditions been normal. For Chile, a policy mistake (a rapidly appreciating real exchange rate which resulted in capital inflows equal to as much as 10.9 percent of GNP in 1981) was compounded by sharply deteriorating terms of trade for her major exports.

Some other countries maintained their debt-servicing obligations throughout the worldwide recession. Some, such as Korea, were in reasonable policy balance when the oil price rapidly rose, and undertook sharp policy adjustments which quickly restored external balance. Turkey was notable for having had highly expansionary monetary and fiscal stances in the 1970's, combined with a severely distorted trade regime and a panoply of controls on private economic activity. The Turkish debt crisis actually started before the second oil price increase, and culminated in a major policy reform program inaugurated in January 1980; Turkish economic performance improved greatly during the worldwide recession.

Other countries had yet different patterns: fiscal and monetary policies had been conservative in much of South Asia so that initial debt levels were very low, while trade policies had been so restrictive that these countries had largely insulated themselves from the world economy at the cost of their own growth; in most of Subsaharan Africa, pervasive controls and regulations on private economic activity, inefficient parastatals, severely overvalued exchange rates, and highly restrictive trade regimes had already extracted a high cost in the form of negative growth rates of per capita incomes in the 1970's; when the terms of trade deteriorated in the early 1980's, output and incomes fell sharply and maintenance of debt-servicing was infeasible.

Thus, the precise combination of internal and external circumstances that led to an inability to maintain voluntary debt-servicing varied from country to country and some countries avoided any interruption whatsoever. Many, however, did not.

Policy Response to Debt Crises _____

Almost always, an inability to maintain voluntary debt-servicing is also a "balance-of-payments crisis," because if borrowers were credit worthy, they could finance current account imbalances through short-term borrowing. Indeed, sizable run-ups of short-term debt are often the precursors of balance-of-payments crises, which occur when no more short-term or other credit is available.

For most of the LDCs, the size of the necessary macroeconomic adjustment in the early 1980's was very large: current accounts which had been in deficit by 3, 5, and even 10 percent of GNP net of interest payments had to shift to 0, 2, and 4 percent surpluses—shifts of as much of 10 percent for individual countries.

The first "emergency" necessary step involved stopping increases in debt by reducing macroeconomic imbalances; in the short run, this inevitably meant curtailing imports. This, in turn, meant either reduced income levels or heightened trade restrictions. As a longer-term measure, it was essential to increase incentives for production of exportables: most LDCs' trade regimes were already distorted in favor of import-competing production, and there was relatively little scope for efficient import substitution. To effect the economically desirable shift would have entailed both a significant change in the real exchange rate and reductions in levels of protection to imports, a necessary but often politically painful step. Note that import liberalization implied that the initial restriction of imports had later to be reversed.

As already mentioned, in 1982-83, it was thought that the debt problem would be relatively short-lived. Except for 1984, however, when falling debt-service ratios resulting from rapidly rising world exports and lower interest rates seemed to validate this forecast, developments have been less favorable than anticipated.

There have been a number of disquieting phenomena. First, despite the policy reforms undertaken and the current account shifts of some LDCs, debt-service ratios have risen. Second, with a very few conspicuous exceptions, growth rates of the heavily indebted countries have been very low. Third, a key assumption in earlier optimistic assessments had been that there could be rapid growth of LDCs' exports, and yet export growth in 1985 was relatively low and, worse yet, protectionist pressures against the exports of developing countries appeared to be increasing. Fourth, some of the LDCs that initially undertook policy reforms appeared to backslide as the political pressures arising from lower incomes and slow growth became irresistible, while simultaneously it became evident that some countries were unable to carry the needed reforms sufficiently far to alter the underlying policy problems that had led to problems in the first place. Finally, even those countries whose exports grew rapidly and whose policy reforms appeared adequate were not able to attract voluntary capital inflows: net flows in the aggregate continued falling, and much of the new lending that did take place was part of rescheduling activities, rather than a resumption of voluntary flows.

To a considerable degree, these five factors constitute a vicious circle: slow growth in the OECD is in part the result of protectionist pressures against the expansion of LDC exports which in turn are used as an argument in LDCs against the needed policy reforms; the failure of policy reforms to go far enough in some LDCs contributes both to their slow growth and to the failure of their exports to grow; that in turn results in the lenders' reluctance to expand voluntary lending which in turn makes it harder to undertake policy reforms and in some cases precludes the needed resources for investment in exportables. Breaking this vicious circle is the challenge for policy.

Prospects for LDC Growth and Resumption
of Voluntary Lending _____

There are some worldwide macroeconomic preconditions that must be met if the debt problems of the LDCs are to be resolved. Chief among them is that developed country markets remain open to the exports of those countries whose policy reforms have realigned incentives sufficiently to generate the needed supply response. It is self-evident that if the LDCs cannot in any event expand their export earnings at a rate sufficient to permit a gradual reduction of the debt-service ratio over time, there can be no satisfactory resolution to the current problems. However, it is on other aspects of the policy challenge that I wish to focus here.

Any analysis of the current situation must start with an appreciation of the necessity for sufficient policy reform, the ways in which the "debt overhang" can impede realization of the benefits, and the interrelationships between these two key aspects of the situation.

Debt-servicing obligations of a significant magnitude can raise two problems for a country. On one hand, there is the necessity to earn (or save) the foreign exchange for debt-service. On the other hand, especially when debt is public, there is a public finance problem, as the government must in one way or another raise the resources.

Earning the foreign exchange for debt-service requires the shifting of incentives toward the production of tradables, primarily exportables in most cases. When incentives are shifted, investible resources need to respond to expand capacity in new lines of activity. Shifting incentives typically entails measures that will increase private rewards to more accurately reflect social returns, and also policies to reduce the "crowding out" by the public sector.

For governments to raise the appropriate resources for debt service almost always entails exactly the opposite policy response: taxes must be raised, or expenditure lowered. While lowering some forms of expenditures, and reducing inefficiencies in the public sector, can and should be part of the longer-term realignment of incentives, in the short run, increasing taxes and/or diverting public resources away from infrastructure maintenance are almost always easier.

When debt-service obligations are high, increasing public resources to service debt will be likely to reduce incentives and resources available to the private sector sufficiently to preclude the necessary investment response. In countries where debt-service obligations have jumped by 4-6 percentage points of GNP while capital inflows have fallen 3-6 percent, in the absence of inflows domestic investment rates of only 10-12 percent of GNP will be feasible. In these circumstances, it can hardly be hoped that investment will be sufficient to increase the supply of exportables sufficiently for growth.

Therein lies the policy dilemma: for countries undertaking adequate policy reforms, additional external financing may have a very high rate of return. It is quite possible that countries having undertaken the necessary reforms may find themselves caught in a low-growth, high-debt-service trap: because capital inflows have diminished while debt-service obligations have increased, domestic savings available to finance new investment is low despite high rates of return on activities newly profitable after policy reform. Simultaneously, because of high debt-service ratios and slow growth, foreign financing for these newly profitable activities is not forthcoming. In these circumstances, exports cannot grow for lack of capacity expansion, debt-service ratios will remain high, and countries may therefore remain uncreditworthy.

Symptoms of such difficulties might be several, but high real interest rates well above international levels would be one of them. Another would be increased national savings rates (before debt servicing) combined with reduced rates of investment. Finally slow growth of capacity in tradables despite high profitability would be observed.

If this "debt overhang" trap were present, the clear policy implication would be that some degree of augmented official capital flows was temporarily warranted, and would have a very high real rate of return. However, the other clear policy implication is that these official flows would be unwarranted in the absence of sufficient policy reform: failure of a country sufficiently to realign its real exchange rate and liberalize its trade regime, to align its incentive structure in ways conducive to economic efficiency, or to control its public sector deficit sufficiently to permit the realization of growth and an improved current account position would render additional capital inflows no more warranted than some earlier borrowing had been.

The risk is that the resources available for truly well-founded policy packages will be inadequate, while other countries, having moved their policies in the right direction but not far enough, will increase their liabilities in ways that will prejudice the success of reform when it does finally occur. The challenge for policymakers and researchers is to determine "how much is enough" by way of policy reform, and to distinguish between cases in which a "debt overhang" phenomenon arises from cases where policy reforms have simply been inadequate to the task. Categorizing all indebted countries, regardless of the degree of policy reform, as being in the same category is clearly a policy mistake.

It is relatively simple to ascertain whether countries are undertaking reforms in the right direction; determining whether these reforms are "enough" is a very different matter, and one that requires the attention of the research and policy community.

8. SHARING THE BURDEN OF THE INTERNATIONAL DEBT CRISIS

STANLEY FISCHER

Department of Economics, MIT, Cambridge, MA 02139, and Research Associate, NBER.

Muddling through was the right strategy to handle the international debt crisis in 1982. Over the next four years, the debtor countries performed miracles on current account as they made massive interest payments amounting frequently to as much as 6 percent of GNP, with very little inflow of funds. But the price in terms of growth has been heavy, the debt problem continues to bedevil many of those countries, and the time for debt relief has arrived.[1]

The initial burden of the debt crisis was borne largely by the debtor countries. In addition, bank shareholders have paid the price of lower stock values for their assets. But because there has been no formal debt relief, debtor-country wage earners bear the burden of unnecessarily low real incomes. Formal debt relief will entail little further burden on bank shareholders, while substantially reducing the burden on wage earners in debtor countries. This should be possible without increasing burdens on taxpayers in the industrialized countries.

Background

There are two major debt crises—the crisis of Africa and that of Latin America and the Philippines. Although the African debt crisis is more serious in human terms, its implications for the financial system are less serious, and I do not discuss it further.

The debt crisis had three causes: imprudent macroeconomic management and borrowing by the debtor countries; imprudent lending by the commercial banks; and the increase in the *ex ante* real interest rate. The rise in the real interest rate to about 6 percent by 1982 increased the real interest burden on borrowers sixfold and completely changed the nature of the debt problem. With a real interest rate of 1 percent, growing out of a debt overhang was easy; with a 6 percent real interest rate, few countries could realistically hope that growth would easily reduce the debt burden without significant current account improvements.

Reprinted from *American Economic Review*, Vol. 77, No. 2, May 1987, pp. 165-170 by permission of the publisher.

It is unlikely that the possibility and effects of an interest rate shock of that magnitude were taken into account when the original loan agreements were entered into.[2] In the first instance, such an increase in the *ex ante* rate over a protracted period had not been seen previously. Second, it is likely that the significance of the shift from fixed to floating rate lending had not been absorbed. In past debt crises when loans were made at fixed interest, real interest rates would rise with deflation. But once the price level stabilized, the real interest burden would be higher only to the extent of the proportional decline in the price level. And it remained possible that inflation would reduce the burden in the future. In this crisis, the real interest rate has risen and stayed high for five years, and shows little sign of falling soon. Now inflation brings no automatic debt relief.

The initial response to the debt crisis in 1982 was to work out debt reschedulings with IMF approval certifying the debtors' macroeconomic policies. That was the appropriate strategy. Something—renewed world growth, a recovery of primary product prices, or a decline in the real interest rate — might turn up while the borrowers made much-needed changes in macroeconomic policy. With the rapid U.S. recovery in 1983-84 and the impressive turnarounds in trade account by the debtors, proponents found justification for their positions.[3] To be sure, the continued high real interest rate was a source of worry, but, in 1985, Gramm-Rudman-Hollings promised improvement on that front.

Developments in the debtor countries were less encouraging. There was indeed an extraordinary turnaround in trade account: in Brazil and Mexico an improvement of the order of 6-7 percent of GNP, compared with the worsening of the U.S. trade account of 3 percent of GNP that is proving so difficult to reverse. But the improvement in debtor country trade accounts was a result of import compression, through real devaluation and restrictive aggregate demand policies. Export volume had risen since 1980, but low dollar prices kept the dollar value of

Table 1
DEBT DATA, DEVELOPING COUNTRIES, WESTERN HEMISPHERE

	1978	1982	1986
Total ($b)	155.8	333.0	382.5
Debt/Exports (%)	217.0	273.1	333.1
Debt Service/Exports (%)	38.2	50.6	46.0
Debt/GNP (%)	31.8	43.5	47.0

Source: World Economic Outlook, International Monetary Fund, October 1986.
Note: Total debt outstanding for all capital-importing developing countries was $399b. in 1978, $763b. in 1982, and $973b. in 1986.

exports virtually unchanged. Investment fell by 5-7 percent of GNP between 1981 and 1985 for the major debtors.

Per capita real GNP was down, as much as 20 percent in some of the debtor countries.[4] The debt-to-exports ratio was not falling despite current account improvements and the rising volume of exports. More concretely, the burden of the debt took the form of transfers from the developing to the developed countries as capital inflows slowed. Whereas in 1981, Latin America and the Caribbean had a net inflow of resources of 2 percent of GNP, in 1984 and 1985 that area was transferring nearly 4 percent of GNP abroad.[5]

The Role of the Banks

By 1984 the commercial banks had become battle weary. Interest receipts from debtor countries exceeded new loans in 1984, 1985, and 1986. The U.S. banks actually reduced their exposure in Latin America in 1985. The banks, the main beneficiaries of the efforts of the IMF and the U.S. authorities' attempts to maintain continued debt servicing, participated in IMF packages with increasing reluctance. The Baker Plan in October 1985 spelled out the conditions for continuing cooperation among the U.S. government, the multilateral lending institutions, and the banks, but still did not succeed in bringing new commercial bank financing of even the modest proportions included in the plan into the developing countries.

Fear of financial collapse in the United States was one of the main motivations for the original approach to the debt crisis. In 1982, the nine large money center banks had over 250 percent of their capital in loans to LDCs; the proportion for all U.S. banks taken together was above 150 percent. By mid-1986, the nine money center banks had sufficient equity and reserves to withstand even the complete loss of Latin American assets (Table 2). The European and Japanese banks, which built up loan loss reserves more rapidly, were even better placed than U.S. banks to withstand losses on LDC debt.

Although banks have increased their loss provisions, they continue to carry LDC debt at face value. The active market in such debt prices it at a significant discount. Sample prices are listed in Table 3. Equity values for the banks are consistent with the prices of debt in the secondary market.[6]

Proposed Solutions

Reform proposals can be distinguished according to whether they propose extending the effective maturity of the debt, changing the nature of claims on the LDCs,

Table 2
U.S. BANK EXPOSURE TO DEVELOPING COUNTRIES (JUNE 1986)

	Nine money center banks	All U.S. banks
To LDCs:		
$b	73.9	112.1
% of Capital	167.2	101.3
% of Assets	11.7	7.3
To Latin America and Caribbean:		
$b	43.2	68.2
% of Capital	97.7	61.6
% of Assets	6.9	4.4

Source: Federal Reserve Board of Governors, Statistical Release E16 (126), October 17, 1986. "Capital" consists of equity, subordinated debentures, and reserves for loan losses.

whether they offer genuine debt relief, and what sort of conditionality they impose (Paul Krugman).

The present strategy and the Baker Plan both deal with the debt crisis by extending the effective maturity of the debt. Interest capitalization would do the same. Any method that reduces the current flow of resources from the debtor countries will help them grow in the short run. But further lending promises little in the way of a lasting solution to the debt problem. So long as real interest rates remain around 6 percent, debtor countries will have great difficulty growing out of their debt problem.

Debt-equity swaps, increased direct investment, proposals to sell shares in the export earnings of the debtors, and indexation of payments to export prices, would all change the form of the debt. None necessarily changes the present value of the debt, though their risk characteristics may make these forms of debt more attractive to the debtors. The recent Mexican agreement takes the IMF part way down the road of providing cash flows that respond to the risks facing the developing countries.

The debt crisis has made it entirely clear that floating rate debt is a poor way of financing a country's development. Innovative methods of financing all give promise that international capital flows can resume without producing the danger of another debt crisis. However, they are being introduced too slowly to resolve the current crisis.

Conditionality is explicit in the Baker Plan and in the present strategy. As IMF conditionality has progressed over the past four years to the sophistication of

Table 3
SECONDARY MARKET LDC DEBT PRICES,
NOVEMBER 14, 1986 (CENTS/$)

Country	Price	Country	Price
Argentina	65.7	Mexico	57.2
Bolivia	7.5	Philippines	73.0
Brazil	75.5	Turkey	98.3
Chile	68.0	Venezuela	74.5

Source: Salomon Brothers, Inc.
Note: Price is average of bid and offer prices.

the recent Mexican package, it has become a viable means of providing useful external constrains on domestic policymakers. Conditionality will be needed if debt relief is granted, both to ensure that the relief is not wasted, and to prevent relief being an entirely pleasant experience.

Debt Relief

There are now two choices. Either the piecemeal approach continues, or there is some form of debt relief. The current approach is certainly more imaginative—provided the Mexican package is not the last of its kind—than that of 1982. But the banks are increasingly reluctant to participate.

The argument that the slow approach is the right one points to the successes of the last four years—there was no financial collapse in the United States, there has been no explicit debt default, Latin America is moving towards instead of away from democracy. Maybe something will still come up; perhaps a U.S. tax increase that takes the real interest rate down by 2-3 percent, perhaps an improvement in the trade climate, perhaps a growth recovery.

Perhaps liberalization of debtor economies will solve the debt problem, as increasing confidence draws flight capital home. High interest rates might attract flight capital home, just as they may entice other capital from abroad. But the interest rates needed to bring home flight capital will not restore investment. Indeed, the notion that flight capital should come home is not consistent with general liberalization, for it is very likely that optimally diversified portfolios for residents of developing countries contain more industrialized country assets than they do at present—even including flight capital. Liberalization is likely to lead to more, not less, capital flight.

The case for debt relief is not that the present evolution cannot continue, but that it should not continue. For four years, the debtor countries have paid the price of low GNP growth and significant falls in real wages as they have made transfers to service the debt. Protectionist pressures in the industrialized countries have made the transfer more difficult. The transfers have been made at a real interest rate that was almost certainly not envisaged when the debt was incurred.

Economic theory has little to say about the appropriate procedures to follow when unanticipated events happen.[7] Formally, the loan contracts do not give the borrower the right to reopen negotiations, nor is there any procedure for establishing whether a particular set of circumstances might reasonably have been anticipated when the contracts were entered into.

Presumably any potentially Pareto-improving changes in debt contracts have already been made. What remains are changes that improve the lot of one party to the contract at the expense of the other. Thomas Walde notes that there is a strong legal presumption in favor of lenders, who gave up real resources in exchange for promises. The IMF and developed country governments have certainly taken the attitude that the debt contracts should continue to be honored, no matter what the burden on the borrowers.

One argument for maintaining current debt contracts is distributional—that the lenders deserve to receive the payments due them. That is a hard argument to support in the present crisis. The lenders had no reason to expect such payments, they too made mistakes, and they are not obviously more deserving than the borrowers. Further, the borrowers have paid a high price for whatever mistakes they made in the past.

The market, reflected in Table 3, has already concluded that the lenders will not receive their claims in full. Shareholders have taken their losses. But the lenders hang on to their claims in the hope of capital gains in the event the borrowers pay in full. Millions of residents of developing countries are being kept at low levels of income for the sake of possible capital gains for bank shareholders. There is no distributional case for the current debt strategy. There is a strong distributional case for debt relief.

Even so, there might be an efficiency argument against relief. It has been contended from the beginning of the debt crisis that only by maintaining existing debts can the existing international capital markets be maintained. It is impossible to be sure, but the evidence from history is strong that default or relief is not the end of the capital markets. Indeed, debt relief that promises to put an end to the uncertainty of the current situation would likely promote future capital flows —albeit, and to the good, in forms other than floating rate debt. It is difficult indeed to believe that international capital will fail to flow to a country offering good rates of return.

Moral hazard is another argument against debt relief. Why grant relief to the badly behaved when the well-behaved, such as Turkey, have made a more serious and successful effort to adjust? Isn't this an invitation to countries in trouble in the future to default? The answers here are simple. No country will get debt relief in the future without going through a protracted period of uncertainty and adjustment. What borrower will in the future become overextended to have the privilege of following in the footsteps of an Argentina or Mexico or Brazil over the past four years? Further, the proposal is for debt relief administered from the center, not for default by the borrowers.

What form should relief take? Relief should only be available in the context of structural adjustment programs adopted by the countries in cooperation with the IMF and, depending on how rapidly it adapts, the World Bank. There would be no general forgiveness of debt, rather in each new negotiation interest and principal payments to commercial lenders would be reduced to 65 percent of the contractual value contingent on a structural adjustment program being agreed with the IMF. If the commercial lenders found such terms inappropriate, they would forego the help of the IMF and their governments in extracting resources from the debtors, and negotiate on their own.

The IMF agreements would be for comprehensive growth-oriented adjustment programs, encouraging investment in both government and private sectors. Other desirable structural adjustments, along the lines of freeing up markets and privatization of sectors that have no inherent government connection, such as nightclubs, hotels, and grocery chains, could be included. So too would the opening up of the economy to imports, and the removal of standard developing country distortions in the form of subsidies.

What would such a scheme cost? The total outstanding debt to financial institutions and other private creditors of all countries with recent debt-servicing difficulties was $336 billion in 1986. Interest payments on this amount appear to be about $28 billion.[8] The annual reduction in the interest bill would be close to $10 billion. For example, Brazil and Mexico would save about $2.5 billion annually, the Philippines and Chile about $600 million. The numbers are between 1 and 3 percent of GNP, enough to make a difference, but not enough to let the debtor countries off the hook entirely.

What would be the consequences for the banks? They would take a loss, but there should be no mass bankruptcies. The losses would be recorded gradually as countries negotiated agreements with the IMF, rather than on announcement of the plan.

Without debt relief, the debt crisis promises to drag on for decades, slowing growth in the developing countries, sapping the energies of policymakers, and tieing up the multilateral lending agencies in endless crisis negotiations. With sensible debt relief, countries and the multilateral institutions can begin to worry about growth-oriented development policies. If the debt relief does not come by agreement, then debtor countries would have to consider taking the first step.

References

Cline, W. R., *International Debt*, Washington: Institute for International Economics, 1984.

Dornbusch, R., "The Debt Problem and Some Solutions," mimeo., Department of Economics, MIT, November 1986.

Krugman, P., "Prospects for International Debt Reform," report to the Group of Twenty Four prepared for UNCTAD, January 1986.

Sachs, J., "The Current Account and Macroeconomic Adjustment in the 1970s," *Brookings Papers on Economic Activity*, 1:1981, 201-68.

_____ , "Managing the LDC Debt Crisis," *Brookings Papers on Economic Activity*, 2:1986, 397-431.

_____ and Kyle, S., "Developing Country Debt and the Market Value of Large Commercial Banks," NBER Working paper No 1470, 1984.

Solomon, R., "A Perspective on the Debt of Developing Countries," *Brookings Papers on Economic Activity*, 2:1977, 479-502.

_____ , "The Debt of Developing Countries: Another Look," *Brookings Papers on Economic Activity*, 2:1981, 593-606.

Walde, T., "Sanctity of Debt and Insolvent Countries, Defenses of Debtors in International Loan Agreements," mimeo., UN, New York, May 1986.

Notes

1. Rudiger Dornbusch (1986) and Paul Krugman (1986) both discuss the case for debt relief, as does Jeffrey Sachs (1986).

2. The *Brookings Papers on Economic Activity (BPEA)*, representative of thinking by well-informed economists, contains only three papers on the international debt between 1977 and 1982. Robert Solomon (1977) contains no suggestion that future interest rate developments might affect the stability of the debt. In the discussion following the paper, the real interest rate receives mention only in the last sentence. In papers in 1981, Solomon and Sachs mention that the debt problem could become

serious if the real interest rate failed to come down—but place no emphasis on this possibility.

3. The best-known scenario is that of William Cline (1984).

4. Argentina and Venezuela suffered the largest income declines.

5. The net transfer is calculated as the current account deficit (representing net capital inflows) minus net investment income, both taken from *World Economic Outlook* (October 1986, p.77).

6. In a study based on 1983 data, Sachs and Steven Kyle (1984) suggested Latin debt was then being carried at about 80 cents on the dollar.

7. Thomas Walde (1986) discusses legal precedents in domestic and international agreements, including force majeure and change of circumstances. The most relevant cases appear to be the Westinghouse and Alcoa vs. Essex cases where price shocks resulted in courts excusing nonperformance.

8. Based on data in *World Economic Outlook*, October 1986.

IV ____ THE GLOBAL LABOR POLICIES: THE FLOW OF PEOPLE _____

9. GROWTH WITH UNEMPLOYMENT: THE PARADOX OF THE EUROPEAN RECOVERY

BRIAN V. MULLANEY

Brian Mullaney is an International Economist at Morgan Stanley & Co. Incorporated. This article first appeared as a Special International Study by Morgan Stanley's Economics Department.

In contrast to the strong employment results in the United States during the current recovery, unemployment remains a serious problem in Europe. The source of the problem is structural in nature, and therefore cannot be remedied through fiscal expansion, as some have suggested. The solution lies primarily in reducing European labor market rigidities, slowing the growth in unit labor costs, and improving competitiveness through industrial restructuring.

Since the 1981 to 1982 recession, the most severe in the post-World War II period, the US economy has staged a remarkable recovery, perhaps the most outstanding aspect of which has been the record-setting pace of job creation. Since hitting bottom during 1982, total employment has grown at a 3% annual rate, and 9 million new jobs have been created. In addition, the US unemployment rate has fallen from its high of 10.7% in 1982 to 7.1% in 1985. Job growth in Canada has also been rapid, with both countries now employing more workers than before the recession.

The record of employment growth in the US and Canada, however, contrasts sharply with that of Western Europe. The European economies, depending on the country, have now experienced between two and four years of post-recession growth; yet, as recent labor market data show in Tables 1 and 2, unemployment has continued to rise, with the aggregate jobless rate increasing from 9.3% in 1982 to 11% in 1985. In addition, total employment has actually fallen during the present recovery period. And, in order to reduce European joblessness to the 1979 level by the end of the decade, over 2 million jobs per year—or 5,800 per day—will need to be created even if the labor force fails to grow.

Reprinted from *Columbia Journal of World Business,* Winter, 1986, pp. 21-26 by permission of the publisher.

Fiscal Policy and Cyclical Employment Growth _____

Why does the enormous disparity in employment growth between North America and Europe exist? An initial reason is that the strength of the cyclical recovery in these two areas has varied considerably. Since 1982, the US and Canada have expanded vigorously at more than a 4.5% pace annually, while Europe has experienced an average growth rate of only 2% to 2.5% during the current business cycle. This differential can, in part, be explained by the divergence in the fiscal policies pursued in these two regions. Both the US and Canada have followed a very expansionary course, while Europe has generally opted for fiscal restraint, resulting in slow growth in domestic demand which has constrained employment expansion.

Tight fiscal policies and sluggish economic growth, however, explain only part of the difficulty. More important causes exist, namely structural problems centering around the functioning of European labor and product markets and the industrial reorganization currently taking place in Europe. Both of these developments have tended to reduce the responsiveness of employment growth to fluctuations in output.

Economic Growth and Unemployment _____

The existence of structural problems in the European labor and product markets can be shown by examining how fluctuations in economic growth impact changes

Table 1
UNEMPLOYMENT RATES

	1970	1980	1981	1982	1983	1984	1985
OECD Europe	3.0	6.2	8.0	9.3	10.3	10.8	11.0
Germany	0.8	3.0	4.4	6.1	8.0	8.6	8.7
France	2.4	6.4	7.8	8.7	8.9	10.0	10.1
UK	3.1	6.8	10.5	12.1	12.9	13.1	13.5
Italy	5.3	7.5	8.3	9.0	9.8	10.2	10.3
Spain	2.4	11.2	14.0	15.9	17.4	20.1	21.5
US	4.8	7.0	7.5	9.5	9.5	7.4	7.2
Canada	5.6	7.4	7.5	10.9	11.8	11.2	10.7

Source: US Labor Department, Organization for Economic Cooperation and Development, and Data Resources, Inc.

Table 2
TOTAL EMPLOYMENT GROWTH
(PERCENT CHANGE)

	1981	1982	1983	1984	1985
Germany	−0.7	−1.7	−1.5	0.1	0.7
France	−0.6	0.3	−0.6	−1.1	−0.5
UK	−0.4	−1.9	−0.6	1.5	1.2
Italy	0.2	−0.3	0.3	0.3	0.5
Spain	−3.2	−1.3	−0.7	−2.9	−1.7
Sweden	−0.2	−0.1	0.1	0.7	1.1
OECD Europe	−1.0	−0.7	−0.8	−0.1	0.2
US	1.1	−0.9	1.3	4.1	2.4
Canada	2.8	−3.3	0.9	2.5	2.7

Source: US Labor Department and Organization for Economic Cooperation and Development

in the rate of unemployment. The relationship between these two variables was initially analyzed by Arthur Okun in the context of the US labor markets.[1] Okun defined a concept called the "GNP gap" as the difference between a country's underlying economic growth potential and its actual growth performance. He went on to show that a highly stable, positive relationship exists between the divergence in potential and actual economic growth and changes in the unemployment rate. This relationship is expressed as a coefficient which measures the percent amount by which the unemployment rate will fall in a year if actual GNP growth exceeds potential by 1%.

Table 3 compares the Okun coefficients for North America and several European nations. Coefficients for the US and Canada are about 0.4, implying that for both of these countries, the actual growth rate of GNP will need to exceed the potential rate by 1% in order to reduce the unemployment rate by 0.4% in a year. As Table 3 shows, actual growth rates for the US and Canada have been well in excess of their potential rates during the current business cycle, thus accounting for the recent declines in unemployment in North America. Further, the divergence between actual and potential GNP growth has historically accounted for most of the change in the jobless rate for these two countries.[2]

Coefficients for European nations, on the other hand, are considerably lower than those for the US and Canada. This implies, for example, that economic

Table 3
EXPLANATION OF UNEMPLOYMENT CHANGES DURING THE CURRENT
BUSINESS CYCLE USING OKUN'S LAW

	(1) Okun coefficient	(2) R2	(3) Actual GNP growth (Annual)	(4) Potential GNP growth	(5) Actual change in unemploy- ment rate	(6) Projected change in unemploy- ment rate
US	0.40	0.83	4.5	2.2	−3.4	−3.2
Canada	0.38	0.66	5.5	2.9	−3.2	−2.7
UK	0.21	0.24	2.9	1.9	+2.0	−0.8
France	0.18	0.42	1.5	2.8	+1.1	+0.6
Italy	0.06	0.08	2.6	2.6	+0.3	0.0
Germany	0.28	0.65	2.5	2.5	+1.2	0.0
Spain	0.26	0.35	2.4	2.9	+5.8	+0.4
Belgium	0.28	0.29	1.1	2.3	+2.2	+0.8

Source: Actual data are from the Organization for Economic Cooperation and Development and the US Department of Labor. Coefficients and potential growth rates are Morgan Stanley estimates.

growth which is 1% in excess of its potential would reduce the unemployment rate in a year by only 0.28% in Germany. Likewise, if British growth were to exceed its potential by 1%, unemployment would fall only 0.21%, and so on. This suggests that European economic growth must exceed potential growth by a greater amount than what the US and Canada must achieve in order to reduce unemployment by a similar magnitude. These lower coefficients also indicate, however, that employment growth is less sensitive to the business cycle in Europe than in the US, signifying that factors are at work which inhibit labor from responding normally to economic expansions.

Labor Market Distortions and Low Okun Coefficients _____

Why is employment less responsive to economic growth in Europe than in the United States? One reason for this is the high degree of inflexibility in the European labor markets. Restrictive labor laws and union pressures make laying off workers during cyclical downturns exceedingly difficult. Employment thus remains relatively stable, and during recessions productivity falls rapidly. The inability to reduce staff during contractions prevents firms from recouping profit margins, typically a prerequisite for an economic expansion. As a result, companies are unwilling to increase employment during recoveries that are perceived as being only temporary.

For example, the present recovery in Europe was led by rapid export growth resulting from depressed currency levels and the strong US expansion. European producers, however, did not behave as if they believed that this was a sustainable situation; so, employment did not increase during this upturn. In contrast, North American labor markets are far more fluid, and unemployment is much more responsive to the business cycle. Although an increased number of people are laid off during recessions, the turnover of the unemployed is rapid, and long-term joblessness is low relative to that of Europe. In addition, during expansions employment growth in the US and Canada is typically robust.

Another example of labor market rigidity is the low degree of geographic mobility among workers in Europe. This immobility hinders the efficient allocation of labor, thus preventing workers from taking advantage of new economic opportunities. Therefore, very severe economic downturns are needed to induce people to relocate and seek new employment. Labor immobility, coupled with rigid regulations regarding hiring and firing, results in reduced labor turnover (longer periods of time spent in the same job). In the US, on the other hand, job turnover is very rapid—93% of workers have been in their present job less than five years, compared with 55% in France, 74% in Germany, 70% in Italy, and 72% in the UK.

Unemployment compensation, comparatively more generous in Europe than in North America, is also a factor. For example, replacement ratios—the average unemployment benefit as a percent of the gross income of a typical production worker—are higher in most European countries than in the United States. Belgium's and France's ratios are four times greater than the American ratio, Germany's and Sweden's are three times larger, and the UK's is 30% higher.

Not only are unemployment benefits more generous in Europe, but their duration tends to be longer. For instance, the replacement ratio for an average unemployed family (a married couple with two children and one-income earner) in the UK remains above 60% for two years, while in the US benefits extend for only six months. Because of this, the average period of time that a worker is unemployed is longer in Europe than in the US. This contributes to higher unemployment. An increased wage level is needed to induce the jobless to accept new positions.[3]

Wage Growth and Unemployment

The most significant contributor to European labor market inflexibility is the rapid wage growth which has emanated from rigid pay-setting practices. Throughout the 1970s, European inflation-adjusted (real) wage growth rose very quickly compared to that of the US and, most importantly, relative to European productivity improvements (Table 4). Consequently, higher unit costs in the manufacturing sector made European goods increasingly uncompetitive in world markets. Further, since wage hikes were larger than what were warranted by productivity gains, labor became less attractive as a factor of production, causing employers to seek ways through which they could reduce their reliance on this resource in the production process. As a result, job growth in Europe has been stagnant for several years, with total employment currently at approximately the 1973 level.

The effects of excessive wage growth are not quickly remedied, and Europe is still bearing the consequences of the rapid wage growth experienced during the 1970s. In order to restore unit costs to their prior levels and to make labor a more attractive input in production, productivity gains will have to be higher than real wage increases for several years. The performance along these lines has been quite good so far in the 1980s (Table 4)—a trend that, if continued, will provide a setting for more rapid job creation.

Table 4
COMPARISON OF REAL WAGE AND PRODUCTIVITY
GROWTH IN MANUFACTURING

	Real hourly compensation (% change)		Output per hour (% change)	
	Avg. annual 1970-79	Avg. annual 1980-84	Avg. annual 1970-79	Avg. annual 1980-84
US	0.0	1.7	2.6	2.6
UK	5.8	1.7	3.1	3.8
France	6.0	2.6	5.3	4.1
Germany	6.1	1.1	4.5	2.6
Italy	7.8	1.7	4.8	4.0
Netherlands	6.4	0.1[*]	6.9	3.9+
Sweden	4.9	−0.3	3.6	4.0

Source: Department of Labor, Bureau of Labor Statistics
[*] Through 1983.

It is important to recognize, however, that much of this recent improvement in output per worker in Europe has resulted from cyclical factors and especially from the shedding of a huge amount of low productivity industrial labor (which has not been employed elsewhere). For example, in the United Kingdom manufacturing productivity has risen 23% since 1980 as a result of a 20% decline in employment (while total output has essentially remained the same). Yet, although the European manufacturing sector is experiencing a strong resurgence in productivity, it is, indeed, questionable whether these improvements can be sustained without having alternative employment opportunities available to those who have been laid off as a result of labor-shedding practices. In addition, unit cost reductions, resulting from the use of labor-saving technologies, can enhance a country's competitive position, but will not create jobs during periods of economic expansion.

Resource Allocation and Okun Coefficients _____

In addition to labor market distortions, policies creating inefficiencies in the product markets weaken the relationship between employment and economic growth, thus leading to lower Okun coefficients. Failing enterprises are supported to a far greater extent in Europe than in the US. In 1983, business subsidies as a percent of GNP in the major European economies were between 3.5 and 7 times the level in the US. Trade protectionism in the agricultural and service sectors is also more widely practiced in Europe than in America.

Aiding declining businesses and industries, either through subsidies or protectionism, leads to a poor allocation of all resources, including labor, and tends to make structural adjustment more protracted. These enterprises are inclined not to be employment-generating during cyclical upturns. Additionally, this support prevents the labor-shedding required during cyclical downturns which would help reallocate workers to the more productive sectors where a country's comparative advantage lies. Moreover, protectionism, by insulating firms from low-cost foreign competition, reduces incentives to decrease expenses, and the high cost structures further worsen the competitive position of these companies.

Rigid domestic capital markets also cause similar allocation inefficiencies in that they inhibit the distribution of funds to the sectors in which Europe maintains a comparative advantage.

Yet, do labor and product market distortions complete our explanation of the disparity in employment trends in Europe and North America? Columns 3 and 4 of Table 3 indicate that in most of Europe, economic growth relative to potential was too slow to prevent a rise in the jobless rate (UK was an exception). Yet,

Columns 5 and 6 show that the actual increases in European unemployment rates exceed those projected using Okun's law, signifying that employment growth is also being affected by other factors. In the UK for example, the rate of economic growth was rapid enough to reduce unemployment; however, a drop in joblessness did not occur—in fact, British unemployment has increased dramatically during the current business cycle.

Industrial Restructuring and Employment Growth _____

Over the past several decades, Europe, like the US, has undergone significant structural shifts in output and employment, moving from an agricultural to an industrial and then to a service-oriented economy. These shifts, however, have been more pronounced in Europe than in the United States, as shown in Table 5. Employment in agriculture has been declining consistently, especially in Spain, Italy, and France. On the other hand, the service sector, over the past 20 years, has been the most dynamic segment of the labor market, a consistent producer of jobs for the European economies.

However, the most important development in recent years has been the restructuring of the European manufacturing sector and the demise of industrial employment. Although jobs in this sector have been declining for a decade, the pace of the decrease accelerated markedly during the recession—a trend that has continued into the present recovery (Table 6). This industrial rationalization is

Table 5
STRUCTURAL CHANGE AND THE SECTIONAL DISTRIBUTION OF EMPLOYMENT
(PERCENT OF TOTAL EMPLOYMENT)

	Agriculture			Industry			Services		
	1965	1974	1984	1965	1974	1984	1965	1974	1984
US	6.3	4.1	3.3	32.8	32.4	28.5	60.9	63.4	68.2
UK	3.8	4.2	3.3	46.5	42.2	32.9	49.6	55.0	64.5
Germany	10.9	7.1	5.6	48.4	46.7	41.3	40.7	46.2	53.1
France	17.8	10.7	7.9	39.1	39.4	33.0	43.1	50.0	59.1
Italy	26.3	17.5	11.9	37.0	39.3	34.5	36.8	43.2	53.6
Sweden	11.3	6.7	5.1	42.8	37.0	29.8	45.9	56.3	65.1
Spain	30.9	23.1	18.0	34.2	37.8	32.7	34.9	39.9	49.3

Source: Data Resources, Inc., and Organization for Economic Cooperation and Development.

long overdue, but the restructuring of the economy has been exceedingly rapid, and is inflicting substantial costs on the labor market.

The direct consequences of industrial rationalization have been staggering. Table 7 displays data for only five European countries (UK, France, Germany, Italy, and Spain); but in these nations alone, the decline in industrial employment has averaged 1.3 million jobs each year since the end of the 1970s. Labor-shedding and economic adjustment of this sort are beneficial if an economy is flexible and dynamic enough to absorb the displaced workers in other segments of the labor force. During the 1960s and 1970s in Europe, these workers found positions primarily in the rapidly expanding service sector. However, given the massive size of recent labor displacements, the modest growth in this sector during the 1980s has not been adequate to prevent an increase in overall unemployment.

Two important indirect effects of industrial restructuring have contributed to the sluggish job growth in the service sector. First, the deep cuts in industrial employment have restrained the expansion of personal incomes which in turn has resulted in reduced private consumption of services. As a consequence, the rate of service sector employment growth has dropped sharply from 2.3% in the early 1970s to 1.3% during the early 1980s.

In line with this is the decline in income resulting from tight fiscal policies. Social and personal services (health care, educational, and governmental) account for about 50% of service sector output. However, the income loss due to restrictive policies and declines in transfer payments has reduced the demand for these ser-

Table 6
EMPLOYMENT GROWTH BY SECTOR
(PERCENT CHANGE)

	Agriculture					Industry					Services				
	1981	1982	1983	1984	1985	1981	1982	1983	1984	1985	1981	1982	1983	1984	1985
Germany	−2.0	−0.9	−0.3	−0.1	0.2	−2.2	−3.6	−3.4	−0.9	−0.3	0.7	−0.2	−0.1	1.0	1.5
France	−3.5	−3.0	−2.3	−2.2	NA	−2.5	−1.6	−2.6	−3.3	NA	1.2	1.7	1.1	0.5	NA
UK	−1.7	0.0	−1.1	−0.8	−1.2	−8.7	−4.9	−4.3	−0.8	−0.7	−1.1	0.0	0.4	3.0	2.2
Italy	−5.8	−7.7	0.2	−4.0	−5.9	−0.7	−1.6	−2.3	−4.2	−2.5	2.7	2.7	2.2	4.5	4.0
Spain	−6.3	0.1	−2.2	−4.3	−1.6	−5.1	−4.2	−1.8	−5.0	−4.7	0.4	2.0	0.7	−1.0	0.2
Sweden	0.0	−0.4	−2.5	−5.2	−4.7	−2.9	−3.5	−1.1	0.4	0.9	1.3	1.5	0.9	1.4	1.0
US	−0.3	1.4	−0.8	−2.0	−2.6	−0.4	−6.4	0.0	5.8	1.0	1.9	1.5	2.0	3.8	2.8

Source: Data Resources, Inc., and Organization for Economic Cooperation and Development.

Table 7
STRUCTURAL CHANGE AND EMPLOYMENT GROWTH CHANGE IN NUMBER OF JOBS BY SECTOR (YEARLY AVERAGES, THOUSANDS)

	Germany		France		UK		Italy		Spain	
	1967-79	1980-84	1965-78	1979-84	1970-79	1979-83	1965-81	1981-84	1965-77	1977-84
Change in										
Labor Force	42.8	98.8	209.6	112.8	145.4	−8.5	109.3	195.7	103.4	33.7
Agriculture										
Employment	−96.4	−11.8	−111.8	−49.6	−14.4	−7.3	−148.2	−102.0	−94.5	−93.6
Industrial										
Employment	−53.7	−278.5	5.5	−161.2	−131.1	−471.0	29.0	−200.7	46.4	−172.1
Service										
Employment	154.6	46.5	233.2	135.6	232.2	30.3	−177.3	241.3	82.7	0.0

Source: Data Resources, Inc., and Organization for Economic Cooperation and Development.

vices. In addition, budget cuts have directly decreased the number of services the government provides and, therefore, the amount of public employment.

Second, the high degree of integration between the service and the industrial sectors has restricted employment expansion in the service area during the current period of industrial restructuring. In Europe nearly one-third of all service sector jobs are directly tied to the goods-producing sector (e.g., transport, communications, consulting, and finance). In order to take advantage of the economies of scale, manufacturing became more reliant on outside service firms to perform functions relating to industrial design, processing, and organizational management, as these activities became more complex.

During the 1960s and 1970s, European industrial sector employment remained stable (although its share of total output fell), and service sector output and employment growth were buoyant. This relative stability of the manufacturing sector allowed the service area to expand rapidly enough to absorb most of the displaced workers from other sectors and newcomers to the labor force (Table 7). With the decline in industrial activity, however, the demand for services derived from the goods-producing industries fell sharply.

This process of industrial restructuring, in addition to increasing unemployment, has caused a staggering rise in long-term joblessness in Europe. In many countries, over 40% of those unemployed have been out of work for more than a year, in contrast with 14% in the US. In France, for example, long-term joblessness in 1984 represented 42% of total unemployment as compared with 17% in 1975. Also, joblessness among the youth in Europe (15 to 24 years of age) is over 21% and rising. This indicates that newcomers to the labor force are discovering that finding employment is very difficult. High youth unemployment could result in a poorly skilled labor force in the future.

Conclusions and Implications _____

The existence of these structural problems in the labor and product markets has significantly weakened the relationship between economic growth and employment expansion in Europe. *As a result, a cyclical upturn in economic activity alone will not be enough to reduce the jobless rate to any significant degree; therefore, an expansionary fiscal policy is not the solution to high European unemployment.* Leaders in Western Europe recognize this and have resisted pressure from the US and others to loosen their restrictive stance. *Decreasing labor, product, and capital market rigidities, on the other hand, would be an important step in improving the capability of European economies to create jobs.*

Most European countries in recent years have begun to address their problems of excessive wage growth and structural change. Furthermore, growth prospects for Europe in 1986 have been enhanced because of the collapse of oil prices. Indeed, actual growth should exceed potential in most countries. Therefore, in 1986 unemployment should decline in Europe, but only slight reductions in jobless rates are expected.

One reason for this is that although employment will increase because of economic expansion, more people will be entering the work force, thereby limiting the extent to which the jobless rate can drop. In fact, workers who had previously dropped out of the labor market are likely to seek employment again because of the improved economic outlook.

A second reason is that the effects of solving the problems of labor and product market rigidities and economic restructuring will not be immediate. Unemployment rates will decline over time once structural problems are remedied and when industrial reorganization is completed. Severe costs, however, are involved in this process. In certain countries, especially Germany, the restructuring appears well advanced. Other countries such as Spain and Italy, however, will require more time to repair the damage caused by the excessive wage gains of the 1970s. Nevertheless, this process is necessary if Europe is to have a more flexible and productive economic structure and, therefore, a more competitive future.

Notes

1. Arthur Okun, "Potential GNP: Its Measurement and Significance," American Statistical Association, Proceedings of the Business and Economics Statistics Section, 1962.
2. This point is verified by the high level of R^2 for the US and Canada in Table 3. R^2 is a statistical measure of the closeness of the relationship between the unemployment rate and the GNP gap. It summarizes the percentage of the variation in the unemployment rate explained by the GNP gap.
3. The literature on this topic is growing. See, especially, P. Minford, *Unemployment: Causes and Cure*, Basil Blackwell, New York, 1983; and R.G. Ehrenberg and R.L. Oaxaca, "Unemployment Insurance, Duration of Unemployment, and Subsequent Wage Gain," *American Economic Review*, Vol. 68, No. 8, p.754–766, December 1976.

10. ACTIVE LABOR MARKET POLICY: AN INTERNATIONAL OVERVIEW

BERNARD CASEY

GERT BRUCHE

The authors are, respectively, Research Fellow and Member of the Policy Information Group, International Institute of Management/Labour Market Policy, Science Centre Berlin, and Research Fellow and Leader of the Policy Information Group, International Institute of Management/Labor Market Policy, Science Center, Berlin.

At the end of 1973, Western industrialized countries experienced a shock in the form of a quadrupling of the price of crude oil. Most were thereby pushed into a recession of a magnitude greater than any downturn experienced since the beginning of the thirties. In an attempt to contain the impact of this downturn and to hold down the growth of unemployment, active labor market policy was accorded a greatly expanded role that involved not only the wider utilization of existing measures, but also the introduction of entirely new instruments. In subsequent years, and despite a partial recovery in the period of 1976-1979, a mixture of demographic pressures and the effects of structural adjustments of national economies to the new conditions of world competition meant that the perceived need for selective interventions remained. However, in response to the changing nature of the problems to be tackled, a transformation in the kind of policies applied also occurred.

In this paper, we present an international overview of the development of labor market policy since the world economic crisis of 1974-1975, covering both European and American experiences.[1] We concentrate primarily on programs which involve public expenditures. Normative measures such as dismissal protection procedures and employment quotas are not treated here; nor do we consider programs for the handicapped, an important component of the activities of the labor market authorities in some countries, but which we regard as more an element of social policy (see Schmid and Semlinger, 1984). Space limitations prohibit any detailed description of program conditions or institutional arrangements (see Bruche, 1983a). We do, however, attempt to portray some of the more general policy trends and equally to pinpoint interventions which seem to us ex-

---

[1]The authors would like to thank Harold L. Wilensky for his comments on an earlier version of this paper and the Bureau of Labor Market Research, Canberra for the opportunity to undertake the work of revision.

Reprinted from *Industrial Relations,* Vol. 24, No. 1, Winter 1985, by permission of the publisher.

ceptional. Our description is essentially qualitative rather than quantitative in nature; even with respect to such relatively straightforward matters as program participation, the data necessary for making meaningful international comparisons are largely unavailable.

The relative importance accorded to active labor market policy varies greatly between countries. An attempt to use a standardized and narrow definition of such interventions (Casey, 1984a) showed that while "low unemployment" Sweden has on occasion spent as much as 2.2 per cent of Gross Domestic Product (GDP) on labor market policy measures, "low unemployment" Austria never allocated more than 0.2 per cent in this direction. The comparable peak figure for the U.S. was just under 0.7 per cent in fiscal year 1978, falling to under 0.4 per cent by 1981. Similarly, the overall economic policy contexts in which such programs were pursued were very different. Austria's labor market policy was at best the adjunct of an expansionary demand management policy, Sweden's at times almost a substitute for it. In France, a low level of expenditure on active labor market programs in the course of the seventies, never more than 0.5 per cent of GDP, went hand in hand with the pursuit of neoliberal fiscal strategy, while the expansionary about-turn of 1981-1983 affected both policy areas. In the U.S., despite an initially countercyclical application of labor market policies, program expenditures followed an essentially procyclical path after 1977 (Casey, 1984a).

If the volume of policy and its context differed widely between countries, this was less true of labor market conditions (see OECD, 1983). Most countries experienced a drop in employment and a sharp rise in unemployment in the first year of the downturn. While employment picked up subsequently, it thereafter grew—and here the U.S. is something of an exception—at a lower rate than in the sixties. At the same time, the labor force itself expanded at a more rapid pace than in the past. Average unemployment rates thus stood considerably higher than at any time since the Great Depression. Coupled with this overall rise in joblessness was an increasing "structuration" of unemployment (Schmid, 1981). The proportion of long-term unemployed rose dramatically. In addition, unemployment was increasingly concentrated among particular categories of persons, notably new entrants and re-entrants to the labor market, and those at the end of their working lives. Thus, youth unemployment rates sometimes stood at two and even three times the overall rate, those of women higher than those of men, and those of older persons higher than those of prime-age workers. The difficulties faced by especially disadvantaged groups such as handicapped persons and ethnic minorities were, of course, substantially exacerbated.

How successful has labor market policy been in this situation? We draw on the principal conclusions of evaluation studies to assess a wide range of programs and program types in terms of their overall efficiency, within their own and within macro-economic terms, and in terms of their equity—the extent to which they redistributed risks of unemployment and improved the situation of the more disadvantaged groups in the labor market. We consider first the "bridging policies" characteristic of the initial years of the downturn; subsequently we look at the more traditional instruments of active labor market policy, such as marginal wage subsidies and job creation and training; and then we discuss the range of measures developed particularly to promote the integration of young persons into work. Thereafter, we examine the various attempts to reduce unemployment by reducing labor supply, considering in turn foreign worker policy, early retirement, and efforts to cut the working week. Finally, we summarize and draw some general conclusions on possible ways forward.

Bridging a "Temporary" Downturn

An important element of the initial reaction of labor market policy to the crisis of 1974-1975 was what can be described as the defense of employment. Because the downturn was then perceived to be of only short duration, the response was one of finding ways to shield the labor market from its effects by means of so-called "job retention" measures or by providing temporary alternative positions for those who did lose their jobs.

Job retention measures. Within the category of job retention measures, two principal forms of intervention can be identified: that involving the maintenance of the employment contract in the absence of production and that involving some form of subsidization of production itself. Measures within the first group can again be subdivided into two types—simple short-time working schemes providing compensation for lost earnings to workers put on short weeks, and schemes whereby nonworked time is put to some "more productive" use, such as retraining. Germany is the most frequently cited example of a country making successful use of the first of these instruments. For the crisis year of 1975 some estimates suggest that without short-time working, the rate of unemployment would have been 0.7 percentage points higher than the 4.7 per cent actually recorded (Schmid, 1982). On the other hand, there is also evidence to suggest that the costs of rehiring and retraining might well have induced many enterprises to hold onto labor, particularly more skilled labor, even without public aid (Flechsenhar, 1980). At the start of 1975, France made a substantial revision of its short-time working system, increasing the share of costs of compensating short-time workers to be borne by the government (rather than by the enterprise); this, no doubt, contributed to the major increase in the relevant instrument's utilization in that year.

Short-time working is popularly considered to be a European phenomenon; the functional equivalent in the U.S. is the temporary layoff which, it is argued, the nature of the unemployment compensation system and the "seniority" provisions of collective bargaining encourage (Moy and Sorrentino, 1981). It is, however, interesting to note that alongside a steep rise in the incidence of temporary layoffs, the number of American workers put onto short weeks—but not enjoying any supplementary compensation for wages lost—jumped dramatically in 1974. Unemployment reached an average of 9 per cent of the labor force in the spring of 1975, while such short-time working affected a further 3 per cent.

In Sweden, where the downturn came later than in the other Organization for Economic Cooperation and Development (OECD) countries, in-firm training was promoted as an alternative to temporary layoffs in 1977-1978. Enterprises received a subsidy for adopting this response; in its peak month the subsidy was being paid for the equivalent of 16 per cent of employment in manufacturing. The quality of training was, however, somewhat suspect. Insofar as job rotation was recognized as training, then despite the scheme's intent, production too was supported. In addition, it has been estimated that only a small proportion of subsidies paid out actually contributed to the avoidance of layoffs (Peterson and Vlachos, 1978). On a smaller scale, Austria made use of a scheme similar to the Swedish one, mainly in response to trade union pressure, since the wage compensation rate under the retraining program exceeded that granted by the short-time scheme (Wösendorfer, 1980).

Direct support of production in order to prevent redundancies characterized the labor market policy of several countries, especially Britain, Sweden, and Austria. Between 1975 and 1979, British textile, clothing, and footwear industries, in particular, were heavily dependent upon this form of intervention (Metcalf, 1982). Other European Community countries, however, protested what they regarded as the "export of unemployment," eventually forcing the scheme to be replaced by a conventional short-time compensation measure. For a while, Sweden sought to subsidize stockpiling as a means of avoiding layoffs, although this program discriminated against enterprises producing "one off" goods and items not easily storable. It also seems to have involved a considerable level of "windfalls" or payments to firms for doing what they had in any case planned to do (Suzuki, 1980). Sweden also brought forward and selectively awarded government orders to provide breathing space for firms in difficulty. During the seventies, Austrian authorities made significant use of loans and credit guarantees to enterprises encountering short-term problems, and offered similar guarantees to firms in a dominant position in local labor markets that were facing structural difficulties.

The importance of job retention policies declined with the bottoming out of the first recession. With the second downturn at the end of the seventies, their use was even more restricted. Production support measures had been abandoned almost entirely. In Austria, recognition of the worsening economic situation was reflected in the acceptance of short-time working in place of in-firm training. Short-time working became very much the dominant enterprise-oriented measure. Its relative success in Europe has been one of the factors promoting legislative initiatives in the U.S. and particularly in Canada to establish similar provisions there.

Provision of temporary positions. Instead of seeking to preserve jobs, another countercyclical policy response of the mid-seventies was the creation of alternative work for those losing their jobs. This was the primary orientation of active labor market policy in the U.S., as characterized by the addition of a new title to the Comprehensive Employment and Training Act (CETA) funding counter-cyclical public service employment (PSE) opportunities. Many other OECD countries similarly introduced or expanded job creation programs at this time, with Sweden setting the lead in terms of the quantitative importance of effort (numbers so employed reaching 1.1 per cent of the labor force). Here too, and in contrast to elsewhere, the number of places in institutional training and retraining schemes was substantially increased to absorb a substantial proportion of the increase in joblessness. The operation of both of these program forms we shall consider in more detail in later sections.

Increasing the Demand for Labor

Employment creation as well as job retention efforts featured in the initial response of governments to the sharp deterioration of the labor market of the mid-seventies. While, however, the significance of programs of the latter kind tended to decline as the increasingly structural nature of the crisis became apparent, the importance of the former grew. Two types of intervention in particular were utilized, the first involving the promotion of additional employment in the private sector via the medium of marginal wage subsidies, the second the creation of temporary jobs in the public and nonprofit sector. In American technical parlance, both are referred to as "direct job creation" measures. Here, however, we shall treat them separately, reserving the second for the following section.

Marginal wage subsidies. The U.S. provides the best-known example of the use of a marginal wage subsidy, and the New Jobs Tax Credit (NJTC) program, which operated in 1977-1978, was also the largest effort of its type undertaken. A major component of the 1977 Economic Expansion Act, it offered enterprises a flat rate tax rebate worth some 20-25 per cent of average wages for each additional employee whose recruitment increased the labor force above 102 per cent of its previous year's level. In 1977 alone, nearly 800,000 man-years of subsidy were approved. Similar "global" marginal wage subsidies were also utilized in Sweden in the periods 1978-1979 and 1981-1982, although both relatively and absolutely their scale was very much smaller. In these two latter cases, the programs were constructed as much to advance the time of recruitments as to increase their number, the objective being to bring forward an anticipated recovery by a few months.

In contrast to these efforts are the considerably more selective programs, such as the marginal wage subsidy for depressed regions which operated in Germany in 1974-1975, the schemes for small firms which have operated in Belgium beginning in 1975 and in Great Britain between 1977 and 1980, and a new Belgian program encouraging the recruitment of a first employee by a one-man firm. Attempts have also been made to specify the recruitment of specific categories of persons. For example, the German program targeted those more than three months out of work; a Canadian employment tax credit covered those with two weeks of joblessness; and the beneficiaries under a Belgian scheme of 1979-1982 were school leavers and the longer-term unemployed. In the Belgian case, and, more importantly, under a recent French program (discussed later), attempts have been made to use such "targeted" marginal wage subsidies to reduce the cost of new recruitments which might be consequent upon reductions in weekly working time.

A considerable body of theoretical literature, as well as pronouncements of bodies such as the OECD, has suggested that marginal wage subsidies could be a relatively effective instrument of employment creation (Rehn, 1982; OECD, 1982a,b). However, evaluations of the various programs practiced, whether short-term, cyclically oriented, or longer term and more selective, all indicate a relatively high "windfall" component. Thus, one study of the NJTC estimates a "net employment effect" (the share of subsidized hirings that were induced only as a result of the program) of some 5-10 per cent, although other investigations are somewhat more favorable (Perloff and Wachter, 1979; Bishop and Haveman, 1979). Despite the very different mechanisms employed (tax relief, exemption from employer social insurance contributions, direct subsidies), levels of support, targeting, and other restrictions, analyses of the multiplicity of European programs come to surprisingly similar conclusions (see Borg *et al.*, 1981; Calame, 1980; Colin and Espinasse, 1980; Goosens and Vuchelen, 1981; Lundin and

Vlachos, 1982; Schmid, 1979). In general, the "net employment effect" is about 10 per cent, with a maximum of some 25 per cent being reached in the case of the German scheme of 1974-1975. This last figure is to be compared to the approximately 45 per cent "net employment effect" estimated to have been necessary for that particular program to have been fiscally neutral. Findings from Sweden and Britain also suggest that the larger the firm the greater the windfall. In very small enterprises, personnel policy is more flexible and more likely to be influenced by short-term stimulants than in large enterprises where decision making is much more rigid and determined by longer-term considerations.

Job creation. Public-sector job creation is often considered as synonymous with active labor market policy and is certainly one of its most visible components. The sharp rise in unemployment recorded in the aftermath of the first oil shock prompted many governments to initiate or expand such programs. In terms of size and of its role as a counter-cyclical stabilizer, the Swedish job creation program is the most well known; in recent years Belgium has increased its efforts to reach a similar scale. The Carter Administration's attempt in 1977 to use PSE as the largest single element of its economic stimulation package is also frequently noted. On the other hand, some countries, notably France and Austria, have as yet scarcely explored the possibilities for such measures.

Despite differences between countries in terms of the use made of job creation programs, certain general trends have become apparent. In the first years of downturn, participants tended to be largely prime-age, male, and relatively short-term unemployed. But the changing structure of unemployment and political pressures in countries such as Germany and America have led to an increasing, if by no means sufficient concentration upon various "problem groups," notably women, young persons, and the long-term unemployed. There has been a concomitant change in the nature of projects supported. Up to the mid-seventies, there was a heavy concentration on construction and land reclamation/protection projects; subsequently, jobs in social services and administration have come to the fore (Auer and Maier, 1984).

Expansion of the job creation effort and change in the nature of the work performed have necessarily meant that new bodies have become involved in the organization and implementation of projects. The relative share undertaken by local and regional government authorities has tended to fall, that of the nonprofit making or voluntary sectors to rise. In some countries, notably Sweden, efforts were made to utilize the private sector as a project organizer, particularly in efforts to promote the integration of young persons into the labor force. Nevertheless, some questions have been asked about whether, at least within the more traditional implementation structures, a saturation point has not been reached (Maier, H., 1982). Equally, and despite the persistence of high levels of unemployment, some governments have been unwilling or fiscally unable to increase the volume of job creation activity. This has led to novel solutions. In Great Britain the principal job creation scheme has been reorganized on a part-time basis, while in that country, and more particularly in the Netherlands, programs for voluntary work for the unemployed have been, or are in the process of being established.

The major expansion of PSE at a time when local administrations were increasingly subject to fiscal retrenchment earned job creation in America the reputation of being subject to a high rate of "substitution." Some estimates suggest that at the end of 1976, as many as 46 per cent of PSE jobs would have existed even without the program (Mirengoff and Rindler, 1978). While tighter program conditions subsequently reduced this proportion substantially, the allegation that such rates obtained was one important reason for the program's ultimate abolition. One reason why substitution might have been a particularly acute problem in America was the almost complete absence of a tradition for this type of measure, coupled with the inability of the implementing agencies to generate genuinely additional projects at short notice. In Sweden and the Netherlands, structures have long existed whereby public construction projects, in particular, are "banked," being brought forward or set back in accordance with the state of the labor market. Although it could be said that a sort of substitution still occurs, this is therefore of a very much more deliberate kind. Finally, in Europe the existence of relatively strong trade unions has limited the possibilities for substitution with respect to the newer social service and administration job creation projects.

Follow-up studies, looking at the subsequent employment histories of job creation program participants are scarce. Surveys from Germany suggest that in 1978, between 30 and 40 per cent of participants were in jobs shortly after completing programs (Spitznagel, 1979), compared to the 32 per cent figure recorded for PSE in the same year. The subsequent deterioration of the labor market and the simultaneous concentration of programs on more disadvantaged groups has, no doubt, lowered these figures somewhat. Certainly this seems to have been the experience of the "post reauthorization" CETA period (Mirengoff *et al.*, 1982).

That for many participants a job creation program provides more an interruption of unemployment than a step towards integration into regular employment has led some governments to experiment with projects which are potentially permanent. This principle lies behind Canada's "Local Employment Assistance Programme," which is targeted on particularly disadvantaged persons, and the Belgian "Third Labour Market," instituted in 1982 for the very long-term unemployed, which offers employment contracts of unlimited duration. When, in 1979, the French government took its first small steps in the area of job creation, it aimed to promote projects which, as well as having innovative organizational structures, would aim to meet previously unsatisfied demands for goods and services, and could eventually be self-financing. This last goal appears to have been achieved in about one-third of the limited number of projects already in existence for more than one year (these were analyzed in 1981; see Gaudin [1982]).

Finally, and with a somewhat similar objective, the labor market authorities in several countries (Belgium, France, Great Britain, the Netherlands, and Sweden) have in the past few years been seeking ways to enable unemployed persons to establish themselves as entrepreneurs, either by granting some temporary income support or by permitting the "capitalization" of unemployment benefits. In France a scheme of the latter sort has been operating since 1979, and some 100,000 persons have taken advantage of it so far, with younger, more highly qualified persons predominating. Surveys suggest that between 60 and 80 per cent of these assisted enterprises were still in existence after a period of one year (Block-Michel *et al.*, 1982).

Promoting Placement Opportunities _____

A complement to strategies aimed directly at increasing demand for labor are efforts to improve the quality or attractiveness of the labor supply. The accelerating process of structural adjustment and the increasing demand for qualified manpower would itself seem to imply an expanding role for occupational training and retraining. So too would the growing problem of long-term unemployment because it increases the danger of dequalification, which further reduces job prospects. For new entrants to the labor market, lack of occupational skills or experience is often the greatest handicap; it is a major reason for the concentration of unemployment among the young. As well as the organization and/or funding of institutionally based training programs, attempts to promote placement chances can involve the offer to employers of financial incentives designed to offset the perceived additional costs, associated with either lower productivity or the need to provide additional training, of hiring particular categories of jobseekers. The following sections examine first the more classical training efforts and then those more narrowly targeted measures designed to enhance the recruitment of various problem groups.

Traditional training programs. The provision of training and retraining is perhaps the most traditional of the functions of labor market policy and that which was already most extensively developed in the European countries well before the onset of the crisis. In this period, its principal tasks had been the upgrading of the skills of persons already employed or the facilitating of the passage of inactive persons into the labor force to help counter labor shortages. The first was particularly important in Germany, where two-thirds of all participants in the extensive program there were involved in such upgrading training; the second was the then most important component of Austrian labor market policy. Only in Sweden had the strategy of retraining redundant workers from declining sectors been implemented on a major scale, forming a key component of the so-called "Rehn-Meidner" model (see Meidner, 1969, 1980).

Despite the justifications that the onset of recession might have given (see Mukherjee, 1974), substantial increases in the volume of training activities were rare. In France, indeed, the expansion of training capacity that had occurred up to 1975 was thereafter almost halted. What was to be observed in many countries, however, was a change in the make-up of trainees. The proportion of unemployed persons increased; in Germany it rose from 11 to 43 per cent between 1970 and 1980. Nevertheless, despite both the growing scale of long-term unemployment and the heavy concentration of joblessness among the unskilled and older persons, it was younger, better-qualified jobseekers who tended to predominate among the participants in most countries' programs. There was also a rise in the proportion of women taking part in labor market training schemes. This trend was linked with a substantially greater emphasis being given to courses providing training in social services and clerical/administrative occupations, rather than the traditional manual occupations which had previously predominated. Finally, there was in many countries a growth in the share of young participants, reflecting in part a tendency to use labor market training increasingly to overcome deficits in the educational system. In France, where this tendency was perhaps most visible, under 25-year-olds constituted some 63 per cent of all labor market trainees by the end of the seventies.

The provision of remedial and basic training to low skilled, long-term unemployed persons, often with only a marginal previous attachment to the labor force, has, on the other hand, been the principal component of CETA, and subsequently, of the Job Training and Partnership Act (JTPA) in America. Even in the absence of their specific targeting, there are good reasons why the U.S. programs serve a very different client group than those in Europe. Under CETA, very much lower training grants were available than in Europe; furthermore, under the JTPA, eligibility for these grants has been severely limited. At the same time, American participants in training schemes are generally excluded from drawing unemployment compensation, although an innovation of the JTPA is a clause suggesting that, for "displaced workers," benefits might continue to be paid and these be set against individual states' "matching" obligations under this subprogram.

Many commentators have noted the very small relative and absolute size of efforts for "displaced workers" in America. Yet, with the exception of the large-scale Swedish retraining programs serving as much as 1.5 per cent of the labor force at any one time, really significant public activities in this sphere are lacking in much of Europe, too. Recent moves by the French government to offer two-year retraining programs to redundant workers from certain "crisis branches" must be interpreted more as an attempt to defuse severe political unrest and reduce the impact of mass dismissals on the unemployment total than as a fundamental redirection of training policy.

Measures for problem groups. Beyond the aim of raising the general level of employment in a noninflationary way and/or promoting the occupational mobility of the labor force, a consistent objective of active labor market policy has been to improve the prospects of certain problem groups. We have already seen how particular categories of jobseekers have come increasingly to dominate traditional labor market programs; here we concentrate upon specifically targeted interventions.

An international overview uncovers instances of the use of wage subsidies to stimulate the hiring of the long-term unemployed, handicapped persons, older persons, ethnic minorities, and women into traditionally male occupations. In almost all cases these are, however, very small efforts. This is because conditions are often drawn very tightly to prevent possible "windfalls," and thus the programs tend to be unattractive to potential employers. Where terms are looser and numbers greater, most employees for whom the subsidy is paid are likely to be hired in any case (Dahme *et al.*, 1980). This appears to have been the case with the American TJTC (Ripley *et al.*, 1982). Finally, research in Germany has suggested that, given the multiplicity of disadvantages employers tend to perceive as being experienced by such categories as the handicapped and long-term unemployed, even the offer of a 100 per cent wage subsidy might well fail to alter hiring decisions in their favor (Schmid and Semlinger, 1980).

Although most of the "classic" problem groups have in practice been neglected, this is not the case for young persons. Programs for them have come to dominate active labor market policy in nearly all of the European countries and in North America, too. Even in the German-speaking countries (Germany, Austria, and Switzerland), where the existence of the "dual apprenticeship system" has served remarkably well to integrate young persons into working life (see Williams, 1981), special programs for young persons have become increasingly important since the end of the seventies (Maier, F., 1983).

The actual programs adopted in Europe share similar goals and content. All attempt to remedy supposed deficits in schooling and provide some sort of work experience or training for young persons. As far as possible, placements in enterprises are sought. Most programs are constructed around the wage subsidy principle, although Belgium presents an interesting exception in its use of a compulsory quota system whereby enterprises are required to recruit additional trainees to a proportion of 3 per cent of the normal labor force. Some indication of the size of youth employment programs can be seen in the fact that in Great Britain, whereas in 1978 one in eight school leavers were passing through the relevant "Youth Opportunities Programme," by 1982 this had become one in two. In France the so-called "National Employment Pacts" and their successors, which concentrate almost exclusively on young persons, have been by far the largest single element of active labor market policy pursued. Even in Sweden the relatively low rates of youth unemployment have, as we have seen, only been achieved thanks to the massive use of job creation programs, including those establishing temporary jobs in private enterprises. Indeed, job creation has been criticized as providing the first introduction to working life for many. Here and elsewhere, it is argued, special youth employment programs involving subsidies to employers have tended to displace traditional "entry jobs," thereby substantially reducing their net employment effect (see Auer, 1983; Delalande, 1981; Metcalf, 1982).

Attempts to remedy these deficits have in the last year or so led to a greater emphasis on longer lasting programs with a higher training content instead of short-term placements. The new British "Youth Training Scheme" and the French "Employment and Training Contracts," programs representing steps to establish labor market institutions that might perform the same functions as the successful German "dual system," bear witness to this. Finally, the governments of Belgium and the Netherlands have sought to expand or strengthen already existing apprenticeship systems, the former by promoting apprenticeship as an alternative to full-time technical schooling, the latter by encouraging the setting up of "equalization funds" to distribute the costs of initial training more fairly among employers.

The increasing concentration of labor market programs upon young persons found in Europe occurred, of course, in America too. Within CETA training and job creation programs, the share of young persons grew in the late seventies, while additional, youth-specific titles were also added. Under the new JTPA this emphasis is continued, with 40 per cent of block grants being reserved for under-21-year-olds. An important difference between American and European youth programs to date, however, has been that while the latter have tended to be enterprise based, the American programs have largely involved classroom training or work experience in specially subsidized projects in the public/nonprofit sectors. Thus, one crucial "integrative" element has been largely absent. It will be interesting to see how far the new "business orientation" of the JTPA serves to change this.

Reducing Labor Supply _____

Until the onset of the first oil crisis, an important task of active labor market policy had been the mobilization of additional manpower—both within individual countries and from abroad—in order to counter labor shortages. However, in Europe if less so in America, the transformation of the situation of shortages into one of surpluses led to a series of more or less conscious efforts to seek relief via a reduction in labor supply. The potential target groups for such a strategy were those sections of the labor force for whom some form of "alternative role" (Offe and Hinrichs, 1977) outside the domestic paid labor force was available: women (as "homemakers"), young persons (as "scholars/students"), older persons (as "retirees"), and foreign workers (as "emigrants"). In practice, the female share of employment rose in almost all countries in the course of the seventies, and only in Switzerland can anything approaching a policy of exclusion with respect to women be observed (see Schmidt, 1984). Similarly, a general expansion of educational opportunities might well have served to reduce younger persons' participation rates, but in most cases this expansion had been introduced prior to the start of the downturn and for other than labor market policy reasons. Reductions in the size of the foreign labor force and early retirement programs, on the other hand, were actively pursued. It is to these two topics we now turn. In the final section, we consider a more recently introduced element of supply reduction strategy, one which seeks not to reduce the number of persons in the labor force, but rather to reduce the number of hours offered by each person and thus to redistribute available work.

Foreign worker policy. Despite persisting high levels of unemployment, in many European countries and in the U.S., the size of the foreign workforce has scarcely fallen or has even increased in the post 1974-1975 period. However, three countries, Austria, Germany, and Switzerland, whose foreign worker policy can be described as being based upon a "rotation of guest workers," were able to use the opportunities this provided to achieve substantial reductions in labor supply. Thus, over the years 1973 to 1978, the size of their respective foreign labor forces fell by between one-quarter and one-fifth, with Switzerland in the fore. Taking the size of the reduction effected as a proportion of the total labor force in 1978, the latter stood as high as 7 per cent in Switzerland and 2-3 per cent in the other two countries. In France, too, somewhat similar efforts were undertaken, although on a more limited scale. While in both Germany and Switzerland the decline in the size of the foreign labor force had halted by 1978 and, indeed, was gradually reversed in subsequent years, in Austria the recession at the end of the decade prompted a further considerable fall in the number of "guest workers." Their total fell by a further one-sixth between 1980 and 1983.

The principal mechanism for reducing their foreign labor forces that the above-mentioned countries utilized was one of stopping the inflow of new job-seekers from abroad. A combination of recession and the restrictive renewal of work and residence permits meant that outflows of foreign workers remained, for a while at least, at a relatively high level. However, with the exception of Austria, the effectiveness of this strategy decreased over the years, in part because those "guest workers" who remained had won rights to long-term or unlimited work and residence permits; in part because it proved difficult to prevent family members from joining those already in the country, and in part because large numbers of children of first-generation foreign residents started entering the labor market (Bruche, 1983b).

It was for such reasons that the governments of France (in 1977-1978) and most recently of Germany (1983-1984) sought to encourage returns to the land of origin by offering financial incentives or "return premia." In both cases, however, take-up rates and numbers affected were rather low. The low level of the premia offered (FF 10,000 per employee in France and DM 10,000 in Germany, both with supplements for family members) makes it questionable whether they indeed served to induce departure (Werner, 1983). It is likely that many who did take advantage of the grant had other reasons for wishing to return home, including a growing feeling of discrimination.

During the period in which certain European governments were applying a strict guest worker policy, the U.S. was experiencing a major inflow of both legal and illegal foreign jobseekers. Although in the European countries, unless resort is made to openly discriminatory measures, the potential for a further cutback in the foreign labor force seems largely exhausted; in the U.S., legislative initiatives have recently been proposed to reduce at least the rate of entry of illegal immigrants. However, the U.S. lacks the procedures for control of residence and employment (via, e.g., the police and social insurance agencies) which substantially contribute to the ability of many European countries to operate a "guest worker" policy. In the absence of such routine controls, any American efforts are unlikely to have any real labor market impact.

Early retirement. If a dominant element of active labor market policy has been the integration of young persons into working life, this has had its mirror image within supply side policy in the increasing exclusion of older persons. Indeed, these two strategies are interrelated. Although in many cases early retirement programs were initially developed as a humane response to the plight of the older long-term unemployed who had little chance of re-entering work, such instruments have increasingly come to be used to shift the burden of unemployment onto the elderly and away from other groups with higher collective bargaining or political priority—namely, prime-aged workers or young persons. The notion of the old "having had their turn" and "having to make way for the young" certainly characterizes much of European labor market policy.

The means by which early retirement is facilitated varies considerably across countries (see Casey, forthcoming; Casey and Bruche, 1983). As an *explicit* element of labor market policy, early retirement has been pursued most extensively in France and Belgium. There, special "bridging payments" are available for workers aged 55 and over who are dismissed for economic reasons. In France, furthermore, the official pension age has recently been lowered to 60. In both countries, and also in Great Britain, public policy has included schemes whereby financial support for early retirement is made conditional upon replacement by an unemployed person. A similar provision has just been legislated for in Germany. While the smaller-scale British scheme has achieved an estimated 80 per cent "real rate of replacement," that of the larger and much more loosely constructed French scheme is only about 50 per cent (Frank *et al.*, 1982).

The public pension systems of several countries allow early (i.e., at 60) benefits to be drawn by older long-term unemployed. Particularly in Germany and Sweden, these provisions have been deliberately utilized, with the support and even the encouragement of the trade unions and the labor market authorities, by enterprises undergoing contraction or rationalization (Russig, forthcoming). Similarly, Dutch provisions for the extended payment of unemployment benefits until pension age led subsequently to pressure for changes in dismissal protection legislation to enable the burden of redundancies to be placed upon eligible older workers. Most recently, such persons have been exempted from the requirement to register as unemployed.

It is, however, not only via instruments of labor market policy that early withdrawals from the labor force have been effected. Instruments originally intended to serve objectives of social policy have also been used. Thus, the effective lowering of the public pension age in Germany to 63, a reform introduced primarily to share the benefits of economic advance, but which actually took effect in 1973, came at a most propitious time. The exit of many older workers (combined with the considerable reduction in the size of the foreign workforce) helped Germany to maintain relatively low unemployment rates during a time of substantial decline in the level of employment. Despite a more favorable overall record on the jobs front, a somewhat similar phenomenon was also found in Austria.

Equally, we should consider in this context the role of disability pension schemes, which have been increasingly "functionalized" to serve labor market policy purposes. In the Netherlands, where labor market prospects are considered alongside medical factors in assessing rights to a pension, the sectoral incidence of disability is significantly related to rates of employment decline (van den Bosch and Petersen, 1983). In Germany, where somewhat similar principles hold, over half of all new pensions to men are made before the age of 60, ostensibly on grounds of poor health. Even in Sweden, despite its "work for all" philosophy, a broad interpretation of "disability" was linked to declining labor force participation of older persons. It is, however, also interesting to note that in Sweden the decline in older persons' participation rates has almost halted since the later seventies. One explanation for this might be the existence, since 1976, of a partial pension scheme which, although not introduced to serve such purposes, has also been utilized by some enterprises as a more humane means of reducing or rationalizing their labor forces (Riksförsäkringsverket, 1984).

In terms of public *policies* regarding retirement, a strong Europe/America dichotomy is apparent. Legislation such as the Age Discrimination in Employment Act (ADEA) was intended to maintain and even extend the employment of older persons. When, however, we look at retirement *practices* in the U.S., the same patterns as found in Europe emerge. First, the effects of ADEA itself, which bans discrimination on grounds of age but justifies it on grounds of performance, are ambiguous. Secondly, at least in those sectors covered by collective bargaining, arrangements to "buy out" older workers with early company pensions are frequent where labor force reductions are planned. Thirdly, the actuarially reduced social security pension, and to a lesser extent the disability pension, are, in a country with only limited unemployment insurance coverage, the only available means of income support for unemployed older persons with few chances on the open labor market (Casey and Bruche, 1983).

Shortening the work week. A de facto lowering of the retirement age has been the form of "worksharing" that has been most extensively realized. Redistributing employment opportunities via a shortening of the standard working week, as demanded by most European (if to a lesser extent Scandinavian) trade unions, has as yet had little impact upon public policy. Many governments have expressed reservations about the effectiveness of such a strategy; some have openly opposed it as likely to result in a decrease rather than an increase in employment. Furthermore, the fact that the costs of a shorter work week are borne more directly by the employer than are the costs of early retirement, in which public agencies often intervene, has stiffened resistance to trade union attempts to realize their objectives via collective bargaining (Hart, forthcoming). Only in France has cutting the work week been included as an important element of government strategy to reduce unemployment, although the authorities in Holland and Belgium have been sympathetic to collective bargaining efforts, subject to certain conditions being met. In France, in 1981, legislation mandated a one-hour cut in the standard working week, wage subsidies were offered to those firms hiring additional workers which had made larger reduction in hours, and limits on overtime working were tightened. In the Netherlands, a 1982 national collective agreement has led to work-time reductions in return for "real" if not "money" wage cuts; in Belgium, publicly supported "worksharing" experiments have been initiated that link cuts in individual work time to an extension of enterprise operating time.

The cut in the work week from 40 to 39 hours that occurred in France at the start of 1982 has been estimated by the Labor Ministry itself to have saved or created some 20,000-70,000 jobs at most, compared to the reduction in labor supply of 300,000 that a simple arithmetical calculation might suggest it would have induced (Délégation à l'Emploi, 1983; Marchand *et al.*, 1983; Frank and Tregoat, 1983). However, a recent empirical study from Great Britain, following up the effects of collectively agreed worktime reductions of a similar order of magnitude which have occurred in that country in the last few years, suggests no positive and possibly even negative employment consequences (Department of Employment, 1983). Even in Holland, where "worksharing" has been combined with "income sharing," provisional estimates indicate that any "employment effect" is more in terms of job saving than job creation (SoZa, 1983). Finally, the French government's attempts to induce accelerated work-time reductions by offering first marginal wage subsidies for new recruitments and then general wage subsidies for all workers affected, have to date proved singularly disappointing; the interest shown by enterprises has been minimal.

More instances are to be found of governmental efforts to promote that more cost-neutral form of "worksharing, " part-time working (see Casey, 1983). Evaluation of a Dutch experiment to offer subsidies to employers to split jobs, however, suggests that this is an ineffective form of intervention. That conclusion is confirmed by recent experience in Britain, where a "Job Splitting Scheme," anticipated to create 100,000 new part-time jobs within 18 months, had generated only some 1,500 jobs within the first year. In an attempt to encourage more voluntary part-time working, a number of governments have taken steps to remedy disadvantages often encountered by part-timers under the provisions of social security and labor law, while for their own employees, certain governments have also introduced automatic rights of transfer to and from such work schedules. However quantitatively successful such efforts might have been, evidence from Belgium and France suggests that they have not succeeded in shifting part-time work away from being an essentially female-dominated form of employment.

Strategic and Political Trends in Policy _____

Despite national differences of context, orientation, and intensity, it is possible to distinguish certain broad trends of policy over the past decade. Anticipating that the recession induced by the first oil crisis would be of only short duration, the first reaction of many European governments (if not that of the U.S.) was to encourage the maintenance of existing jobs, often via short-time work, in some cases even via the subsidy of production itself. Alongside traditional short-time work programs were schemes promoting a more productive use of idle time by subsidizing in-plant training and provisions for temporary support of production itself. At the same time, governments used job creation and labor market training programs to provide "temporary parking places" for those finding themselves without work.

A subsequent recognition that the oil crisis marked a fundamental break with the past that required restructuring of production meant that the appropriateness of job retention strategies increasingly came into question. In addition, as the economic situation stabilized or improved, the construction of many programs meant that the level of their utilization in any case declined. A gradual reorientation of labor market policy then ensued; concern was increasingly directed to those out of work rather than those threatened by unemployment and to improving the position of certain problem groups in the labor market—women and especially young persons. On the one hand, this led to the adaptation of traditional labor market programs, as illustrated by the growing share of job-creation programs in the service, as opposed to the construction sector and the increasing share of young persons in institutional training programs. On the other hand, it led to the creation of new or almost totally new schemes, such as the sponsoring of job-creation projects in the private sector and the creation of new forms of temporary employment/training and work experience contracts.

Alongside the increasing efforts to mitigate youth unemployment was the emergence and development of measures to encourage the exclusion of older persons from the labor market. This phenomenon was most pronounced in Europe, but in all of the Western industrialized countries there has been a tendency towards a decline in the "actual" if not the "normal" age of retirement that cannot be disassociated from the universal deterioration in the labor market. Furthermore, particularly the German-speaking countries made use of the opportunity to reduce the size of their substantial foreign labor forces to limit the burden of unemployment facing their own citizens. More recently in Europe, a new component of supply-reducing policy has come to the fore, that of cutting weekly working time. While many governments have been wary of embracing such a strategy, this is the area where much future activity is likely to be concentrated.

Changes in emphasis within active labor market policy over time have been matched by changes in the intensity with which it has been pursued. In the first years after recession, active labor market policy was seen by some as providing a "third way" (between fiscal and monetary policy) or non-inflationary means of restoring full employment. Organizations such as the OECD applauded and, indeed, actively advocated its utilization. Subsequently, its limitations, too, were realized and its potential was viewed more cautiously, if also more realistically. In this respect, the more recent publications of the OECD (1982a) can be compared instructively to their predecessors (OECD, 1976, 1978).

On the other hand, judgments about the role of active labor market policy have often been influenced as much by political as scientific reasoning, a process which has not been helped by the relative absence of evaluation research in many countries outside the U.S. Changes in the make-up of governments involving a shift to the right have often resulted in efforts to wind down active labor market policy. The experience of the first years of the Thatcher Administration in Great Britain or the Reagan Presidency bear testament to this. Shifts to the left often imply the reverse, as occurred in France in the period immediately after Mitterrand assumed power. However, even governments for whom intervention was originally anathema have subsequently found themselves obliged to take action, and/or have actively committed themselves to expanding active labor market policy. Thus, the British Conservatives are now administering a totality of labor market programs far larger in scale than that of their Labour predecessors. The Christian Democrat/Liberal coalition in Germany has, in its first year in office, been responsible for an increase in the volume of participation in training and more especially boosted job creation to record levels, whereas the previous Social

Democratic/Liberal coalition had been cutting back such programs at the end of its life. Equally, in the course of 1982, the same American president who had abolished PSE on accession to office accepted and even participated in the initiation of an "employment creation" package and was arguing for a portable wage subsidy for the long-term unemployed. This suggests that active labor market policy also serves symbolic purposes, enabling governments to demonstrate a response to politically unacceptable levels of joblessness.

Are Efficiency and Equity Obtainable? _____

Beyond pure symbolic functions, what is the potential of selective labor market policy for achieving the goals of efficiency and equity? In order to answer this, we shall briefly consider the main categories of intervention described so far.

In situations of short-term declines in demand, there is some justification for efforts to maintain existing jobs, taking care, however, that the programs utilized do not simply subsidize employers' hoarding practices or involve, whether disguised or not, support for continued production. Even where enterprises are facing problems of a more structural nature, steps might be taken to "smooth" the process of adjustment *if*, simultaneously, major efforts are also made to identify and facilitate transition to alternative employment opportunities. The danger with all job maintenance strategies is, of course, that support has often continued to be provided when the requirements of structural change would dictate otherwise. Such behavior has its attractions since job losers are a much more identifiable group than those who might be employed in newly created jobs elsewhere. In short, if requirements of efficiency are to be met, very strict limitations must be put on periods of program entitlement.

Despite their continued advocacy in both political and academic circles, experience shows that the efficiency of marginal wage subsidy programs in increasing demand for labor is suspect. At least with respect to large enterprises, the programs often seem to result in huge "windfalls." Insofar as such measures are to be repeated, there is a good argument for restricting them to very small enterprises.

Job creation programs have, in recent years, been increasingly revised to meet the target of equity. They tend to be the measures in which the various problems groups are best, if not yet adequately represented. At the very least, they allow temporary respite from the demoralizing circumstances of long-term unemployment. If, as a result of "substitution," their economic efficiency is occasionally open to question, they can nevertheless be defended for tending to lead to public services being provided in a more labor-intensive manner than otherwise would have been the case. There is also an argument for attempting to use a combination of job creation and unemployment compensation funds to facilitate small business start-up. In the current large pool of unemployed persons, a significant reserve of creative potential may lie waiting to be tapped.

Of the more traditional active labor market policy measures, job training seems to come closest to achieving equity and efficiency simultaneously. As the OECD commented, "Raising the productivity of workers (via training) increases their competitive edge in the labor market and improves their income stream over the life cycle. At the same time, it represents an investment by society in the capacity of the work force to adjust to structural change and contribute to future economic growth" (OECD, 1982a, p. 98). Most countries, however, have a long way to go in establishing structures that actually meet this aspiration. Not only is there the requirement that the volume of training capacity be increased, but also that provision be made for the greater participation of disadvantaged groups. Regarding youth training and work experience, there is also a strong argument for fundamental reform of labor market institutions to smooth the transition from school to work. Given the nonspecific nature of such initial training, efforts to increase the volume of apprentice training will necessitate steps to distribute its costs more fairly between the trainee and his employer and between firms which train and those which profit from the training activities of others (see Casey, 1984b).

With respect to the various supply-reducing measures considered, our comments are more succinct. In Europe, if not in the U.S., the effectiveness of policies that reduce the foreign labor force is not in doubt, although some observers question whether the same room for maneuvering will exist in the future as has in the past. However, on the grounds of equity, a restrictive "guest worker" policy has little to recommend it. Equity reasons also suggest there are limits to the extent to which an early retirement strategy can be pursued. As one French observer has put it, society is in danger of creating for itself a new problem group of persons without a proper role, neither workers, nor unemployed, nor retirees, too young to be considered as old, but too old to be treated or accepted as young (Gaullier, 1982). Furthermore, when most demographic predictions are pointing to a substantial increase in dependency rates, the future costs of such a policy are likely to become unbearable. In those countries where early retirement has been most extensively pursued, financing has already come under strain and retrenchment has been necessary.

Finally, despite the appeal to equity of such slogans as "more free time for all in place of unemployment for many" (the slogan of the German Metal Workers Union during the 1984 strike), there is little to encourage belief in either the efficiency or the efficacy of a "worksharing" strategy as expressed in the more simplistic demands for a cut in the standard working week or the small, step-like reductions achieved in certain European countries. "Worksharing," to be effective, will require first an element of "income sharing" and, second, arrangements whereby shorter individual working time is linked to at least the maintenance of capacity utilization time. There is also scope for more voluntary part-time working, particularly if it permits more imaginative schedules than the conventional half-time roster. In addition, working-time reductions for older workers in the form of partial retirement opportunities might be considered. These have the multiple advantages of reducing "pension shock," of providing for work adjustment, and of facilitating workforce reductions or rejuvenations. Since partial retirees still contribute to their own upkeep, this policy is also less expensive than full early retirement options. Indeed, in the future partial retirement might provide a way of extending the working life of older persons beyond the present normal retirement age.

With many of the same constraints upon the utilization of macro-economic levers obtaining as in the past, and with the prospect of unemployment continuing at present high levels well into the foreseeable future, active labor market policy would appear to have a continued role to play. Despite the astonishing economic recovery and growth of employment experienced in the U.S. in 1984, this applies as much to America as it does to Europe. Although economic growth brings more jobs than any form of employment promotion scheme ever can, disadvantaged groups benefit employment last and least from such growth (Bendick, 1982). Equity, if not other considerations, dictates intervention on their behalf. Should a return to the growth rates of the fifties and sixties occur, certain types of programs will become less relevant, but this will not be the case for all. The more "classical" instruments of labor market policy, particularly programs for training and retraining, can continue to play an important part in promoting the process of structural change. The argument of such interventions, however, will then be in terms of their contribution to macro-economic efficiency.

References

Auer, P. *Strategien der Arbeitsbeschaffung in drei Ländern: antizyklische, problemgruppen-orientierte und experimentelle ArbeitsbeschaffungsmaBnahmen.* Discussion Paper IIM/LMP 83-22, Wissenschaftszentrum Berlin, 1983.

Auer, P. and H. Maier, "Strategien der Arbeitsbeschaffung in der Bundesrepublik und im Ausland: Erfahrungen aus fünf Ländern," *Mitteilungen aus der Arbeitsmarkt-und Berufsforschung*, 2/1984, forthcoming.

Bendick, M. "Employment, Training and Economic Development." In J. Palmer and I. Sawhill, eds., *The Reagan Experiment*. Washington, DC: Urban Institute Press, 1982, pp. 247-269.

Bishop, J. and R. Haveman. "Selective Employment Subsidies: Can Okun's Law Be Repealed?," *American Economic Review*, LXIX (May, 1979), 124-130.

Bloch-Michel, C. *et al.* "Création d'enterprises par les demandeurs d'emploi," *Bilan de l'Emploi 1982*. Paris: Ministère des Affairs Sociales et de la Solidarité Nationale, 1983, 55-70.

Borg, S., L. Eriksson, and A. Read. "Erfarenheter av nyrekryteringsbidraget— sammanfatting och kommentarer," *Meddelande fran utredningsenheten*, No. 15, Solna: AMS, 1981.

Bruche, G. *Die Administration arbeitsmarktpolitischer Programme. Ein internationaler Vergleich (Frankreich, Niederlande, Osterreich, Schweden, USA)*. Discussion Paper IIM/LMP 83/10, Wissenschaftszentrum Berlin, 1983a.

_____. "Ausländische Arbeitnehmer." In M. Schmidt, ed., *Pipers Wörterbuch zur Politik—Bd. 2, Westliche Industriegesellschaften*. München: Piper & Co., 1983b, pp.40-47.

Calame, A. *Impact and Costs of Wage Subsidy Programmes: Experiences in Great Britain, Sweden and the USA*. Discussion Paper IIM 80-1a, Wissenschaftszentrum Berlin, 1980.

Casey, B. *Governmental Measures to Promote Part-Time Working: Experiences in Belgium, France, Great Britain, the Netherlands and the Federal Republic of Germany*. Discussion Paper IIM/LMP 83-26, Wissenschaftszentrum Berlin, 1983.

_____. *The Development of Labour Market Policy: a comparison of trend and volume of interventions in Austria, France, the Netherlands, Sweden and the USA in the period since the world recessions of 1974/75*. Mimeo, Wissenschaftszentrum Berlin, 1984a.

_____. "De Nieuwe wet op het industrieel leerlingswezen: een stap in de juiste richting," *Economisch en Sociaal Tijdschrift*, XXXVIII, No. 4 (1984b), 461-474.

_____. "Recent Trends in Retirement Policies and Practices in Europe and the USA." In J. Birren *et al.*, eds., *Aging and Technological Advances*. New York: Plenum Press, forthcoming.

Casey, B. and G. Bruche. *Work or Retirement? Labour Market and Social Policy for Older Workers in France, Great Britain, the Netherlands, Sweden and the USA*. Aldershot: Gower Press, 1983.

Colin, J.F. and J.M. Espinasse. "Les subventions à l'emploi. Un essai d'analyse," *Travail et Emploi*, No. 1 (June, 1980), 37-49.

Dahme, H.J., D. Grunow, and F. Hegner. "Aspekte der Implementation sozialpolitischer Programme." In R. Mayntz, ed., *Implementation politischer Programme, Empirische Forschungsberichte.* Königstein: Athenäum, 1980.

Delalande, F. "Les Pratiques d'embauche des employeurs dans le cadre des pactes rationaux pour l'emploi," *Travail et Emploi,* No. 10 (October-December, 1981), 63-72.

Délégation à l'Emploi. "La Réduction du Temps de Travail," *Travail et Emploi,* No. 19 (March, 1983), 25-29.

Department of Employment. "Shorter hours through national agreements," *Employment Gazette,* (October, 1983), 432-436.

Flechsenhar, H. *Kurzarbeit als Mabnahme der betrieblichen Anpassung.* Frankfurt: Harry Deutsch, 1980.

Frank, D. *et al.* "Entreprises et contrats de solidarité de préretraite-démission," *Travail et Emploi,* No. 13 (July-September, 1982), 75-90.

Frank, D. and J.J. Tregoat, "Une politique active en matière d'emploi et du lutte contre le chômage a marqué 1982," *Bilan de l'emploi 1982.* Paris: Ministère des Affairs Sociales et de la Solidarité Nationale, 1983, 15-36.

Gaudin, J. "Les emplois d'utilite collective: Premières caractérisation issues d'une analyse d'expériences ressortissant au domaine socioéconomique," *Travail et Emploi,* No. 12 (April-June, 1982), 35-48.

Gaullier, X. *L'avenir à reculons: chômage et retraite.* Paris: Les Editions Ouvrières, 1982.

Goosens, K. and J. Vuchelen. "Het bedrijfseconomische karakter van het Plan De Wulf," *Cahiers Economiques de Bruxelles,* No. 98 (2e trimestre, 1981), 203-228.

Hart, R. *Working Time: A Review of Problems and Policies within a Collective Bargaining Framework.* Paris: OECD, forthcoming.

Lundin, T. and V. Vlachos. *Lönesubventioner som ett sysellsättningspåverkande medel. En intervjuundersökning.* Lund: Nationalekonomiska Institutionen, 1982.

Maier, F. *Jugendarbeitslosigkeit in der Bundesrepublik Deutschland: ein ungelöstes Problem.* Discussion Paper ILM/LMP 83-23, Wissenschaftszentrum Berlin, 1983.

Maier, H. "ArbeitsbeschaffungsmaBnahmen als Instrument aktiver Arbeitsmarktpolitik in den 80er Jahren." In F.W. Scharpf *et al.,* eds., *Für eine aktive Arbeitsmarktpolitik. Erfahrungen und neue Wege.* Frankfurt: Campus, 1982, pp. 119-140.

Marchand, O., D. Rault, and E. Turpin. "Des 40 heures aux 39 heures: processus et réaction des entreprises," *Economie et Statistique,* No. 154 (April, 1984), 3-15.

Meidner, R. *The Role of an Active Manpower Policy in Contributing to the Solution of the Dilemma Between Inflation and Unemployment.* Paris: OECD, 1969.

_____. *Begriff, Ziel und Rahmenbedingungen des schwedischen Modells einer selektiven Arbeitsmarktpolitik.* Discussion Paper IIM 80-4, Wissenschaftszentrum Berlin, 1980.

Metcalf., D. *Alternatives to Unemployment: Special Employment Measures in Britain.* London: Policy Studies Institute and Anglo-German Foundation, 1982.

Mirengoff, W. and L. Rindler, *CETA: Manpower Programs Under Local Control.* Washington, DC: National Academy of Sciences, 1978.

Mirengoff, W. *et al. CETA—Accomplishments, Problems and Solutions.* Kalamazoo, MI: Upjohn Institute for Employment Research, 1982.

Moy, J. and C. Sorrentino, "Unemployment and Lay-off Practices in 10 Countries," *Monthly Labor Review*, CIV (December, 1981), 3-13.

Mukherjee, S. *There's Work to be Done.* London: Manpower Services Commission/HMSO, 1974.

OECD. *Ministers of Labour and the Problems of Employment*, Vols. I and II. Paris: 1976 and 1977.

_____. *A Medium-Term Strategy for Employment and Manpower Policies.* Paris: 1978.

_____. *The Challenge of Unemployment: A Report to Labour Ministers.* Paris: 1982a.

_____. *Marginal Employment Subsidies.* Paris: 1982b.

_____. *Employment Outlook.* Paris: 1983.

Offe, C. and K. Hinrichs. "Sozialökonomie des Arbeitsmarktes und die Lage 'benachteiligter' Gruppen von Arbeitnehmern." In C. Offe, ed., *Opfer des Arbeitsmarktes zur Theorie der strukturierten Arbeitslosigkeit.* Darmstadt: Neuwied, 1977, pp. 3-61.

Perloff, J. and M. Wachter. "The New Jobs Tax Credit: An Evaluation of the 1977-78 Wage Subsidy Program," *American Economic Review*, LX (May, 1979), 173-179.

Peterson, J. and V.I. Vlachos. *En gransking av utbildningsbidraget för permitteringshotade.* Lund: Nationalekonomiska Institutionen, 1978.

Rehn, G. "Anti-inflationary Expansion Policies (with Special Reference to Marginal Employment Premiums)." *Occasional papers of the Swedish Institute for Social Research*, 4/1982.

Riksförsäkringsverket. *Delpension och rörlig pensionsålder: en uppföljning och utvärdering.* Stockholm: Riksförsäkringsverket, 1984.

Ripley, R. *et al. The implementation of the Targeted Jobs Tax Credit. Final Report.* Mimeo. Columbus, OH: Ohio State University, 1982.

Russig, H. "Redundancy and the Public-Private Mix." In M. Rein and L. Rainwater, eds., *Public-Private Interplay in Social Protection: a Comparative Study*. White Plains: Sharpe, forthcoming.

Schmid, G. "The Impact of Selective Employment Policy: The Case of a Wage-Cost Subsidy Scheme in Germany 1974-75," *Journal of Industrial Economics*, XXIII (June, 1979), 339-355.

_____. *Strukturierte Arbeitslosigkeit und Arbeitsmarktpolitik*. Frankfurt: Athenäum, 1981.

_____. *Zur Effizienz der Arbeitsmarktpolitik: ein Plädoyer für einen Schritt zurück un zwei Schritte vor*. Discussion Paper IIM/LMP 82-3, Wissenschaftszentrum Berlin, 1982.

_____. *Arbeitsmarktpolitik für Behinderte: Erfahrungen aus der Bundesrepublik Deutschland, GroBbritannien, Schweden und den USA*. Discussion paper IIM/LMP 84-10, Wissenschaftszentrum Berlin, 1984.

_____ and K. Semlinger. *Instrumente gezielter Arbeitsmarktpolitik: Kurzarbeit, Einarbeitungszuschüsse, Eingliederungsbeihilfen*. Meisenheim: Anton Hain, 1980.

Schmidt, M. *Der Schweizerische Weg Zur Vollbeschäftigung: Eine Bilanz der Beschäftigung, der Arbeitslosigkeit und der Arbeitsmarktpolitik*. Frankfurt: Campus, 1984.

SoZa. "Conclusie uit enqête van Sociale Zaken," *NRC Handelsblad* (28.12.1983).

Spitznagel, E. "Arbeitsmarktwirkung, Beschaftingungsstrukturen und Zielgruppenorientierung vol allgemeinen MaBnahmen zur Arbeitsbeschaffung." *Mitteillungen aus der Arbetismarkt-und Berufsforschung*, 2/1979, 198-216.

Suzuki, M. *Langerstödet: en studie av des effekter på sysselsätting och lageruppbyggnad*. Mimeo. Höghskolan i Växjö, 1980.

Van den Bosch, F. and C. Petersen. "Een economische analyse van de non-participatiegraad: de invloed van arbeidsongeschiktheid." In F. van den Bosch and C. Petersen, eds., *Economie en arbeidsongeschiktheid: analyoc en beleid*. Deventer: Kluwer, 1983, pp. 149-164.

Werner, H. "Ausländerbeschäftingung und Ausländerpolitik in Frankreich." *Mitteilungen aus der Arbeitsmarkt- und Berufsforschung*, 4/1983, 360-377.

Williams, S., ed. *Youth Without Work: Three Countries' Approaches to the Problem*. Paris: OECD, 1983.

Wösendorfer, J. *Beurteilungskriterien für das Arbeitsmarkt-förderungsgesetz. Untersuchung der aktiven Arbeitsmarktpolitik in Österreich*. Wien: Österreichisches Institut für Arbeitsmarktpolitik, 1980.

V _____ THE INFORMATION SOCIETY: THE FLOW OF INFORMATION _____

11. PARAMETERS OF THE POST-INDUSTRIAL SOCIETY: COMPUTOPIA

YONEJI MASUDA

The emerging information society will be completely different from industrial society, argues Masuda. Indeed, we can look forward to "Computopia" on Earth, if only we understand and direct the underlying social forces. Masuda was author of the Japanese *Plan for an Information Society: A National Goal Toward the Year 2000*, published as early as 1971. This reading is taken from his most recent book, *The Information Society as Post-Industrial Society* (World Future Society, Bethesda, MD, 1981 and 1983), and provides us with a rare glimpse of Japanese thinking about the future.

What is the image of the information society?

1. The information society will be a new type of human society, completely different from the present industrial society. Unlike the vague term "post-industrial society," the term "information society" as used here will describe in concrete terms the characteristics and the structure of this future society. The basis for this assertion is that *the production of information values and not material values will be the driving force* behind the formation and development of society. Past systems of innovational technology have always been concerned with material productive power, but the future information society must be built within a completely new framework, with a thorough analysis of the system of computer-communications technology that determines the fundamental nature of the information society.

2. The developmental pattern of industrial society is the societal model from which we can predict the overall composition of the information society. Here is another bold "historical hypothesis": *the past developmental pattern of human society can be used as a historical analogical model for future society.* Putting the components of the information society together piece by piece by using this historical analogy is an extremely effective way for building the fundamental framework of the information society.

Reprinted from *The Information Society as Post-Industrual Society*, 1983, by permission of the publisher.

Table 1 presents the overall framework of the information society based upon these two premises. This table presents the overall composition of the information society based on a historical analogy from industrial society. Let me explain each of the major items.

1. The prime innovative technology at the core of development in industrial society was the steam engine, and its major function was to substitute for and amplify the physical labor of man. In the information society, "computer technology" will be the innovational technology that will constitute the developmental core, and its fundamental function will be to *substitute for and amplify the mental labor of man.*

2. In industrial society, the motive power revolution resulting from the invention of the steam engine rapidly increased material productive power, and made possible the mass production of goods and services and the rapid transportation of goods. In the information society, "an information revolution" resulting from development of the computer will rapidly expand information productive power, and make possible *the mass production of cognitive, systematized information, technology, and knowledge.*

3. In industrial society, the modern factory, consisting of machines and equipment, became the societal symbol and was the production center for goods. In the information society the *information utility* (a computer-based public infrastructure) consisting of information networks and data banks will replace the factory as the *societal symbol,* and become the production and distribution center for information goods.

4. Markets in industrial society expanded as a result of the discovery of new continents and the acquisition of colonies. The increase in consumption purchasing power was the main factor in expansion of the market. In the information society, "the knowledge frontier" *will become the potential market,* and the increase in the possibilities of problem-solving and the development of opportunities in a society that is constantly and dynamically developing will be the primary factor behind the expansion of the information market.

5. In industrial society, the leading industries in economic development are machinery and chemicals, and the total structure comprises primary, secondary, and tertiary industries. In the information society the leading industries will be the *intellectual industries,* the core of which will be the knowledge industries. *Information-related industries* will be newly added as *the quarternary group* to the industrial structure of primary, secondary, and tertiary. This structure will consist of a matrix of infor-

Table 1
PATTERN COMPARISON OF INDUSTRIAL SOCIETY AND THE INFORMATION SOCIETY

	Industrial society	Information society
Innovational technology		
Core	Steam engine (power)	Computer (Memory, computation, control)
Basic function	Replacement, amplification of physical labor	Replacement, amplification of mental labor
Productive power	Material productive power (increase in per capita production)	Information productive power (increase in optimal action-selection capabilities)
Socioeconomic structure		
Products	Useful goods and services	Information, technology, knowledge
Production center	Modern factory (machinery, equipment)	Information utility (information networks, data banks)
Market	New world colonies, consumer purchasing power	Increase in knowledge frontiers, information space
Leading industries	Manufacturing industries (machinery industry, chemical industry)	Intellectual industries, (information industry, knowledge industry)
Industrial structure	Primary, secondary, tertiary industries	Matrix industrial structure (primary, secondary, tertiary, quaternary/systems industries)
Economic structure	Commodity economy (division of labor, separation of production and consumption)	Synergetic economy (joint production and shared utilization)
Socio-economic principle	Law of price (equilibrium of supply and demand)	Law of goals (principle of synergetic feed-forward)
Socio-economic subject	Enterprise (private enterprise, public enterprise, third sector)	Voluntary communities (local and informational communities)
Socio-economic system	Private ownership of capital, free competition, profit maximization	Infrastructure, principle of synergy, precedence of social benefit
Form of society	Class society (centralized power, classes, control)	Functional society (multicenter, function, autonomy)
National goal	GNW (gross national welfare)	GNS (gross national satisfaction)
Form of government	Parliamentary democracy	Participatory democracy
Force of social change	Labor movements, strikes	Citizens' movements, litigation
Social problems	Unemployment, war, fascism	Future shock, terror, invasion of privacy
Most advanced stage	High mass consumption	High mass knowledge creation
Values		
Value standards	Material values (satisfaction of physiological needs)	Time-value (satisfaction of goal achievement needs)
Ethical standards	Fundamental human rights, humanity	Self-discipline, social contribution
Spirit of the times	Renaissance (human liberation)	Globalism (symbiosis of man and nature)

mation-related industries on the vertical axis, and health, housing, and similar industries on the horizontal axis.

6. The economic structure of industrial society is characterized by (1) a sales-oriented commodity economy; (2) specialization of production-utili-

zing divisions of labor; (3) complete division of production and consumption between enterprise and household. In the information society (1) information, the axis of socioeconomic development, will be produced by the information utility; (2) self-production of information by users will increase; information will accumulate; (3) this accumulated information will expand through synergetic production and shared utilization; and (4) the economy will change structurally from an exchange economy to a *synergetic economy*.

7. In industrial society the law of price, the universal socioeconomic principle, is the invisible hand that maintains the equilibrium of supply and demand, and the economy and society as a whole develop within this economic order. In the information society the *goal principle* (a goal and means principle) will be the fundamental principle of society, and the synergetic feedforward, which apportions functions in order to achieve a common goal, will work to maintain the order of society.

8. In industrial society, the most important subject of social activity is the enterprise, the economic group. There are three areas: private enterprise, public enterprise, and a third sector of government ownership and private management. In the information society the most important subject of social activity will be the *voluntary community*, a socioeconomic group that can be broadly divided into local communities and informational communities.

9. In industrial society the socioeconomic system is a system of private enterprise characterized by private ownership of capital, free competition, and the maximization of profits. In the information society, the socioeconomic system will be a voluntary civil society characterized by the superiority of its infrastructure, as a type of both public capital and knowledge-oriented human capital, and by a fundamental framework that embodies the *principle of synergy and social benefit*.

10. Industrial society is a society of centralized power and hierarchical classes. The information society, however, will be a multi-centered and complementary voluntary society. It will be horizontally functional, maintaining social order by *autonomous and complementary functions of a voluntary civil society*.

11. The goal of industrial society is to establish a Gross National Welfare Society, aiming to become a cradle-to-grave high welfare society. The information society will aim for the *realization of time value* (value that designs and actualizes future time) for each human being. The goal of

society will be for everyone to enjoy a worthwhile life in the pursuit of greater future possibilities.

12. The political system of industrial society is a parliamentary system and a majority rule. In the information society the political system will become a *participatory democracy*. It will be the politics of participation by citizens; the politics of autonomous management by citizens, based on agreement, participation, and synergy that take in the opinions of minorities.

13. In industrial society, labor unions exist as a force for social change, and labor movements expand by the use of labor disputes as their weapon. In the information society, *citizen movements* will be the force behind social change; their weapons will be litigation and participatory movements.

14. In industrial society there are three main types of social problems: recession-induced unemployment, wars resulting from international conflict, and the dictatorship of fascism. The problems of the information society will be future shocks caused by the inability of people to respond smoothly to rapid societal transformation, acts of individual and group terrorists such as hijackings, *invasions of individual privacy*, and the crisis of a *controlled society*.

15. The most advanced stage of industrial society is a high mass-consumption stage, centering on durable goods, as evidenced by motorization (the diffusion of the automobile). The most advanced stage of the information society will be *the high mass knowledge creation society* in which computerization will make it possible for each person to create knowledge and to go on to self-fulfillment.

16. In industrial society, the materialistic values of satisfying physiological and physical needs are the universal standards of social values; but in the information society, seeking the *satisfaction of achieved goals* will become the universal standard of values.

17. Finally, the spirit of industrial society has been the renaissance spirit of human liberation, which ethically means respect for fundamental rights and emphasis on the dignity of the individual, and a spirit of brotherly love to rectify inequalities.

The spirit of the information society will be the *spirit of globalism*, a symbiosis in which man and nature can live together in harmony, consisting ethically of *strict self-discipline and social contribution*.

Figure 1
THE TRANSFORMATION PROCESS FROM INDUSTRIAL SOCIETY TO INFORMATION SOCIETY

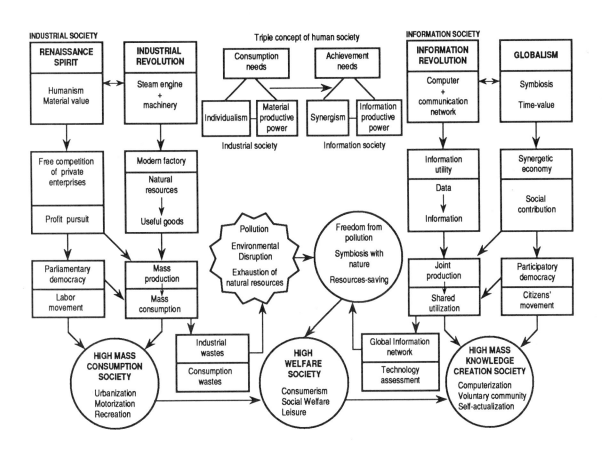

A Vision of Computopia

Looking back over the history of human society, we see that, as the traditional society of the Middle Ages was drawing to a close, the curtain was rising on the new industrial society. Thomas More, Robert Owen, Saint Simon, Adam Smith, and other prophets arose with a variety of visions portraying the emerging society. The one that is of special interest to me is Adam Smith's vision of a *universal opulent society*, which he sets out in *The Wealth of Nations*. Smith's universal affluent society conceives the condition of plenty for the people, economic conditions that should free the people from dependence and subordination, and enable them to exercise true independence of spirit in autonomous actions.

Smith presented *The Wealth of Nations* to the world in 1776. Strangely, James Watt's first steam engine was completed in the same year, but although the Industrial Revolution was under way, Smith's grand vision of a universal society of plenty was still far off when he died in 1790. His vision seems to be half-realized two centuries later, as society reaches Rostow's High Mass Consumption stage. The High Mass Consumption stage means that the material side of Smith's vision, of people having wealth in plenty, is partially accomplished, at least in the advanced countries. The wider vision he had, of individual independence and autonomy that would follow, has clearly not been realized, because the axis around which the mass production and consumption of industrial goods turns in industrial society comprises machines and power. Capital investments are necessarily immense, with the result that the concentration of capital and corresponding centralized power are the dominating factors. This is the fundamental structure of all industrial societies, something that transcends the question of a society being capitalistic or socialistic.

Industrial societies are characterized by centralized government supported by a massive military and administrative bureaucracy; and in capitalist states supranational enterprises have been added that make the modern state dependent on the trinity of industry, the military, and the government bureaucracy. In industrial societies the individual has freedom to take social action in three ways. A person is able to participate indirectly in government policy by voting in elections once every few years. He or she has the freedom of using income (received as compensation for subsistence labor) to purchase food and other articles necessary to sustain life, which implies freedom to use time on weekends and holidays as one likes. This freedom of selection, however, is freedom only in a limited sense, quite removed from the voluntary action selection that Adam Smith envisioned.

As the twenty-first century approaches, however, the possibilities of a universally opulent society being realized have appeared in the sense that Smith envisioned it, and the information society that will emerge from the computer communications revolution will be a society that actually moves toward a universal society of plenty.

The most important point I would make is that the information society will *function around the axis of information values rather than material values*, cognitive and action-selective information. In addition, the information utility, the core organization for the production of information, will have the fundamental character of an infrastructure, and knowledge capital will predominate over material capital in the structure of the economy.

Thus, if industrial society is a society in which people have affluent material consumption, the information society will be a society in which *the cognitive creativity of individuals flourishes throughout*. And if the highest stage of industrial society is the high mass consumption society, then the highest stage of the information society will be the *global futurization society*, a vision that greatly expands and develops Smith's vision of a universal opulent society; this is what I mean by "Computopia." This global futurization society will be a society in which everyone pursues the possibilities of his or her own future, actualizing his or her own self-futurization needs by acting in a goal-oriented way. It will be global, in which *multi-centered voluntary communities of citizens participating voluntarily in shared goals and ideas flourish simultaneously throughout the world*.

Computopia is a wholly new long-term vision for the twenty-first century, bearing within it the following concepts.

Pursuit and Realization of Time Value

My first vision of Computopia is that it will be a society in which each individual pursues and realizes time value. In Japan, the advanced welfare society is often talked about, and people are now calling for a shift of emphasis from rapid economic growth to stable growth, stressing social welfare and human worth, sometimes expressed as a shift from a GNP society to a GNW society, i.e. gross national welfare. The current idea of an advanced welfare society, however, tends to place the emphasis on the importance of living in a green environment where the sun shines. Obviously, in seeking to escape from the pollution and congestion of cities, and from the threat of a controlled society, this concept is significant, as indicative of our times. Yet it does not embrace a dynamic vision of the future, which I feel is its greatest weakness. The disappearance of pollution and congestion or even escape from the cities will not alone bring satisfaction. The need for self-realization is of a very high dimension that must be actively satisfied. The future society, as I see it, will be a society in which each individual is able to pursue and satisfy the need for self-fulfillment.

The self-realization I refer to is nothing less than the need to realize time value, and time value, of course, involves painting one's own design on the invisible canvas of one's future, and then setting out to create it. Such self-fulfillment will not be limited merely to individuals all pursuing their own self-realization aims, but will expand to include mini-groups, local societies, and functional communities.

Freedom of Decision and Equality of Opportunity

The concepts of freedom and equality grew out of the Puritan revolution (1649-60), which occurred in England around the end of the Middle Ages. Initially, the ideas of freedom from absolute authority and legal equality underlay these concepts, backed by the theories of social contract and individual consent as the basis of political authority, theories that maintain that freedom and equality are natural rights for all people. These two ideas provided the theoretical base for the formation of modern civil society.

As the capitalist economic system came into being, freedom and equality developed conceptually to include "freedom to work at something of one's own choice," "equality of ownership," "freedom to select an occupation," and "industrial equality," more commonly referred to as free competition.

The information society will offer new concepts of freedom and equality, embodying freedom of decision and equality of opportunity.

As I have said, the information society will be a society in which each individual pursues and realizes time value. In this type of society the freedom that an individual will want most will be *freedom to determine voluntarily the direction of time value realization in the use of available future time.* Call it "freedom of decision." Freedom of decision is the freedom of decision-making for selection of goal-oriented action, and refers to the right of each individual to determine voluntarily how to use future time in achieving a goal. This will be the most fundamental human right in the future information society.

"Equality of opportunity" is *the right all individuals must have, meaning that the conditions and opportunities for achieving the goals they have set for themselves must be available to them.* This will guarantee that all individuals have complete equality in all opportunities for education, and the opportunity to utilize such opportunities for action selection. Guaranteed equality of opportunity will, for the first time, assure that the people will share equally the maximum opportunities for realizing time value.

Flourishing Diverse Voluntary Communities

A society composed of highly educated people with a strong sense of community has long been a dream of mankind, and several attempts have been made to bring it into being. Recently, communes have been formed by young groups, and a number of cooperative communities have been formed in Japan. One was the *Yamagishi-kai*, formed after the war. The rapid growth of information-productive power built around the computer will see some big advances and developments beyond the ideas and attempts of the past. There will be enhanced independence of the individual, made possible for the first time by the high level of the information-productive power of the information society. The development of information-productive power will liberate people by reducing dependence on subsistence labor, with rapidly increasing material productive power as the result of automation, thus increasing the amount of free time one can use. There will also be an expanded ability to solve problems and pursue new possibilities, and then to bring such possibilities into reality; that is to say, it will expand one's ability for futurization.

The development of this information-productive power will offer the individual more independence than can be enjoyed now.

Another point to be noted is the autonomous expansion of creativity that will follow. The keynote of Utopian societies in the past has been the establishment of communal life through the common ownership of the means of production, based more or less on the prototype of primitive communism. This type of society has inevitably operated with a relatively low level of productive power; but the future information society will ensure more active voluntary communities, because humans will be liberated from dependence on subsistence labor, and because of the expanded possibilities for future time-value realization.

As a consequence, Utopian societies will move on from being merely cooperative societies, where most time must still be given to sustaining existence, to become dynamic and creative voluntary communities. It is people with common goals who will form the new voluntary communities, communities that will always be carried on by voluntary activity and the creative participation of individuals; individual futurization and group futurization will be harmoniously co-ordinated with societal futurization. In the mature information society of the future, nature communities, non-smoking communities, energy conservation communities, and many other new types of voluntary communities will prosper side by side.

Interdependent Synergistic Societies

A synergistic society is one that develops as individuals and groups cooperate in complementary efforts to achieve the common goals set by the society as a whole. The functioning societal principle is *synergism*, a new principle to replace the free competition of the current capitalistic society.

In the future information society, information utilities, whose structure of production is characterized by self-multiplication and synergy, will take the place of the present large factories, and become the societal symbol of the information society. These information utilities will be the centers of productive power, yielding time value that will be the common goal of voluntary communities, because of the *self-multiplication* that characterized production in the information utility.

Unlike material goods, information does not disappear by being consumed; and even more important, the value of information can be amplified indefinitely by constant additions of new information to the existing information. People will thus continue to utilize information which they and others have created even after it has been used; and, at macro-level, the most effective way to increase the production and utilization of information will be for people to *work together to make and share societal information.* This economic rationality means that the information utility itself will become part of the infrastructure. It will be the force behind the productive power that gives birth to socioeconomic values, and corresponding new socioeconomic laws and systems will come into being as a matter of course. *Synergistic feedforward* will function as the new societal principle to establish and develop social order, with the resulting societies becoming voluntary communities.

Functional Societies Free of Overruling Power

The history of the rule of man over man is long, continuing right into the present, simply changing form from absolute domination by an aristocracy linked with religion in feudal society to economic domination of enterprises in capitalist society, and to political domination by the bureaucracy in both socialist and capitalist society. The future information society, however, will become a *classless society*, free of overruling power, the core of society being voluntary communities. This will begin as informational and local communities which a limited number of people steadily develop and expand.

A voluntary community is a society in which the independence of the individual harmonizes with the order of the group, and the social structure is a multi-centered structure characterized by mutual cohesion. By "multi-centered" I mean that *every individual and group in a voluntary community is independent, and becomes a center.* "Mutual cohesion" means that *both individuals and groups that constitute the centers share a mutual attraction to form a social group.* Behind this mutual attraction lies the common goal, the spirit of synergy, with the ethics of self-imposed restraints. In other words, as individuals pursue their own time value, they work synergetically as a group to achieve a shared goal, and all exercise self-restraint so that there will be no interference with the social activities of others. This social structure is the overall control system of a voluntary community.

In the political system, democracy based on participation of the citizens will be the general mode of policy-making, rather than the indirect democracy of the parliamentary system. The technological base to support this participatory democracy will consist of (1) information networks made possible by the development of computer-communications technology; (2) simulation of policy models; and (3) feedback loops of individual opinions; with the result that policy-making will change from policy-making based on majority versus minority rule to policy-making based on the balance of gain and loss to individuals in the spectrum of their areas of concern, both in the present and in future time. In policy-making by this means, the feedback and accumulation of opinions will be repeated many times until agreement is reached, to insure the impartial balance of merits and demerits of the policy decision as it affects individuals and groups with conflicting interests.

The present bureaucratic administrative organization will be converted into a *voluntary management system of the citizens*. Only a small staff of specialists will be needed to carry out administrative duties, officers who are really professionals responsible for the administration functions. The bureaucratic organization of a privileged class will disappear. In this voluntary civil society, ruling, coercion, and control over others will cease. Society will be *synergistically functional*, the ideal form that the information society should take.

Computopia: Can It Become a Reality? _____

Can these visions of Computopia be turned into reality? We cannot escape the need to choose, before it is established, either "Computopia" or an "Automated State." These inescapable alternatives present two sharply contrasting bright and dark pictures of the future information society. If we choose the former, the door to a society filled with boundless possibilities will open; but if the latter, our future society will become a horrible and forbidding age.

As far as present indications go, we can say that there is a *considerable danger that we may move toward a controlled society*.

This is seen in the following tendencies.

During the first 15-20 years of their availability, computers were used mainly by the military and other governmental organizations and large private institutions. Medium and small enterprises and individuals were generally barred from using computer-communications technology, since large-scale computers at the early stage of automation were extremely costly. This situation caused a significant delay in democratic applications of computers. Initially, they were used mainly for automatic control and labor-saving purposes, rather than "problem solving" applications. The development of automatic control of separate systems to integrated real-time control systems covering broad areas is increasing the danger of a controlled society.

The utilization of computers for major scientific and technological applications, such as space development, has led us to neglect the need for coexistence with nature, while our impact on nature has grown immeasurably. The development of "big" science and technology has operated in such a way as to further increase the imbalance between human and nature systems.

If computerization continues in this direction, the possibility of a controlled society increases alarmingly.

However, I believe and predict that the catastrophic course to an "Automated State" will be avoided, and that our choice will be to follow the path to "Computopia." I give two logical reasons for my confidence.

The first theoretical basis is that *the computer as innovational technology is an ultimate science.* By "ultimate science" I mean a science that will bring immeasurable benefits to humanity if wisely used, but which would lead to destruction if used wrongly. Nuclear energy, for example, can be an extremely useful source of energy, but it could kill the greater part of the human race in an instant. The computer may, in one sense, be more important, as an ultimate science, than atomic energy.

If computers were to be used exclusively for automation, a controlled society, the alienation of mankind, and social decadence would become a reality. But if used fully for the creation of knowledge, a high mass-knowledge-creation society will emerge in which all people will feel their lives to be worth living. Further, an on-line, real-time system of computers connected to terminals with communication lines would turn society into a thoroughly managed society if utilized in a centralized way, but if their utilization is decentralized and open to all persons, it will lead to creation of a high mass-knowledge-creation society. Similarly, if data banks were to be utilized by a small group of people in power to serve their political purposes, a country would become a police state; but if used for health control and career development, every person can be saved from the sufferings of disease, and be able to develop full potentialities, opening up new future opportunities and possibilities.

The computer thus confronts us with these alternatives: an "Automated State" or a "Computopia." So it is not the *forecasting* of the state of a future information society, but our *own choice* that is decisive. There is only one choice for us—the road to Computopia. We cannot allow the computer, an ultimate science, to be used for the destruction of the spiritual life of mankind.

The second theoretical basis of my confidence is that *the information society will come about through a systematic, orderly transformation.* Information-productive power will develop rapidly to replace material productive power, a development that will bring about a qualitative conceptual change in production, from production of material goods to the production of far-reaching systems that include everything from production systems for material goods (such as automated factories), to social systems (wired cities, self-education systems), to political systems (direct citizen participation systems), and even to ecological systems.

Obviously, information-productive power centering on the computer communications network will be the powerful thrust to bring about societal systems innovations. New social and economic systems will be created continuously, and society as a whole will undergo dynamic changes: not the drastic social changes of the past, typified by the power struggles of ruling classes, wars between nation-states, and the political revolutions of mass revolt, but a *systematic, orderly transformation*. As old socioeconomic systems gradually become ineffectual and unable to meet the needs of the times, they will atrophy, and new, responsive socioeconomic systems will take their place, in the way that a metamorphosis takes place with an organism, the useless parts of the body atrophying and other parts developing in response to the new demands.

Moreover, this systematic transformation of the societal structure will be brought about by citizen action, *changing means- and goal-oriented modes of action into cause-and-effect modes of action*. I have pointed out that human modes of action will become goal-oriented in the information society: these modes of goal-oriented action will evolve to the point where they function as a goal principle, to become the principle of social action. When this happens, social action will be logical, means-oriented action for the pursuit of common goals. So we can replace the term "goal-means-oriented action" with the term "cause-effect relationship," following the idea of Max Weber, who changed this concept of goal-means relationship into a concept of cause-effect relationship. In the information society, the social actions of citizens in general will become goal-means relationships that operate as cause-effect relationships.

The Rebirth of Theological Synergism of Man and the Supreme Being _____

The final goal of Computopia is the *rebirth of theological synergism* of man and the supreme being, or if one prefers it, *the ultimate life* force — expressions that have meaning to both those of religious faith and the irreligious. This can be called the ultimate goal of Computopia. The relation existing between man and nature was the beginning of civilization. For many thousands of years man was completely encompassed by the systems of nature, which he had to obey or be destroyed by them. Five or six thousand years ago, man succeeded in harnessing these systems of nature in a limited way to increase agricultural production, and the first civilizations were built. This marked the beginning of man's conquest of nature. But with the Industrial Revolution the conquest of nature meant the destruction of nature, and now nature's retaliation has begun, the sequel to man's relation with nature that turned into destruction.

Now, a new relationship is beginning. At last, man and nature have begun to act together in a new ecological sense, on a global scale, in synergistic society. At the base of this conversion of human society into an ecological system is the awareness of the limitations of scientific technology. It means awareness that scientific technology is simply the application of scientific principles, and that these cannot be changed by man; nor can he create new principles to work and live by. It is also a new awareness of the commonality of man's destiny, in that there is no place where man can live except on this earth, which first gave him life; from this very awareness is emerging the idea of a synergistic society where man and nature must exist in true symbiosis.

This is the assertive, dynamic idea that man can live and work together with nature, not in a spirit of resignation that says man can only live within the framework of natural systems; but man and nature will work together as one. Put another way, man approaches the universal supra life, with man and god acting as one.

"God" does not refer to a god in the remote heavens; it refers to nature with which we live our daily lives. The scientific laws that we have already identified and are aware of are simply manifestations of the activity of this supreme power. The ultimate ideal of the global futurization society will be for man's actions to be in harmony with nature in building a synergistic world.

This synergism is a modern rebirth of the theological synergism which teaches that "spiritual rebirth depends upon the cooperation of the will of man and the grace of God," however it may be expressed. It aims to build an earthly, not a heavenly, synergistic society of god and man.

When we open the book of history, we see that, when man brought about the accumulation of wealth and an increase in productive power, various choices had to be made. The Greeks built magnificent temples to Apollo and carved beautiful statues of Venus. The Egyptians built gigantic pyramids for their Pharaohs, and the Romans turned the brutalities of the Colosseum into a religious rite. The Chinese built the Great Wall to keep out the barbarians. Now man has made the fires of heaven his own, and left footprints on the craters of the moon.

We are moving toward the twenty-first century with the very great goal of building a Computopia on earth, the historical monument of which will be only several chips one inch square in a small box. But that box will store many historical records, including the record of how 4 billion world citizens overcame the energy crisis and the population explosion, achieved the abolition of nuclear weapons and complete disarmament, conquered illiteracy, and created a rich symbiosis of god and man, without the compulsion of power or law, but by the voluntary cooperation of the citizens to put into practice their common global aims.

Accordingly, the civilization to be built as we approach the twenty-first century will not be a material civilization symbolized by huge constructions, but will be virtually an *invisible civilization*. Precisely, it should be called an "information civilization." *Homo sapiens*, who stood at the dawn of the first material civilization at the end of the last glacial age, is now standing at the threshold of the second, the information civilization after ten thousand years.

12. GLOBAL ISSUES: INFORMATION TECHNOLOGY AND THE THIRD WORLD

JUAN RADA

Information technology is changing the technological profile of manufacturing and the service industries. The main effect on the less developed
countries will be to increase the obsolescence of their industries, services,
and development strategies.   Juan Rada is with the International
Management Institute, Geneva and this paper was first read to the
IFAC seminar, Vienna, Austria, March 1983.

Introduction

The effects of information technology on North-South relations, the international
division of labor and development, is a subject of growing interest to specialists as
well as policy-makers (Mitterand, 1982).   I will attempt to review here the
reasons for this interest by analyzing aspects of the effects of the technology in
some of these areas. In a brief article all aspects cannot be covered, and the in-
tention is to highlight some of the main issues.

Since the beginning of the debate in developed countries about the effects of
information technology on their societies and economies, consideration has been
given to potential impacts, both positive and negative, on developing countries. In
the early stages of discussions and research, the main concern was related to the
assessment of economic effects, especially the potential erosion of one of the
developing countries' perceived comparative advantages, namely low labor costs
(Rada, 1980).

This concern remains central today, but it is qualified by a number of considerations as the understanding of the effects of technology grows. Such considerations include questions of quality, product cycle, change in the function of
products, and a better understanding of the behavior and structure of the suppliers of the new type of equipment. In addition, the early concern was especially
centered around the erosion of advantages of offshore assembly, especially in
those countries with export-oriented economies —which, of course, constitute a
rather exceptional group of developing countries.

Reprinted from *The Information Technology Revolution*, pp. 571-589 published by the MIT
Press by Tom Forester.

From the almost exclusive focus on automation in manufacturing and economic effects, new and important elements have been added. From an economic point of view, two of these deserve special attention. The first concerns attempts to understand the effects of automation within developing countries, particularly in those cases where development is geared primarily toward the internal market. This is the case, for instance, with most of the Latin American economies (UNIDO/ECLA, 1982).

The second relates to one aspect of the effects of information technology that, although implicit in early research, was somehow overlooked in terms of its real importance: namely, that it allows the transportability of services to an extent and depth not dreamed of some years ago. This has opened up new questions, especially for developing countries.

Although I shall focus on these two points, the social, cultural, and political effects of automation are of equal, if not of greater, importance. Lately, substantial attention has been paid to these points, particularly in the context of searching for alternative development strategies. This search is not new, but it differs from earlier attempts in its desire to see whether, given the nature of the technology, some entirely new concept of development can be pursued, heavily based on human resources, information, and knowledge-intensive activities: in brief, to determine how developing countries can appropriate information technology in a qualitatively different form, and aim at some sort of leapfrogging.

These views are based on a prospective assessment of the form human activities could take as a result of the changing technological profile of society. This view has been developed out of a mechanical extrapolation of the potential of the technology and is most creatively expressed in works such as Alvin Toffler's *The Third Wave*.

In other words, would it not be better for LDCs to aim at societal models that will truly consider the prospective "information society," rather than to evolve (if possible) through the traditional lines? This view might be tempting for many, but often fails to acknowledge not only the unequal distribution of resources and knowledge, but also the fact that "informatization" is the *consequence* of development and not its cause, although the technology can be used for development purposes.

This is not to negate the fact that development needs to be conceived in a completely different form in order to account for the current technological mutation, which indeed questions the very core of currently pursued development strategies. Such questioning, however, involves developed as well as developing countries, since a global approach will sooner or later be necessary to readdress the direction that current changes seem to be taking. The starting point in this discussion is to list briefly the main areas of the economic impact of information technology (IT).

IT: The Main Areas of Impact

Effects in production.

1. Substitution of mechanical components (e.g. watches)
2. Substitution of electromechanical components (e.g. cash registers and calculators)
3. Substitution of electric and older electronics (e.g. computers)
4. Upgrading of traditional products, creating entirely new capabilities (e.g. word processors)
5. Upgrading of control systems and substitution by electronic ones (e.g. machine tools)
6. New products (e.g. games)

In the case of products, the use of electronics can alter the very function of the product. A good example is cash registers, which, from being only adding machines, have become data entry terminals, potentially part of a system of accounting, control, and ordering. Other products, such as machine tools or word processors, if supplied with the adequate hardware and software, can communicate to other machines, data bases, or computers.

Effects in manufacturing processes.

1. Increase in the flexibility, adaptability, and economy of production (e.g. CAD/CAM)
2. Incorporation of skills and functions into equipment (e.g. CNC machines or robots)

In the case of processes, the important developments are essentially two. First there is the programmability, which leads to flexibility, since the same oquipment can be reprogrammed to perform a different task rather than changing the machine. This in turn leads to the second important point, which is that there is a great resistance to obsolescence and thus an extension of the life-cycle of manufacturing processes. Robots, for example, are very resistant to obsolescence since in most cases it is sufficient to change the program and/or the "hand" to use the equipment for a different operation. This has an important capital-saving effect. In addition, there are savings on downtime for retooling and changing tasks.

Effects in the office.
1. Automation of routine clerical work (e.g. data and word processing)
2. Increase in the efficiency and effectiveness of communications, especially in those areas where work is less formalized, such as in professional and managerial areas.

Automation in the office or, more accurately, the use of electronic tools as aids or facilitators of the work is and will have a far-reaching effect on economic activities in general and especially in the production of services. In developed countries the percentage of the labor force working in offices or information activities is constantly growing, in some cases reaching 50 percent. The office sector has traditionally been under-capitalized and its productivity has been low as compared with manufacturing and agriculture.

It is not known how the current process of rapid diffusion of electronic technology in the office, in either clerical or managerial activities, might affect companies' competitiveness, productivity, and the international division of labor.

It is safe to say at this stage that, increasingly, most employees, whether in agriculture or in manufacturing, are concerned with information-processing activities rather than production. In fact, the absolute number of people employed in manufacturing has been decreasing in the US since 1964 and in Europe since the early 1970s. This trend will continue, as it did with agriculture in the past. The decrease in the labor content of agriculture was accompanied by substantial reductions in hours worked and important increases in output.

Effects in services.
1. Transportability of services (e.g. remote access to data bases, banks, archives, etc.). This also leads to new services (e.g. Prestel)
2. Increase in self-service (e.g. gas stations, banking, etc.)

These in turn lead to the replacement of human-to-human services by machines. The impact of information technology on services is perhaps the most important in the long run because it is creating entirely new possibilities that are different from past activities. This point will be discussed later.

The Re-invention of Industry

The first question to ask in terms of the impact of information technology on developing countries is how technology affects developed ones. This question is pertinent owing to the fact that it is in these countries that the technology was first used to increase productivity in manufacturing and services. This problem has been extensively studied, and the main conclusion is that a re-invention of industry will be necessary, that is, a radical change in the technological profile of productive activities.

This change naturally affects countries that have geared their efforts toward industrialization either through import substitution for the internal market or through exports.

The basic hypothesis is that the industrial utilization of IT leads to an erosion of developing countries' comparative advantages and international competitiveness, especially in traditional industries. The main reasons for this are as follows.

Decrease in the relative importance of labor-intensive manufacturing and cost of labor. This is essentially due to the automation of production, which tends thereby to erode the competitiveness of low labor costs. A good illustration is the comparison of Hong Kong and the US in the manufacturing of electronic devices. Table 1 shows that when the process is manual the difference in cost is about 1 to 3, decreasing drastically with semi-automatic processes and automatic ones. While this example refers to components, a similar process is taking place for systems and consumer products. In the case of TV sets, the chairman of Electronics Industry of Korea stated that owing to the automation of assembly and technological change,

> the manufacturing costs of a TV set in Korea and that of the US are practically comparable to each other. Rapid advancement of industrial technology is eliminating labor-intensive portions of the electronics industry; this tends to make it harder for Korea to earn enough foreign currency to import expensive new technology. [Kim, 1980].

It should be mentioned that TV sets as a product have changed substantially in the last few years and are bound to change more in the future when they become digital and the CRT (cathode-ray tube) is replaced by some other form of

Table 1
MANUFACTURING COST PER DEVICE (US$)

Process	Hong Kong	US
Manual	0.0248	0.0753
Semi-automatic	0.0183	0.0293
Automatic	0.0163	0.0178

Source: Global Electronics Information Newsletter, No. 25, October 1982.

display. In other areas preliminary evidence shows similar trends. For instance, the expansion of automation in Japan has contributed to a recent reduction of investment in the Asia/Pacific region involving firms in electronics, assembly parts and textiles (*Business Asia,* 1982).

In the case of garments, a trend to systems optimization and automation is clearly underway. Although not yet a "perfect fit," Hoffman and Rush (1982) conclude that: "Although it has not happened yet, to a great extent there is a feeling among the large producers that a large share of offshore production will be brought back [to the developed countries]."

Value-added is pushed out of assembly and into components as integration increases. This occurs at the product level, while in systems value-added, it is pushed upwards toward servicing. This process is proper to the industries where electronics has substituted other components in products (as described above) and implies that functions previously obtained by assembling pieces are incorporated in the electronic component itself.

In this category fall, for instance, calculators, telexes, sewing machines, and precision engineering in general. In the case of electronic components the amount of value-added obtained in offshore assembly has been decreasing constantly. The dutiable value of components imported under the US tariff arrangements, that is, the value-added in offshore plants to US products diminished from 57 percent in 1974 to 39 percent in 1978 (USITC, 1979).

The main explanation for this is the increasing value of the parts produced in the US as a result of the growing complexity of devices. This process has continued since: one only needs to see that in 1978 the level of technology was LSI (large-scale integration) rather than the current VSLI (very large-scale integration). As the level of integration of components increases, the value-added obtained in front-end operations also increases. Furthermore, the assembling of chips is being automated and moved, in the case of sophisticated devices, to "clean rooms."

Changes in product cycles. Product cycles in many areas have been considerably condensed while process cycles have increased, owing to the resistance to obsolescence of programmable machines and equipment. Typically, product cycles have been shortened in some industries (e.g. office equipment) from 12 to three or four years. This has led to a concentration of manufacturing investment in capital-intensive flexible manufacturing, and partly explains the erosion of the advantage of developing countries in so-called "mature" or "semi-mature" products.

In other words, the "product cycle" view of international trade needs review, since formerly mature industries or products are being completely revitalized. A case in point is a European company that closed a plant in South America because the short product cycle did not justify the investment. In the past, the payback time was far longer with a more stable technology. At the time of mechanical or electromechanical technology, local manufacturing was justified because of the large amount of value-added obtained in assembly; and, because of the longer cycle, there was a relatively small incidence of amortization and development cost in the final cost of products (Cohen, 1981).

Quality considerations. These are growing in importance as markets become more segmented and competition increases under conditions of low growth. This in itself leads to what has been called the "hands-off" approach in manufacturing or automation, coupled with a change in the skill-mix at the shopfloor. One of the main reasons why Japanese manufacturers in the field of semiconductors make very limited use of offshore facilities in developing countries is precisely the perception that the required level of quality cannot be obtained.

Quality has a cost, and requires an infrastructure and substantial managerial know-how. In some cases the old manufacturing system of assembly is inconsistent with quality requirements and new methods have to be used, notably modular or group-work schemes, with emphasis on a highly multi-skilled labor force. This phenomenon highlights the dilemma for export as well as import substitution strategies.

The elements mentioned above are the tip of the iceberg of current change. Further down the inevitable question is: What about access to technology, its production and application? Three comments are necessary here.

First, almost by definition, advanced and rapidly changing technology is not properly documented and therefore its transfer tends to have peculiarities. In fact, transfer of technology in the area of concern of this paper takes place essentially through three main mechanisms:

1. mobility of personnel, which take with them their own knowledge (this is the so-called "Silicon Valley syndrome"). This accounts for a large part of transfers in the US;
2. second sourcing, which is the agreement between two producers to manufacture fully compatible products. This might or might not entail full exchange of technology. An agreement of this nature implies a partner that can produce at similar technical, economic, and quality standards;
3. cross-licensing agreements, which assumes a mutual exchange of technology.

In brief, transfer tends to take place among established or important producers, and furthermore, the technology is tightly guarded as trade secrets. Many companies in the software area, for instance, do not patent or copyright their products because it entails disclosure of valuable information.

The second comment is that the issue is access not only to a given technology but to the *process of technological change*, because of the dynamism of it. This leads to a number of questions that I shall not discuss in this paper, notably about the innovation environment. The point that I wish to make is that access to the process of technological change in advanced areas (and not only IT) seems to take place essentially, as European companies have discovered, with participation in the equity of companies. The possibility of some developing countries doing this is relatively small, as some exploration has shown, essentially because of the high mobility of the personnel and also because of political considerations. In this respect one should simply mention that in many areas of electronics civilian applications have surpassed military ones, creating an additional obstacle to prospects for transfer of technology.

The third comment refers to production and applications. In terms of production, few LDCs are in a position even to raise the question. Some have implemented policies in this field (i.e. India and Brazil), but their performance cannot be evaluated at this stage, except to say that they at least provide the countries with the capacity to follow the technologies closely. Success will depend largely on the targeting of market segments and technologies (e.g. uncommitted logic arrays and custom circuits in general). At the systems (e.g. minis, micros, etc.) and software level, the situation is different. The assembly of equipment from components that are bought practically off-the-shelf is taking place in many countries, and this is likely to continue for some time to come. But as the level of integration of components grows, the amount of software incorporated into chips (firmware) will also grow, taking value-added away from the assembly of systems.

To illustrate this further, the trend in microcomputers is to incorporate into the hardware as many "utilities" as possible, such as word processing, Visicalc, and others, in a similar fashion to what happened with the pocket calculator. At the beginning the calculator featured four arithmetic operations; as integration increased, more were added, making the machine more useful and also less expensive. This trend implies that, in the not-too-distant future, the source of value-added will go to systems software, design, and service in a far more pronounced way than today.

The assembly of systems will continue, especially when protected by tariff barriers, incentives of industrial policies, or both (i.e. Brazil). These types of equipment will be used largely in internal markets, and are unlikely to make a dent internationally. In addition, systems in developing countries tend to be far more expensive than in the international marketplace, making less economical their application, especially when labor costs are lower. In one Latin American country the cost of word processors and microcomputers was, respectively, double and triple that of the US. This is explained by a number of reasons, the most important being that suppliers have to cover maintenance, software development, and overheads, selling a rather limited amount of equipment as they operate as "profit-centers." Installation and use of the equipment is also more costly in some cases because of expensive auxiliary installations (i.e. electrical generators), sub-utilization, or lack of adequate skills, especially managerial ones.

Optimization of systems and office/service automation. One of the most important effects of IT is that it leads to the optimization of business activities as a result of rapid and timely processing of information and the relative ease of communications. I prefer to use the term "service automation" rather than "office automation" because it truly accounts for the nature of the change. The impact of office automation is measurable not at the work-station level (as is done with word processors), but rather at the level of total systems performance, mainly because of the effects on management information systems and managerial effectiveness. To illustrate the point, consider that secretaries account for only 7 percent of the total clerical costs in the US and spend only 20 percent of their time typing.

It is not, then, in the work station that the effects of office automation are to be found, but rather on the synergies, greater numbers of options, faster response, and more informed decisions that are derived from it. This is not to negate the important productivity increases at the work station but to treat them as one, and perhaps not the most important, component of current improvement. Research conducted at IMI-Geneva shows precisely this, and furthermore confirms the optimization of systems that takes place within companies utilizing IT.

The effects of these processes on the international division of labor and developing countries is yet unknown, but it is possible to make some tentative hypotheses. First, given the composition of the labor force in the advanced countries and also within manufacturing companies, an improvement in systems performance will further reinforce the advantages derived from automation and product change. For instance, in pharmaceuticals today, typically only about 30 percent of the labor force is employed in production, and the proportion is expected to decrease from current levels by as much as 40 percent by 1990. This implies that manufacturing is decreasing in importance (as measured in total cost) while performances at the systems level and innovation are becoming the key to profit, growth, and survival.

Second, and most important, is the increase in productivity of services, which for the most part are information-processing activities. The transport ability of services is the most important long-term effect of the technology; thus, more efficient production of them reinforces the great advantage that developed countries have in this area. I shall elaborate on this point later.

Changes in skill-mix and conditions for absorption of technology. I mentioned earlier that important changes in skills accompany the product/process changes. In some cases there are significant skill-saving effects (e.g. CNC machine tools), which can be beneficial to developing countries. In general, the trend seems to be toward higher skills, especially at the systems and design level and not the least in software. Most of the developing countries' labor forces have low skills, or skills of a mechanical nature that in many cases are being substantially altered (for instance, for interface types of work). This again calls for a more active policy on the part of the developing countries in terms of training and education. The absorption of technology is also changing, not only for the reasons stated above about transfer, but also because knowledge tends to be of a more abstract nature.

It is not by chance that much innovation in electronics has taken place around universities (Stanford, Berkeley, MIT, and now Cambridge in the UK). This means that the links between scientific and technological knowledge are becoming tighter, and the neat categories of the past that distinguished invention from innovation are not always tenable.

The need for scientific policies is obvious, especially in areas where these types of knowledge are closely related to technological development (e.g. physics of materials in electronics or genetic engineering), but these policies require a clear focus. It is true that current and future technological progress is based on science, but at the same time innovation does not necessarily require a sophisticated scientific base, as Japan has proven so convincingly during the 1960s and the early 1970s. This is particularly true in relation to process and systems innovation.

In the first case changes tend to be incremental (unless the product changes), and in the second case (systems) changes tend to be of a conceptual and organizational nature. A classical example of this latter type of innovation is self-service, which has boosted productivity in many sectors with little "hardware" investment of R&D work. Credit cards, marketing systems, financial services, leasing and rental operations are other examples. In this respect it would be interesting to compare innovation in banking with the familiar innovation curves in electronics; we would probably find, to our surprise, that they would not differ much.

The skill-mix is changing while new skill requirements are emerging, particularly in software, systems design, and (an almost forgotten one) management and organization. Two different companies or countries with similar skills and other endowments may perform quite differently simply because of differences in their management and organization which lead to varying degrees of technology absorption. Often, skills of different natures can be obtained through training and retraining, but a precondition is the action that creates the *need* for them: that is the answer to the questions what and why, the know-what and know-why. If these two questions are not answered, obtaining know-how will make no difference to performance—on the contrary, it will not even be possible to obtain the proper know-how.

These changes are to an extent already occurring in LDCs, but in some fields the die is cast while in others selectional decisions can still be made. Developing countries can obtain immense benefits from technology if it is applied in the context of a development strategy. For instance, IT is capital-saving in manufacturing and services (lower entry barriers) per unit of output. This leads to the traditional dilemma of technologically induced labor-saving effects, since capital intensity tends to increase.

The main issue for developing countries in terms of employment/technology lies in the field of agriculture rather than computerization in manufacturing or services. The reasons are rather simple. The number of computers currently in use has a practically insignificant effect on the overall volume of employment when they do cause displacement. The two largest users of computers in the developing world are India (about 1000) and Brazil (about 10,000), which in the context of their economies is minimal. The applications to which they are put remain traditional, and they tend to optimize administrative systems that in turn create beneficial effects in the rest of the country's economy.

An illustrative case is the informatization of the postal check system in Algeria, where 176 people were made redundant through voluntary retirement. The general effects can be seen in Table 2. Examples like this illustrate the trade-off between employment and the use of technology and show how beneficial IT can be when applied in critical bottlenecks, especially in relation to infrastructure and services. It needs to be done with the normal criteria of appropriateness of technology, that is, selectivity. It is in the fields of administrative services and infrastructure that the short-term benefits can be realized rather than in totally new types of applications, which will take a long time to mature and are heavily dependent on equipment performance and characteristics of the human-machine interface.

Capital-saving effects also take place in manufacturing and agricultural applications, together with skill-saving effects. The real challenge in this field is to combine traditional and low technologies with advanced ones, and much needs to be done here.

Table 2
COMPUTERIZATION OF THE POSTAL CHECK SYSTEM IN ALGERIA, 1974-7

	Manual 1974	Computerized 1977
No. of operations	24,360,000	33,620,000
Volume (millions DA)	109.5	210.8
No. of accounts	452,000	709,000
Waiting time at centers before processing of document	15 days	2 days
Payment at cash desk	3-6 hours	2 min.
Saturation ratio	95%	50%
Employment	856	680

Source: Secretariat d'Etat au Plan, Commissariat National a l'Informatique. "L'Informatique en Algerie." Algiers, 1978.

Developing countries are far more heterogeneous than developed ones, and sometimes this shorthand concept masks tremendous differences. In some countries (e.g. Southeast Asia) companies are combining advanced technologies with lower labor costs, and future developments will depend on the competitive reaction of developing countries' producers. Others are following a policy of technological upgrading in the exporting industries, and even authorization for acquiring foreign computerized equipment depends in some cases on potential export performance. Furthermore, many developing countries have large pools of educated labor in areas most appropriate to current change, such as software, and great potential exists in this field. I insist on the word "potential" since production or export of software is not as easy as it might sound; in some cases import substitution of software might be far more economical than attempting exports.

Possible policies and measures to maximize the benefits of IT for developing countries are not only necessary but urgent. But this should not mask the equally urgent need to search for different development models, South-South cooperation, regionalism, and, most importantly, some sort of social command of technology. *Command* of technology differs substantially from *control* in the sense that it maintains the relative autonomy of action and creativity at the technological and scientific level, but provides a direction for the application of that creativity based on fundamental human and social needs. A policy of this nature will emerge only if, at country, regional, and global levels, the priorities of IT are identified as being based on a normative concept of development.

Notwithstanding short-term policies and strategies, the fact remains that the gap between developed and developing countries will increase, as will the gaps *within* developing countries, which is one of the important structural causes of their present state. The gap between countries has been shown in many ways. For our purpose what matters is the situation in IT, which can be seen from Tables 3 and 4.

Three important conclusions can be derived from this purely quantitative check. First, the participation of developing countries in the process of "informatization" is indeed small. Second, the gap is likely to grow by a factor of two during the 1980s. It should be said that telecommunications investments are far more predictable than computer investments, owing to longer planning cycles. If anything, the figures in Tables 3 and 4 are optimistic, and would probably need to be adjusted downwards in the light of the severe financial problems of developing

Table 3
VALUE OF DATA PROCESSING EQUIPMENT* (US $1000)

	1978	%	1983	%	1988	%
Developed countries (US, W. Europe and Japan)	110	83	180	82	250	80
Other countries (incl. centrally planned economies)	22.5	17	40	18	61	20
Total	132.5	100	220	100	311	100

*Micros are not included
Source: Diebold. Europe, 1979.

Table 4
WORLDWIDE TELECOMMUNICATIONS EQUIPMENT MARKET* (US $1000)

	1980	%	1985	%	1990	%
Developed countries	36	90	53.5	89	75.4	86
Developing countries	4	10	6.7	11	12.1	14
Total	40	100	60.2	100	87.5	100

*Includes telephone, telegraph, telex, data communications, satellite communications, mobile radio and radio telephone, radio paging, and cable TV.
Source: Arthur D. Little, Inc.

countries that had large telecom and informatic projects (e.g. Nigeria and Mexico).

More precise "informatic indicators," particularly in terms of data and satellite communications are revealed in the data of Table 5. The gap in transmission and satellites is even larger when one considers the entire telecom market (Table 4), and it points to a qualitative difference in priorities for investment and the type of emerging infrastructure. The telecommunications infrastructure, especially in data transmission, is the one that will largely determine the "multiplier effects" of information technology, particularly in terms of knowledge and information-intensive activities.

The third conclusion that can be drawn from Tables 3-5 is that investment in the field of communications and transmission equipment increases almost mechanically the possibility of optimizing systems, increasing office and service productivity, raising the efficiency of production, and furthering conditions for capital-saving effects (e.g. optimization of stocks). This implies that the relative position of developing countries in terms of leapfrogging into the "information age" is even lower than thought if taking traditional indicators of the "industrial age." This is why I stated earlier that IT is the consequence rather than the cause of development, and leapfrogging can be possible only within a global rather than a purely national or regional strategy.

It should be understood that the process of "informatization" of society is one in which greater amounts of knowledge and information are incorporated into goods and services. This also means that knowledge and information activities acquire a dynamism of their own right and become sources of wealth creation and value-added (e.g. design, programming and R&D). As the amount of information and knowledge incorporated into products, processes, and services increases, the

Table 5
TRANSMISSION AND SATELLITE MARKETS (US$ MILLION)

	Telegraph, telex & data transmission		Satellite communications	
	1980	1990	1980	1990
Africa	48.4	97.3	3.0	10.5
Latin America	106.5	189.0	14.3	34.9
North America	2481.4	6000.5	122.8	463.7
Europe	733.9	1984.1	59.0	189.2

Source: Arthur D. Little, Inc.

relative amount of energy, materials, labor, and capital decreases. Technologies diffuse through society precisely because they are factor-saving, and IT saves simultaneously in all directions while increasing the capacity to create and process information, and therefore contributing to the accumulation of knowledge.

The empirical evidence shows precisely that the current process is one where greater amounts of information and knowledge are going into production, and not, as some might suggest, that we shall live off information exchanges (Gershuny and Miles, 1983; Jonscher, 1983). Indeed, the greater consumers of robots or even computers are those industries such as automobiles or telecommunications that a few years ago were considered "traditional" sectors.

The nature of the technology calls for a more detailed understanding of "knowledge and information-intensive activities." I have chosen here to examine the services (there are other aspects, such as knowledge and information transfers), because perhaps the most far-reaching effect of technology is that it allows the transportability of services: instead of going to a bank or library, we can transport the bank or library to our own terminals in our offices or homes.

Services Revisited

The impact of IT on services is vast. It is not possible here to account for all the elements involved, among other reasons because the understanding of services and the data available are limited.

Until recently, interest in the service sector has been due mainly to the tendency for the share of services to rise in total output and employment and the implications of this for the growth of output, employment, and productivity. Two elements make a review necessary: first, the role of services in international trade, and thus on domestic economies, and second, the impact of IT on the production, commercialization, and distribution of services.

The first problem one encounters is that of definition, because the service sector is too heterogeneous in terms of its production and consumption. In this context I simply take the current, albeit imperfect, measurement of trade in nonfactor services or service products. This area includes shipping, insurance, banking, other trade-related services and private and public-related services. In this category, the situation of developing countries can be seen in Table 6.

In areas such as private services, where transportability is increasing, the balance of trade was –$2911 million in 1978 and –$4635 million in 1980. While international trade in goods is either stagnant or decreasing, trade in services has been growing. The case of the UK is illustrative, with private invisible exporters earning a total of £26,472 million in 1981, up 13 percent from 1980, which in itself

Table 6
BALANCE OF TRADE IN NON-FACTOR SERVICES, BY SELECTED
GROUPS OF COUNTRIES, 1977-80 (US $MILLION)

Selected oil exporters	1977	1978	1979	1980
EEC	9,551	13,400	10,183	10,164
EFTA	2,632	3,920	4,623	4,892
US	3,792	3,793	1,408	3,852
LDCs	−20,270	−25,711	−36,701	−42,528
	−18,987	−23,909	−33,623	−38,803

Source: UNCTAD Secretariat, based on IMF statistics; UNCTAD, "Trade and Development Report." Geneva, 1982.

was a record. A large percentage of the above figure was earnings from investments abroad.

One interesting category is consulting engineers, who exported £214 million in 1976 and £425 million in 1980; this is the type of service that is becoming highly transportable (Committee on Invisible Trade, 1982). These figures give a general view of the type of volume involved. In general, developing countries have high deficits in this field, although the two largest deficits belong to West Germany and Japan. The interest here is to see how IT affects this area, which is a dynamic and expanding one in international trade and one that accounts for the greatest percentage of labor in the developed economies as well as a growing percentage of output.

For the decade 1970-80, as recorded in the balance of payments statistics, world services exports grew at an average annual rate of 18.7 percent. The value of service exports in 1980 was of the order of $350 billion. The growth figure is lower than that for world exports of merchandise, but the latter figures are inflated by the upsurge in oil prices (Office of the United States Trade Representative, 1983).

The application of IT to the transportation services has had four main effects on the economy (besides increases in self-service and replacement of human-to-human services by goods):

1. an increase in the transparency of markets owing to the availability of information; for example, the listing of suppliers in data bases with their prices, or teleshopping that is being applied first to industrial products.

This change tends to increase competition since it provides exposure to a wide range of choices;

2. blurring of borders between service providers (i.e. between retailing and banking) and industry and services (i.e. telecommunications and computing);

3. lowering of the barrier to entry in many services: this happens because, once the infrastructure is in place (the data highways), the cost of marketing services is reduced to plugging into networks. For instance, a software producer utilizing Prestel in the UK has theoretically as many retailing points as there are terminals. Furthermore, he/she can transport the product through the telephone lines. In the past, this would have required representatives in many places and an investment in bricks and mortar. Similarly, the use of telebanking allows small banks to compete with large ones, with the added advantage that they have fewer fixed assets to depreciate. The analogy here is the lower barrier to entry into the market for a farmer when a main road passes in front of his land;

4. internationalization of services and specialization in its production. It is this point that I wish to develop further here.

The process of internationalization took place first in mining and agriculture and later in manufacturing. Today it is the turn of services, in accordance with the changes of the structure of the economies. The analogy that could help to clarify the current phenomenon is the effect that the steamboat or the development of railroads had on trade in the last century. The economic transport of bulk cargo destroyed the "natural" barrier to trade internationally and within countries. This was instrumental in the integration of national economies and the development of an international one in tangible goods. This in turn made evident the comparative advantages in the production of goods since distance was no longer an overwhelming impediment to international trade.

The decreasing cost of transmission in telecommunications, the convergence with computers, and the increase in productivity in the production of services is creating similar conditions, but this time in intangibles. Thus, if a European consults a data base in the US he is importing an intangible service, while the US is exporting one. Current change is then making evident the comparative advantages in the production of services, especially those that are knowledge- and information-intensive. One should qualify this statement, by saying that little is known about economies of scale (or scope) in the production of services or the relative factor intensity of their production.

The concentration of knowledge and information-intensive services in developed countries is a fact, and the gap is more pronounced than in manufacturing. The question here is not simply one of import-export but also of job creation, patterns of investment, and production, inasmuch as the latter is becoming also knowledge-intensive. To illustrate this, one can take the example of what the machine-tool industry will look like in the future. Machine tools could be linked via telecommunications to machining data bases, and what will happen to them will be similar to computers: the generation of revenues will be based on software and services rather than hardware. At that point producers will be making "machine packages" rather than discrete pieces of equipment. A manufacturer will buy the entire "package," including the link and servicing. This in itself will change the nature of technology transfer.

Tables 7 and 8 show the concentration and possible consequences of this trend, based on a rather narrow set of criteria, namely, data bases and Canadian imports of data processing services by 400 foreign subsidiaries operating in Canada. Another study (Price Waterhouse Associates, 1981) shows that the trends identified remained valid. (It should be clear that Canada is in a rather exceptional geographical position, and also has special telecommunication arrangements with the US. This means that these types of effects are more pronounced in Canada.)

Table 7
REFERENCE DATA BASES AND RECORDS:
GEOGRAPHICAL DISTRIBUTION, 1975-9

Area	1975	1977	1979
US			
No. of data bases	177	208	259
No. of records (millions)	46	58	94
Other developed economies			
No. of data bases	124	154	269
No. of records (millions)	6	13	55
Total			
No. of data bases	301	362	528
No. of records (millions)	52	71	149

Source: M. E. Williams, "Data Bases and On-line Statistics for 1979," ASIS *Bulletin*, December 1980.

Table 8
COST TO CANADA OF IMPORT OF DATA PROCESSING
AND COMPUTER SERVICES

	1975	1978	1980	1985
Cost of imports of services	$155m	--	$560m	$1.5b
Proportion of outside services required	30%	--	41%	52%
Est. job losses	4,400	7,500	11,000	23,000
Data processing jobs represented in losses	--	6%	8%	14%

Source: Consultative Committee on the Implications of Telecommunications for Canadian Sovereignty (Clyne Report), "Telecommunications and Canada," Canadian Government Publishing Center, March 1979.

It is not possible to go into the details of the implications of this emerging phenomenon, especially in the longterm. It should be clear, however, that this is not simply a question of international flows of machine-readable data or transborder data flows, but also a question of industrial and development policy, since the entire production infrastructure is changing in technological profile via an increase in information and knowledge-intensity of products, processes, and services.

In order to respond to current changes, maximize benefits, and minimize negative impacts, we need to assess how the strategic sectors of developing countries are being affected by technological change in the short and long terms. If policies are not thereby adjusted, the negative effects will outweigh potential benefits since development strategies will be built on quicksand. This should be the first step toward the search for regional and global approaches. A proposal of this nature should not impede the application of the technology now, but could give it better direction. It is also in the best interests of developed countries to search for solutions since interdependence is a growing reality.

Conclusions _____

IT is an expanding reality with far-reaching consequences for the relationships within and between countries. In this context it should be clear that we are at the beginning of the development of IT, not in the middle or at the end.

From the point of view of developing countries, four general conclusions seem to be valid.

1. An erosion of their advantages in low labor costs and "mature industries" is taking place because of changes in products and manufacturing

processes. The final outcome of this trend will depend largely on the LDCs' response at the macro and micro level.

2. Developments of the service sector and in particular of value-added services depend on the industrial base, as it is not an autonomous sector. This means that a deterioration of the industrial base will inevitably affect the creation and development of services. In turn, as the service content of industry increases, the lack of development in services could further affect the possibilities of industrial development.

3. The use of IT in developing countries is limited, and the gap in this field is increasing. With few exceptions, most LDCs have not developed policies to confront the challenge at the different levels required (e.g. skills).

4. A new reality and opportunity is emerging with the internationalization of services. Redressing trends here seem to be a priority, essentially because the situation is still in a state of flux. The lower barrier to entry in services offers some developing countries opportunities that were impossible to imagine with tangible products, among them the possibility of reaching consumers directly.

The final outcome of the effects of IT in developing countries and the global realities will depend largely on the willingness of the actors to approach the problems and opportunities in a global context. The command of technology based on human needs seems to be a priority for what remains of the century.

References

Business Asia (1982), March 12.

Cohen, E. (1981), "Modificaciones provocadas por la microelectronica en el rol de las empresas transnacionales electronicas en los nacionales electronicas en los paises en vias de desarrollo. Analisis de dos casos en el area de maquinas de oficina." Primer Seminario Latinoamericano sobre Microelectronica y Desarrollo, Buenos Aires (mimeo).

Gershuny, J. and Miles, I. (1983), *The New Service Economy* (London).

Hoffman, K. and Rush, H. (1982), "Microelectronics and the Garment Industry: Not Yet a Perfect Fit," in IDS Bulletin, *Comparative Advantage in an Automating World*, vol. 13, no. 2.

Jonscher, C. (1983), "Information Resources and Economic Productivity," *Information Economics and Policy*, vol. 1, no. 1.

Kim, W.H. (1980), "Challenge to US Domination: The Promise of Technology for Newly Industrialized Countries," in *Financial Times Conference: World Electronics Strategies for Success* (London), p. 99.

Mitterrand, F. (1982), *Report to the Summit of Industrialized Countries: Technology, Employment and Growth* (Paris).

Office of the United States Trade Representative (1983), *A US National Study on Trade in Services* (Washington, DC).

Price Waterhouse Associates (1981), "Review of Economic Implications of Canadian Transborder Data Flows," as reported by *Transnational Data Report*, vol. 4, no. 6.

Rada, J. (1980), *The Impact of Microelectronics* (Geneva), chap. 7.

UNIDO/ECLA (1982), "Expert Group Meeting on Implications of Microelectronics for the ECLA Region," Mexico City, June 7-11, 1982. *Conference Proceedings* (Vienna).

USITC (1979), *Competitive Factors Influencing World Trade in Integrated Circuits* (Washington, DC), p. 14.

13. SOME QUESTIONS FOR THE INFORMATION SOCIETY

MICHAEL MARIEN

In this survey, the author takes a critical look at the notion of the "information society" and various versions of it. He then poses some tough questions which deserve careful consideration by all of us. Marien is the editor of *Future Survey*, a monthly abstract of material on futures-related topics, and this essay concludes *De Informatiemaatschappij* (Natuur en Techniek, Maastricht, Netherlands, 1983). It also appeared in the *World Future Society Bulletin*, September-October 1983.

The cluster of technologies described as the "communications revolution" has resulted in the new social condition presently called the Information Society. This article seeks to provide an overview and some sense of the range of future possibilities by providing an interrelated set of broad questions, as well as some brief and tentative answers. It is hoped that this initial inventory of questions will stimulate a better list, continuously updated and addressed in depth as new conditions generate new questions.

In addition to urging better questions, this article also urges better answers. Most of the questions raised here can only be roughly and tentatively answered, even when applied to present conditions. When considering the future, there are of course no firm answers, but only rough estimates, probabilities, and speculations. We should not be ashamed of such fuzziness and imperfection, nor should we turn away from questions about the future. As noted by French political philosopher Bertrand de Jouvenel (1967), it is natural and necessary to have visions of the future.

But three types of preconception should be avoided. The first, and most widespread, is the uncritical, euphoric stance that is expressed by commercial interests, which invariably emphasize only the positive attributes of new technology. This same preconception is frequently found in the narrow world view of the technician (who cannot imagine any negative consequences), and in the Utopian passion of wanting to help people with this or that technology.

A second type of over simplified view is the opposite of the first: the hypercritical, pessimistic stance that perceives all modern technology as a human dis-

Reprinted from *World Future Society Bulletin*, Sept./Oct. 1983, by permission of the publisher.

aster, or focuses solely on growing corporate or government control of information systems. This pessimistic stance can bring forth some important truths (e.g., see Schiller, 1981; Woodward, 1980), but it seldom offers guidance for positively shaping an Information Society.

The third over-simplified view acknowledges both of these positions, and concludes that there are opportunities for good and evil, centralization and decentralization, freedom and oppression, wealth and poverty. But this balanced view is often expressed superficially, merely concluding, for example, that we must choose between Computopia or a Big Brother society. The reality, however, is likely to be complex and ambiguous, requiring many critical choices over time and incorporating elements of simultaneous euphoria and gloom that fluctuate in their balance.

Because ambiguity and uncertainty are highly probable, it is important that we continually ask the right questions, supply the best possible answers, and share these answers across national boundaries. The following questions illustrate the type of concerns that ought to be addressed, and the type of answers that might follow.

Will We Live in an Information Society?

The first question is too often assumed as a given. It is now a fact that in the industrially developed nations of the world the bulk of the labor force is engaged in some manner of producing or disseminating information. Yet, ironically, these very nations are *under*developed insofar as being information societies. Moreover, this dominant characteristic of the society and its labor force will not necessarily continue into the future.

Fashions, values, or insights may change, or society itself may change in such a way that "information society" is clearly inappropriate as a societal label. The term "information society" has only been used for about a decade, superseding the less specific label "service society," and the even more ambiguous "post-industrial society." Information Society was apparently first used in Japan in the late 1960s (Kohyama, 1968), and was the focus of the *Plan for an Information Society* (Masuda, 1981). Forerunners to "information society" include the terms "age of cybernation" (used widely in various forms during the 1960s), "electronic age," and "age of information" (both proposed by Marshall McLuhan in 1964); "knowledge society," described by Peter Drucker in 1969, and the ungainly "technetronic society" suggested by Zbigniew Brzezinski in 1970.

But societal labels come and go, and hundreds have been proposed in recent years. Why should "information society" necessarily last to 2000, or even to 1990?

A new variant might come into usage, such as "telematic society" (proposed by Nora and Minc, 1980, and adopted by James Martin, 1982), or even "the age of Infoglut," which focuses on the pervasive condition of information overload (Marien, 1982). Unemployment caused by the automation of office work and other informational services may be extensive and, if not compensated by an equal number of new jobs in the information sector, could result in a labor force no longer dominated by information-related occupations. The major activity of society would then be some other occupation, or even involuntary idleness—the lack of any occupation—a condition that already characterizes some Third World nations.

It should also be acknowledged that there are other concurrent technological revolutions that could have an even greater impact on society than the new information technologies. The biological revolution could retard the aging process and lengthen human life spans so that we become, essentially, a "Society of Immortals" (albeit a crowded one). Advances in solar cell technology could bring a "soft path" revolution in energy use. The spread of armaments in general, and nuclear weapons in particular, could lead to a cataclysmic detonation of weapons, either through accident or design. (Either instance, ironically, could be seen as a profound failure of communication.) In fact, the EMP or electromagnetic pulse, of a single high-altitude nuclear blast could burn out a nation's electrical systems (Broad, 1983). In the wake of such a grim scenario, "information society" would seem in retrospect to be the ultimate illusion of modern man.

Although the nuclear threat is growing, most experts still think it unlikely that we will experience a nuclear Armageddon. Nevertheless, there is an increasing possibility of serious disruption by war or terrorism (O'Heffernan et al. 1983). If we survive, it is likely that we will have an information society of some sort, although we might not call it that. An intelligent approach to assessing the future would acknowledge the potential for changing images. We must consider the many ways in which we may not have an information society, as well as the many ways in which it may be realized, if we hope to shape such a society to the greatest benefit of the greatest number of people.

Will We Experience a Communications Revolution? _____

Similar to the first question, a "revolution" in communications is widely assumed. But this, too, should be posed as a question. The phrase "revolution" has been used promiscuously in recent years, even among those whose scientific training would seemingly inhibit rash statements about technical and social developments. Consider, for example, the proclamation in the late 1960s about the Green

Revolution—new crops that would solve the world's hunger problems. Similar assertions were also made at that time about communications. In 1970, Isaac Asimov, the prolific author of science fiction and popularized science books, announced a Fourth Revolution of electronic communications (following speech, writing, and the printing press), which when truly established would bring worldwide electronic literacy, the library of mankind available to any person at any time, a personal immediacy to justify the sense of a global village, lessened differences among people, and cities spreading out and disappearing. Shortly thereafter, in 1972, the Carnegie Commission on Higher Education also proclaimed a Fourth Revolution brought on by electronics. A decade later, there are still intimations of such a revolution in higher education and the entire world. But one can hardly say that it has taken place.

Remarkable developments have occurred in the cluster of technologies comprising the "communications revolution." These include not only the notable reductions in computer size and cost, combined with dramatically enhanced capability, but also the expanded use of satellites, cable television, home information services, and the many applications of microchips. And the string of inventions has by no means run its course; in the words of Adam Osborne (1979), an innovative designer and manufacturer of computers, these new technologies are "running wild."

It is impossible to forecast the ultimate configuration of this rapidly evolving cluster of complementary and competing technologies, or to assess their multiple impacts on human life. The best that can be done is to engage in systematic technology forecasting and assessment. Developments in technology can to some degree be anticipated, especially by procedures of collective thinking such as the Delphi method, which assembles expert forecasts, refining and revising them with two or more rounds of questioning (e.g., Pelton, 1981). The potential impacts of individual technologies can be assessed (e.g., Nilles, 1982, on the personal computer, Tydeman et al., 1982, on teletext and videotext, and Wise et al., 1980, on microcomputers). The French government has sponsored a study of the impacts of computerization on society (Nora and Minc, 1980), and the Science Council of Canada (1982) has expressed concern about planning for an information society. Wilson Dizard (1982) has described what the US should do to understand and control the potentially dehumanizing and anti-democratic effects of this "massive technocratic drive."

Unfortunately, no effort has been made to collect all of these forecasts, assessments, speculations, and warnings to determine what is known and not known, identify areas of agreement and disagreement, and establish the range of proven polices that might be pursued. Ironically, in the midst of an inchoate revolution in communications technology, this relatively simple act of communication between researchers and responsible policy-makers has not occurred.

A cautious approach to the "communications revolution" would be to withhold such a label for the present. In contrast to the changes wrought by other technological revolutions in the past 200 years—railroads, the telegraph, telephones, electric power, automobiles, radio, and television—the new cluster of communications technologies has yet to shape the lives of most people profoundly. Still, these new technologies are likely to be immensely influential in the next few decades, if nuclear weapons have not obliterated much or all of humanity, and if a worldwide economic collapse (which would probably retard the development of the information society) is avoided. The development and dissemination of new technologies will probably not be as rapid or as widespread as many enthusiasts today believe. But the "revolution" will proceed, for there is little or no public opposition, and governments at best have only been able to influence—not control—it. The nature of the revolution—how it affects the way we communicate and our lives in general—remains problematic.

Will We Communicate Better? _____

The question of whether we will communicate better—and even whether we are communicating better today than we did in the recent past—appears obvious and simple. But it is a complex question with deep significance, and little or no attention has been paid to it. The failure to consider this question may stem from the trained incapacity of communications experts to consider big questions, or from the twin assumptions that new technologies of communication will necessarily improve communication, and that all attempts to communicate are realized. Rather, it is important to recognize that, while error-free communication is an ideal, non-communication in modern society appears to be widespread (Marien, 1982). Examples include failed communications (important messages not sent or received), flawed communications (wrong messages sent as a result of unintentional error or intentional lying or distortion), miscommunication (messages not understood or believed, or resulting in an unintended effect), and junk communication (trivial messages that are received, but are of no importance).

The new communication technologies will greatly multiply capacities for storage, transmission, and manipulation of information. But will they improve human communication, or inadvertently make it more difficult? To sketch some tentative answers to this question, it is useful to briefly examine a few prospects in eight general situations in which people communicate.

Work

Major changes in the workplace are likely, with many jobs eliminated and new jobs created. Robots in factories will presumably perform many tasks that are dangerous or boring. Automation of office work will displace a large part of the female labor force (Menzies, 1981), but, presumably, will also enable better communication within and among organizations, and allow some degree of decentralization of workplaces to rural areas and individual homes (as suggested by the romantic image of the "electronic cottage," proposed by Alvin Toffler).

Commerce

Relationships between buyers and sellers may be improved with the advent of teleshopping (the display of wares on the home video screen), which would give consumers better information on alternative products. Credit cards activated by thumbprints should be a further advance toward a cashless society.

Health

Computerized communications already offer physicians better access to medical knowledge, and the computerization of personal medical histories (with proper safeguards, one hopes) can supply valuable patient information. Individuals will also have much better access to medical information for their own self-care, with new devices to monitor body processes, worn on the wrist or implanted in the body. Microprocessor implants, for example, could detect the first sign of malignant cells being generated. New developments in microelectronics promise at least some degree of hearing for the deaf and sight for the blind, and computers might even act as psychotherapists (Evans, 1980).

Entertainment

Many people will surely have more electronic options for their pleasure, including videogames and simulated experiences, 100-channel cable television, cheap collector dishes enabling access to increasingly sophisticated communication satellites, and various videodisk and videocassette recordings. Some or all of these will be accompanied by greatly improved presentation in the home, such as wall-size television displays, improved high-definition pictures, and stereo sound. It remains to be seen, however, whether this will result in an abundance of high-quality options or merely a multiplication of banality, a vibrant free market between entertainers and audiences or cultural monopoly and control by governments and information conglomerates.

Education

It is doubtful that any information utility will be a completely free service, as Utopians imagine. Nevertheless, the potential for electronic access to the world's knowledge and for computer programs of instruction, multiple cable television channels devoted to education, instructional videotapes and more, offer enticing possibilities for an education revolution, both within and outside of schools and colleges, that would affect the learning of both children and adults. But the general caveat for all aspects of the communication revolution—not as much, nor as soon — is especially applicable to education. Educational institutions serve many functions other than learning, and they are difficult to change. Extensive self-directed adult learning is possible, but serious utilization of information abundance must compete with the many enticements of non-serious entertainment. Indeed, the mind-deadening influence of television is a major explanation for the steady decline in test scores among American high school students over the past 20 years. Sober analysis of who is learning what as a result of the new technologies will be required. It may well be found that information technology will further widen existing divisions between the rich and poor, and create a new generation gap between the computer-literate young and their print-literate elders.

Politics

Equal caution should be applied to predictions of enhancements in political communications. The new communications technologies offer many promising ways to make societies more democratic: e.g., electronic plebiscites and opinion polls, teleconferencing with representatives, cable television channels devoted to legislative proceedings, and better voter information on candidates. But these possibilities will not necessarily be realized, and could be more than offset by a dossier society utilizing a centralized data bank, improved surveillance capabilities, new lie detector technology, and narrow-casting of political messages enabling candidates to say different things to different groups of voters. Automatic language translators might facilitate intercultural communication and lessen the tensions of world society, but Western and particularly American culture may very well increase its dominance over the Third World, leading to more angry but unheeded calls for a New World Information Order (MacBride et al., 1980; Smith, 1980).

Intergroup Relations

Both within and between nations, the new abundance of information, and its further fragmentation to meet the needs and interests of myriad racial, ethnic, religious, intellectual, political, commercial, and leisure interests, is unlikely to facilitate intergroup harmony and sharing. Mass broadcasting lacked diversity and generally aimed at the lowest common denominator; but it did at least provide a shared experience. The de-massification of the media enhances the virtue of greater variety, but the dark side of this trend is a chaos of specialized interests. And to the degree that one finds ample entertainment and education in the home, people will spend more time in their living rooms, and less time with their neighbors or in public places.

Families

Relations between men and women, husbands and wives, and parents and children may be enhanced by the imminent spread of mobile telephones and the possible development of two-way wrist video devices (popularized for many years in the "Dick Tracy" comic strip). But the multitude of specialized entertainments may nevertheless serve to strain these intimate relations. Another important factor affecting communications within families will be the amount of leisure time available, which may or may not be improved by productivity increases at work and decentralization of workplaces (thus reducing commuting time or enabling more work at home). Involuntary leisure forced by unemployment often places a major strain on family relationships.

To summarize this cursory survey of basic communication nexuses, it is difficult to say whether human communication has been improving or will improve in the future. It appears likely that the new communications technologies will produce overall improvements in work, commerce, health, and entertainment. These technologies also offer considerable potential for improving education and politics, but we should be very cautious in making forecasts and assessments. Communications between groups and within families could improve, but are perhaps more likely to worsen. In all these areas, considerable monitoring will be required to provide a reasonably comprehensive answer to the question of whether we are communicating better.

Will Our Lives Be Better? _____

Will the new information technologies lead to improvements in the quality of life? One must immediately ask, improvements for whom? There will surely be winners and losers, within and among nations. Economic abundance may result from the information revolution; Paul Hawken, for example, postulates that we are in the midst of a tumultuous transition from the mass economy of the industrial age to the "informative economy," where information increasingly replaces mass as a factor in production, resulting in better goods and services. But this does not necessarily lead to more equal sharing, or to enhancement of the *median* benefit. Will all nations benefit from an expanded economic pie (as some argue), or will rich nations increase their share of a relatively limited economic pie (as argued by others)? Will illiterate peasants of the Third World benefit in any way from the new abundance of information? Even within the richer nations, the unemployed and underemployed may not benefit, unless economies expand enough to fund a more generous welfare state.

One must also ask how "quality of life" is measured, which is no simple matter. There may be a growing maldistribution of work, with the current worldwide problem of surplus, unemployable populations aggravated by further advances in automation. The promise of many technologies, and information technology in particular, is that they will be labor-saving, allowing more people to have more leisure. But what is to be done with those who have involuntary leisure forced upon them? And among the employed, voluntary leisure in a technological age can prove illusory, as pointed out by the Swedish economist, Steffan Linder (1970). Many professionals today find their workloads increasing, rather than decreasing. New ways to process information may only add to the chaos, much as superhighways have inadvertently led to more traffic congestion.

Besides economic indicators of quality of life, one must also assess political and human indicators. Will information technologies increase or decrease the threat of nuclear war? Can we maintain and expand democratic forms of governance (Wicklein, 1981)? Will non-democratic governments be strengthened by the new technologies (as now seems likely)? Will we spend more time in pleasant and productive interaction with people, or will our interaction with machines increase to the point where computers become our most important teachers and our best friends?

Who Has to Learn What? _____

Every society requires a minimum standard of competence for its members. The information society will demand a new standard of literacy, well beyond merely knowing how to use a computer. To survive in any civilized fashion, we must learn to cope with what Alvin Toffler refers to as our "blip culture" of immense diversity, contradictory fragmented images, and shattered consensus. The new literacy will require the ability to distinguish between knowledge and mere information, and to seek out wisdom amid abundant knowledge (Work, 1982). Lifelong learning has been extolled for many years, but the new economic literacy will require an ability to learn, and a willingness to retrain for new occupations.

Finally, the new civic literacy must include an understanding of global affairs, for the new technologies of communications, combined with such problems as pollution, access to ocean resources, monetary chaos, and the arms race, are accelerating the process of globalization.

But, in contrast to these needs, what do we in fact know? Victor Ferkiss (1969) asserts that technological man does not yet exist, and neoprimitive man continues to be trapped in a technological environment, in which things—not human beings—are in control. In introducing his notion of "meaning lag," Canadian sociologist Orrin Klapp (1982) warns that meaning formation (the limited human capacity for processing information) is slow and inefficient, compared with the speed and amount of information now accumulating in society.

We must recognize that we live in an Age of Ignorance, where the learning needs of all age groups are outracing their attainments. Our nation is indeed at risk. However, the most important learning needs are not among children, but among adults — especially our political, intellectual, scientific, corporate, and religious leaders — the decision-makers who will be shaping the information society over the next two decades. Their decisions, for better or worse, will largely determine whether the information society is humane, just, productive, free, participatory, and safe, or whether it is a society characterized by greater inequalities, more centralization, accelerating dangers, and further alienation.

Such a reorientation of educational priorities is unlikely, though — at least during the next few years. We still fail to recognize our widespread ignorance and the need to focus on adult learning because the academic degrees that many of us hold convince us that we are well educated as individuals and as societies. We wish to appear knowledgeable and sophisticated, and this image is reinforced by the sophisticated technologies at our individual and collective command — tools such as computers and automobiles that many are able to use, although comparatively few really understand them very well. The citizens of the industrialized countries live in a society that is *developed* in manufacturing era terms — but *overdeveloped* when assessed by humane and ecological measures, and *underdeveloped* as an information society. Our society is underdeveloped because of the gap between our present abilities and our need to learn new skills and shape new worldviews. This "ignorance gap" appears to be growing.

As with the previous questions about the information society, this question also points to the need for empirical research—in this instance, research into what people in all age groups in all nations know. And some global standard of information society literacy must emerge from this sobering assessment.

Who Will Address These Questions? _____

The questions raised here are presumably of central importance to all individuals and nations. They could be considered as a matter of national security, deserving the funding equivalent that is now invested in a single battleship or aircraft, let alone the modern arsenals that every nation seems compelled to have. Worldwide, an estimated $650 billion was spent on military preparations during 1982 (Palme, 1982). It is doubtful whether even 0.01 percent of this amount ($65 million) has been devoted worldwide to considering questions about the information society. Annual spending on this aspect of national security is probably less than 0.001 percent ($6.5 million). Whatever the figure, our societal investment priorities appear to be grossly distorted.

Several hundred books have been published in recent years, dealing with some aspect of the information society. Yet there is little communication among those who address some aspect of this subject. This is largely due to our obsolete industrial era colleges and universities, which encourage attention to small and "manageable" questions, technical questions that result in "hard" answers, and questions that conform to the configurations of the established disciplines and professions.

The fragmentation of perspectives increasingly found in the wider society is reflected in the subject of communications itself, which is studied by the professions of journalism, education, and information science (formerly library science), and such cross-disciplinary areas as computer science, management science, behavioral science, language and area studies, and future studies. Adding to this intellectual tumult, researchers in the social sciences often specialize in the economics, politics, and sociology of information and communications. Occasional government studies attempt to provide some overview, but little or no effort has been made by governments, foundations, research institutes, or leading universities to try systematically to overcome the rampant bureaucratization of knowledge in general and thinking about communications in particular.

People in all nations need the best and most up-to-date answers to the most important questions about the information society. The "national security" benefits of stimulating inquiry, refining and synthesizing the plethora of observations and policy proposals, and encouraging public understanding and dialogue would certainly be great. The cost, in contrast to these benefits, would be miniscule.

Ideally, we need schemes such as the World Brain, proposed by H. G. Wells in 1938, to bring together the scattered mental wealth of the human race and make it universally accessible. Such a reorientation of education and information has been updated by the concept of WISE, the World Information Synthesis & Encyclopedia (Kochen, 1975). Similarly, to deal intelligently with questions of the future, we need an on-going surmising forum, as advocated by Bertrand de Jouvenel, to bring together and debate the many "futuribles" about what might happen and what ought to happen.

Will anything of this sort take place? Appeals to higher and wider vision, such as this essay, are easy to make. Creating and sustaining the institutions needed to promote such vision will be far more difficult. Even with the help of such coordinating and synthesizing organizations, the evolution to an information society will not be an easy one, but only will be made a little less turbulent than it would otherwise be. Continuing the status quo of informational chaos greatly heightens the likelihood that we will not realize a viable and humane outcome. Most countries have avoided choices, with the expectation of muddling through (Nanus, 1982). In such an event, the information society will arrive stillborn—if it arrives at all—owing to our failure wisely to generate and employ information.

References

Asimov, Isaac (1970), "The Fourth Revolution," *Saturday Review*, 24 October, 17-20.

Broad, William J. (1983), "The Chaos Factor," *Science* 83, 4:1, Jan-Feb 1983, 40-9; also "Nuclear Pulse," *Science,* vol. 212, May 29/June 5/June 12, 1981, 1009-1012, 1116-1120, and 1248-1251.

Brzezinski, Zbigniew (1970), *Between Two Ages: America's Role in the Technetronic Era.* New York: Viking.

Carnegie Commission on Higher Education (1972), *The Fourth Revolution: Instructional Technology in Higher Education.* New York: McGraw-Hill.

De Jouvenel, Bertrand (1967), *The Art of Conjecture.* New York: Basic Books.

Dizard, Wilson P. (1982), *The Coming Information Age: An Overview of Technology, Economics, and Politics.* New York: Longman.

Drucker, Peter F. (1969), *The Age of Discontinuity: Guidelines to Our Changing Society.* New York: Harper & Row.

Evans, Christopher (1980), *The Micro Millennium.* New York: Viking (published in Britain in 1979 as *The Mighty Micro.*)

Ferkiss, Victor (1969), *Technological Man: The Myth and the Reality.* New York: George Braziller.

Forester, Tom (ed.) (1980), *The Microelectronics Revolution.* Cambridge, MA: MIT Press, 1980.

Hawken, Paul (1983), *The Next Economy.* New York: Holt, Rinehart and Winston.

Klapp, Orrin E. (1982), "Meaning Lag in the Information Society," *Journal of Communication*, 32:2, Spring, 56-66.

Kochen, Manfred (ed.) (1975), *Information for Action: From Knowledge to Wisdom*. New York: Academic Press.

Kohyama, Kenichi (1968), "Introduction to Information Society Theory," *Chuo Koron*, Winter 1968; cited by Yoneji Masuda in Yoshihiro (ed.), *Changing Value Patterns and their Impact on Economic Structure*. Tokyo: University of Tokyo Press, 1982, p. 174.

Linder, Steffan Burenstam (1970), *The Harried Leisure Class*, New York: Columbia University Press.

MacBride, Sean, et al. (1980), *Many Voices One World: Communication and Society, Today and Tomorrow*. New York: Unipub (final report of the UNESCO International Commission for the Study of Communication Problems).

Marien, Michael (1982), "Non-Communication and the Future," in Howard Didsbury Jr (ed.), *Communications and the Future*. Bethesda, MD: *World Future Society*.

Martin, James (1981), *Telematic Society: A Challenge for Tomorrow*. Englewood Cliffs, NJ: Prentice, Hall (first published as *The Wired Society* in 1978).

Masuda, Yoneji (1981), *The Information Society as Post-Industrial Society*. Bethesda, MD: World Future Society.

McLuhan, Marshall (1964), *Understanding Media: The Extensions of Man*, New York: McGraw-Hill.

Menzies, Heather (1981), *Women and the Chip: Case Studies of the Effects of Informatics on Employment in Canada*. Toronto: Institute for Research on Public Policy.

Nanus, Burt (1982), "Developing Strategies for the Information Society," *The Information Society Journal*, 1:4, 339-56.

Nilles, Jack M. (1982), *Exploring the World of the Personal Computer*. Englewood Cliffs, NJ: Prentice-Hall.

Nora, Simon, and Minc, Alain (1980), *The Computerization of Society: A Report to the President of France*. Cambridge, MA: MIT Press (first published in France in 1978).

O'Heffernan, Patrick, Lovins, Amory B. and Lovins, L. Hunter (1983), *The First Nuclear World War*. New York: William Morrow.

Osborne, Adam (1979), *Running Wild: The Next Industrial Revolution*. Berkeley, California: Osborne/McGraw-Hill.

Palme, Olaf (1982), "Military Spending: The Economic and Social Consequences," *Challenge*, 25:4, September-October, 4-21 (chapter 4 of the report of the

Independent Commission on Disarmament and Security Issues, *Common Security: A Blueprint for Survival*. New York: Simon & Schuster).

Pelton, Joseph N. (1981), "The Future of Telecommunications: A Delphi Survey," *Journal of Communication*, 31:1, Winter, 177-89.

Schiller, Herbert I. (1981), *Who Knows: Information in the Age of The Fortune 500* Norwood, NJ: Ablex.

Science Council of Canada (1982), *Planning Now for an Information Society: Tomorrow is Too Late*. Hull, Quebec: Canadian Government Publishing Centre (report no. 33).

Smith, Anthony (1980), *The Geopolitics of Information: How Western Culture Dominates the World*. New York: Oxford University Press.

Toffler, Alvin (1982), *The Third Wave. New York: William Morrow*.

Tydeman, John, et al. (1982), *Teletext and Videotext in the United States: Market Potential Technology, Public Policy Issues*. New York: McGraw-Hill.

Wells, H.G. (1938), *World Brain*. New York: Doubleday, Doran.

Wicklein, John (1981). *Electronic Nightmare: The New Communications and Freedom*. New York: Viking.

Wise, Kensall D., et al. (1981), *Microcomputers: A Technology Forecast and Assessment to the Year 2000*. New York: Wiley-Interscience.

Woodward, Kathleen (ed.) (1980), *The Myths of Information: Technology and Post-Industrial Culture*. Madison, Wisconsin: Coda Press.

Work, William (1982), "Communication Education for the Twenty-First Century," *Communication Quarterly*, 30:4, Fall, 265-9.

ANNOTATED BIBLIOGRAPHY

ANNOTATED BIBLIOGRAPHY

I. THE GLOBAL TRADING SYSTEMS: THE FLOW OF GOODS _____

Adkins, Roger L. "Competitive Decline: Views of Two Disciplines." *Journal of Economic Issues* 21, no. 2 (June 1987): 869-876.

This paper is a comparison of the viewpoints and biases of management and economists in an attempt to explain U.S. competitiveness in international trade. On this issue of vital concern, both perspectives are valid and each would do well to learn from the other.

Balassa, Bela. "Policy Responses to Exogenous Shocks in Developing Countries." *American Economic Review* 76, no. 2 (May 1986): 75-78.

This paper compares the different policies employed by developing countries in response to external shocks occurring in the 1973-78 and 1978-83 periods and reviews their economic effects.

Baldwin, Robert E., and T. Scott Thompson. "Responding to Trade-Distorting Policies of Other Countries." *American Economic Review* 74, no. 2 (May 1984): 271-276.

This paper is a discussion of the responses to unfair trade practices that are permitted by GATT and their effectiveness. The authors then propose some changes to improve the rules so that free trade will continue.

Clark, Don P. "Regulation of International Trade in the United States: The Tokyo Round." *Journal of Business* 60, no. 2 (1987): 297-306.

This research tests the Marvel-Ray tariff formation model by applying it to the determinants of the Tokyo Round tariff reductions. The author found support for the model.

Cooper, Richard N. "Dealing with the Trade Deficit in a Floating Rate System." *Brookings Papers on Economic Activity* 1, (1986): 195-207.

The management of the U.S. macroeconomic policy in 1986 is discussed, faced with the large trade and federal budget deficit and the confines of the floating exchange rate system.

Czinkota, Michael R. "U.S. Trade Policy and Congress." *Columbia Journal of World Business,* Twentieth Anniversary Issue (1966-1986): 71-77.

This article details the trade policies of the current administration and Congressional activity in the area of trade legislation. The problems are examined and suggestions for future policies are addressed.

Czinkota, Michael R. "International Trade and Business in the Late 1980s: An Integrated U.S. Perspective." *Journal of International Business Studies* (Spring 1986): 127-134.

This study integrates the key issues of international business and trade identified by experts from business, policy, and academia and provides suggestions for future research.

Hufbauer, Gary. "The Long View of Trade Policy." *Harvard International Review* 9, no. 3 (February-March 1987): 6-9.

The author speculates on how government regulations, the macroeconomic climate, and foreign policies will influence the future world trading system.

Jackson, John H. "Perspectives on the Jurisprudence of International Trade." *American Economic Review* 74, no. 2 (May 1984): 277-281.

The author details and compares the costs and benefits derived from the current legalistic system for regulating international trade. Although the comparison is imprecise, the benefits appear to outweigh the costs.

Kindleberger, Charles P. "International Public Goods Without International Government." *The American Economic Review* 76, no. 1 (March 1986): 1-13.

This discussion centers on international public goods, and the position of the current administration. The author presents ideas culled from political philosophy and sociology, which can be used in this realm of economics.

Landefeld, J. Steven, and Kan H. Young. "The Trade Deficit and the Value of the Dollar." *Business Economics* 20, no. 4 (October 85): 11-17.

The trade deficit is due to a variety of factors, with the strong dollar being one component. A decline in the dollar is one factor necessary for increasing our competitiveness; however, the effect across industries would vary and trade improvement would take time.

Landefeld, J. Steven. "International Trade in Services: Its Composition, Importance and Links to Merchandise Trade." *Business Economics* 22, no. 2 (April 1987): 25-31.

The author discusses the nature and importance of services trade, its relationship to merchandise trade, and stresses that they are complements rather than substitutes.

Lawrence, Robert Z., and Robert E. Litan. "Why Protectionism Doesn't Pay." *Harvard Business Review* (May-June 1987): 60-67.

The authors reject the protectionist solutions to the current trade deficits by refuting several of the underlying assumptions. They go on to suggest policies to effectively deal with the deficit.

Lindell, Erik. "Foreign Policy Export Controls and American Multinational Corporations." *California Management Review* 28, no. 4 (Summer 1986): 27-39.

The author examines the effects on U.S. exporters of the foreign policy controls instituted in the years 1976-86 as well as implementation difficulties and corporate objections.

Mills, D. Quinn. "Destructive Trade-offs in U.S. Trade Policy." *Harvard Business Review* (November-December 1986): 119-124.

The author contends that the present trade deficit is a result of government policies designed to gain geopolitical advantages abroad. He presents several measures that can be adopted to overcome prior problems.

Rosen, Howard. "World Trade in the 1980's: The Decade of Transition." *Harvard International Review* 9, no. 3 (February-March 1987): 13-15.

The effects on international trade of three major external shocks, the debt crisis, fluctuating exchange rates, and slow growth in industrialized nations, are discussed and related to future prospects.

Shilling, A. Gary. "U.S. Imports: Sailing Through a Narrow Passage." *Business Economics* 20, no. 4 (October 1985): 18-23.

The rise in U.S. imports has led to a call for increased protectionist measures from hard-hit industries. The author contends that such measures, if instituted, would cause serious economic repercussions abroad.

Srivastava, Rajendra K., and Robert T. Green. "Determinants of Bilateral Trade Flows." *Journal of Business* 59, no. 4 (1986): 623-640.

This research goes beyond the previously studied trade determinants of distance and economic size and found political instability of the exporter and cultural similarity to be of significance for manufactured goods.

Strauss, Robert S. "US Trade and International Economic Policy: A Strategy." *Harvard International Review* 9, no. 3 (February-March 1987): 16-18.

International trade plays a vital role in the U.S. economy. Top level political leadership is necessary to begin the needed system reforms for future growth.

II. THE GLOBAL TECHNOLOGY TRANSFER: THE TECHNOLOGY FLOW _____

Baily, Martin Neil, and Alok K. Chakrabarti. "Innovation and U.S. Competitiveness." *The Brookings Review* 4, no. 1 (Fall 1985): 14-21.

This research explores the crucial role of innovation in the area of U.S. competitiveness in world trade. The authors suggest several policies to build upon this strength.

Brada, Josef C., and Dennis L. Hoffman. "The Productivity Differential Between Soviet and Western Capital and the Benefits of Technology Imports to the Soviet Economy." *Quarterly Review of Economics and Business* 25, no. 1 (Spring 1985): 6-18.

The authors' research indicates that there is no productivity difference between Western and Soviet equipment utilized in the Soviet Union; however, the primary benefit of Western capital is an increase in technological progress.

Derakhshani, Shidan. "Negotiating Transfer of Technology Agreements." *Finance and Development* 23 (December 1986): 42-44.

The author presents four factors to consider in developing a technology transfer agreement that will be equitable for all parties concerned. These factors are: the locus of control, the amount and importance of personal interaction, the degree of initial involvement of the seller, and the relationship stability between the supplier and the recipient.

Dickson, David. "Europe Tries a Strategic Technology Initiative." *Science* 229 (July 1985): 141-43.

The French proposal to form a European Research Coordination Agency (Eureka) for collaborative efforts among European nations on advanced technological research projects has elicited a variety of responses. The arguments for such a joint effort have been political as well as technological and have as much focus on the military dimension as the civilian.

Djeflat, Abdelkader. "The Management of Technology Transfer: Views and Experiences of Developing Countries." *International Journal of Technology Management* 3, Nos. 1-2 (1988): 149-165.

The transfer of technology, from the developing countries' viewpoint, is empirically studied by investigating contractual agreements, the importing process and channels, and negotiation issues.

Haddad, Jerrier A. "Technology and Human Values." *Science and Engineering* 52 (February 1986): 239-241.

The author explores the areas of technology and human values and the question of whether they are the antithesis or dependent on the other. He argues that in fact they are intertwined, and both must be understood in today's world.

Mansfield, Edwin, Anthony Romeo, Mark Schwartz, David Tecce, Samuel Wagner, and Peter Brach. "New Findings in Technology Transfer, Productivity, and Economic Policy." *Research Management* (March-April 1983): 11-20.

This analysis of international technology transfer presents findings on the speed of transfers, the value of product life cycles, the costs, the effects of the patent system, the rate of innovation, productivity, and public policy.

Negroponte, John D. "Science and Technology Cooperation with Latin America." *Department of State Bulletin* 87 (October 1987): 50-52.

This report examines the feasibility and potential benefits of cooperation with Latin America in space, science, and technology. The private sector is deemed crucial to success in this area, as well as effective application of technology to specific production objectives and long-term, adequate funding for program stability and consistency.

Rugman, Alan M. "Strategies for National Competitiveness." *Long Range Planning* 20, no. 3 (June 1987): 92-97.

The author argues that a focus on technology for international competitiveness is not an appropriate viewpoint for all nations. Instead, he proposes that each country examine their own specific advantages and build upon these unique areas of expertise to improve competitiveness.

Sciberras, E. "Government Sponsored Programmes for International Technological Exchanges and Applied Collective Research." *R&D Management* 17, no. 1 (1987): 15-23.

This research finds that the success of collaborative efforts among firms in the areas of R&D and innovation depends greatly upon the industry and the nation. Government sponsorship is of assistance when their objectives and the firm's competitiveness are compatible.

Wallender, Harvey W. III. "Developing Country Orientations Toward Foreign Technology in the Eighties: Implications for New Negotiation Approaches." *Columbia Journal of World Business* (Summer 1980): 20-27.

This paper is a discussion of the trends affecting technology transfers and the implications for negotiating and establishing value on the basis of the local environment.

"West-East Technology Transfer: Impact on the USSR." *OECD Observer* no. 136 (September 1985): 18-24.

The transfer of technology to the USSR has faced a number of obstacles and overall has had a relatively minor impact on economic growth and development.

III. THE GLOBAL TRADING SYSTEMS:
THE CAPITAL FLOWS _____

"A Closed Circle for the Developing Countries? Debt and Financial Flows." *OECD Observer* 14-18.

This paper is an overview of the interrelationship of debt and financial flows to and from developing countries, along with the current reversal of flow activity.

Decoodt, Patrick. "The Debt Crisis of the Third World: Some Aspects of Causes and Solutions." *Columbia Journal of World Business* 21, no. 3 (Fall 1986): 3-9.

The current debt crisis is the result of numerous factors, on the part of both debtor and creditor nations, which this research attempts to analyze. Some proposals for a resolution are then presented.

Engel, Charles. "The International Monetary System: Forty Years After Bretton Woods." *Journal of Monetary Economics* 17 (1986): 441-448.

This review is of the volume containing nine essays on international monetary problems. The consensus is that reform is necessary to overcome the LDC debt crisis and flexible exchange rates, however, few new solutions are proposed.

Feldstein, Martin. "U.S. Budget Deficits and the European Economies: Resolving the Political Economy Puzzle." *American Economic Review* 76, no. 2 (May 1986): 342-346.

The author explains the direct and indirect impacts of U.S. fiscal policies on the European economy. Although it would appear that a strong dollar benefits European trading partners, it has actually led to a decline in trade and a rise in inflation.

Frenkel, Jacob A. "The International Monetary System: Should it be Reformed?" *American Economic Review* 77, no. 2 (May 1987): 205-210.

The author argues that deficiencies and lack of coordination of international macroeconomic policies are the cause of exchange rate problems rather than the failure of the international monetary system and presents ideas for reform.

Gramley, Lyle E. "The Effects of Exchange Rate Changes on the U.S. Economy." *Business Economics* 20, no. 3 (July 1985): 40-44.

This article addresses the interconnection between international economic developments and domestic economic growth, interest rates, and inflation. The implications for the future are discussed as is the need for reduction of the Federal deficit.

Heller, H. Robert. "The Debt Crisis and the Future of International Bank Lending." *American Economic Review* 77, no. 2 (May 1987): 171-175.

To effectively overcome the current debt crisis, it is necessary to focus on the long-term implications of a solution. It is advantageous for all parties involved, banks, debtor nations, industrialized countries and international organizations, to cooperate in this matter.

Kenen, Peter B. "Exchange Rate Management: What Role for Intervention? " *American Economic Review* 77, no. 2 (May 1987): 194-199.

Exchange rate management is viewed positively, however intervention is not. The author presents various official positions on intervention and then looks at intervention as a method of changing expectations.

Khan, Mohsin S., and Nadeem Ul Haque. "Capital Flight from Developing Countries." *Finance and Development* 24, no. 1 (March 1987): 2-5.

The magnitude and reasons behind the outflow of private capital from developing countries are discussed, as well as the short- and long-term consequences and possible corrective policy measures.

Khan, Mohsin S. "Developing Country Exchange Rate Policy Responses to Exogenous Shocks." *American Economic Review* 76, no. 2 (May 1986): 84-87.

The author presents the major external shocks occurring from 1976-86 and their effects on the exchange rates. The response policies of developing countries are analyzed and compared as to their outcomes.

Knight, Malcolm, and Paul R. Masson. "Transmission of the Effects of Fiscal Policies Among Industrial Countries." *Finance and Development* 24, no. 1 (March 1987): 41-44.

This paper examines the influence of fiscal policy shifts by large industrial countries combined with U.S. tax incentives for investment spending on the international rise in real interest rates and exchange rates from 1980-85.

Koromzay, Val, John Llewellyn, and Stephen Potter. "Exchange Rates and Policy Choices: Some Lessons from Interdependence in a Multilateral Perspective." *American Economic Review* 74, no. 2 (May 1984): 311-315.

The floating exchange rate system of the last ten years has not allowed countries to create domestic policies independently of international factors. This paper considers the constraints of the system, the interdependence of national policies, and the effect of the system on these policies.

Lanyi, Anthony. "Issues in Capital Flows to Developing Countries." *Finance and Development* 24, no. 3 (September 1987): 27-30.

Sources of external financing to developing countries and the influences on demand factors are identified. Donor coordination and possible future policies are discussed.

Lemgruber, Antonio Carlos. "New Directions in LDC Debt." *Business Economics* 22, no. 1 (January 1987): 22-25.

The rescheduling of LDC debt is divided into three stages, 1982-84, 1985-86, and the third stage, which is just beginning. Suggestions are made for appropriate new directions in the current uncertainty.

McKinnon, Ronald I. "Planning for Currency Stability." *Harvard International Review* 8, no. 1 (November 1985): 7-11.

The overvalued dollar, leading to hardship in American industries, has increased pressure for trade protectionist policies. This would further compound the problem; rather, the solution proposed here is monetary coordination among the U.S., the European bloc, and Japan.

Park, Sung Sang. "Can the World Economy Survive with High Interest Rates?" *Columbia Journal of World Business* (Fall 1985): 53-58.

A comparison of the U.S. high interest rate policy after 1980 with the low rate policy of Japan, illustrating the detrimental effects on U.S. economic performance.

Rybczynski, T. M. "The International Monetary System: Retrospect and Prospect." *Business Economics* 20, no. 4 (October 1985): 24-29.

The fixed exchange rates of the Bretton Woods era and the following floating rates have left the system in an uncertain position. Various alternatives for the future are discussed, along with the need for international coordination of policies.

Sachs, Jeffrey. "Managing the LDC Debt Crisis." *The Brookings Review* 2 (1986): 397-431.

A strategy proposal for managing the debt crisis from the viewpoint of a creditor nation, emphasizing an individual analysis by country to determine the need for debt relief or restructuring.

Sachs, Jeffrey. "The Uneasy Case for Greater Exchange Rate Coordination." *American Economic Review* 76, no. 2 (May 1986): 336-341.

The 1985 accord by the G-5 (United States, France, Japan, Germany, and United Kingdom) finance ministers to unite in moving towards a managed exchange rate system is presented in light of the theoretical viewpoints concerning exchange rate coordination.

Weaving, Rachel. "Measuring Developing Countries' External Debt." *Finance & Development* 24, no. 1 (March 1987): 16-19.

Up-to-date information is important for proper debt management. Sources for international statistics on developing countries' debts are detailed here.

Whitman, Marina v.N. "Assessing Greater Variability of Exchange Rates: A Private Sector Perspective." *American Economic Review* 74, no. 2 (May 1984): 298-304.

This article reviews the impact and increasing disillusion with flexible exchange rates. The need exists for some type of international coordination to reduce volatility.

Williamson, John. "Exchange Rate Management: The Role of Target Zones." *American Economic Review* 77, no. 2 (May 1987): 200-204.

International policy coordination for exchange rates is necessary, and one proposal is the target zone. This method calls for major countries to negotiate mutually consistent exchange rate target zones. The author argues that it provides the benefits of rate flexibility without the problems inherent in unmanaged floating.

IV. THE GLOBAL LABOR POLICIES: THE FLOW OF PEOPLE _____

Ethier, Wilfred J. "Illegal Immigration: The Host-Country Problem." *American Economic Review* 76 (March 1986): 56-71.

The author initially looks at three key parameters of migration, which are whether or not it is of temporary or permanent nature, the involvement of skilled or unskilled labor; and the legality issue. He then addresses the neglected area of illegal migration of unskilled labor in an attempt to formulate a workable theory, examining the policies of border enforcement and internal enforcement. This theory is developed from the perspective of the host-country.

Fitoussi, J. P., and E. S. Phelps. "Causes of the 1980s Slump in Europe." *Brookings Papers on Economic Activity*, 2 (1986): 487-520.

The authors theorize that U.S. fiscal and monetary shocks have been the cause of much of the current European unemployment. They then present possible policy measures to aid in the correction of the problem.

Galor, Oded. "Time Preference and International Labor Migration." *Journal of Economic Theory* 38 (1986): 1-20.

A theory of labor migration pattern is established in this research. Within the framework of a two-country world with differing time preferences, labor will migrate from the high (low) time preference country to the low (high) time preference country if both countries under (over) invest in relation to the Golden Rule. If both countries are on opposite sides of the Golden Rule, bilateral migration will occur. The steady-state welfare implications of labor mobility are also analyzed.

Haveman, Robert H., and Daniel H. Saks. "Transatlantic Lessons for Employment and Training Policy." *Industrial Relations* 24, no. 1 (Winter 1985): 20-36.

Employment and training programs in various countries were evaluated and important lessons for governmental policies, evident in these programs, are assembled here.

Huang, Wei-Chiao. "A Pooled Cross-Section and Time-Series Study of Professional Indirect Immigration to the United States." *Southern Economic Journal* 54 (July 1987): 95-109.

This research investigates the motivating factors for foreign professionals employing indirect methods of immigration to the United States. Economic considerations were not found to be the predominant determinant. Rather, professional opportunities, working conditions, and political and social considerations also play a significant role. U.S. immigration policies exert considerable influence on professional indirect immigration.

"Job Creation in a Changing Economy." *OECD Observer* (January 1987): 8-11.

The Ministerial Level meeting of the OECD Manpower and Social Affairs Committee in 1986 developed three central objectives for labor market policies for the remainder of the decade, which are discussed in this article. These are higher rates of job creation, more flexibility in expanding labor markets, and equitable and efficient adjustment policies to assist the unemployed in finding jobs. The primary objective of these policies is to reduce unemployment levels in OECD countries.

Jones, Ronald W., Isaias Coelho, and Stephen T. Easton. "The Theory of International Factor Flows: The Basic Model." *Journal of International Economics* 20 (1986): 313-27.

The authors employ "the basic model" relating capital exports to labor immigration to further investigate an optimum strategy for restricting the simultaneous movement of these two factors. Ramaswami's argument, comparing two policy options, is discussed, and then an expanded range of options is applied to the basic model. The options are based primarily on the wage rates paid to foreign labor.

Masterson, Bob, and Bob Murphy. "Internal Cross-Cultural Management." *Training and Development Journal* 40 (April 1986): 56-60.

The increasing number of foreign employees in American companies has underscored a need for cross-cultural management techniques at home as well as in other countries. A variety of cultural issues are presented along with techniques for increasing awareness of cultural differences and skills for interacting with foreigners for optimum results. The integration of culture, company, and individuals is of prime importance for success.

Shulman, Seth. "Engineers and Immigration." *Technology Review* 90 (January 1987): 15.

Allegations that U.S. companies are hiring foreign engineers at lower wages leading to the loss of jobs by American engineers have been brought to Congress. Although immigration laws have been tightened in general, further protection for engineers is being sought. Statistics to back up the lost jobs claim are difficult to find; therefore, it is difficult to determine if the allegations are true and how widespread the problem has become.

V. THE INFORMATION SOCIETY:
THE FLOW OF INFORMATION _____

Cooney, S., and T. J. Allen. "The Technological Gatekeeper and Policies for National and International Transfer of Information." *R&D Management* 5, no. 1 (1974): 29-33.

> *Personal communication has been found to have a significant impact on the transfer of technical information. The implications for international policies are presented and improvements are suggested.*

Freeman, Harry L. "International Telecommunication Policy: The Critical Choices." *Telecommunications* (April 1986): 42-46.

> *A variety of national and international issues that must be addressed to set the appropriate course for the future of worldwide telecommunications networks are discussed in this article.*

Karunaratne, Neil Dias. "Analytics of Information and Empirics of the Information Economy." *The Information Society* 4, no. 4 (1986): 313-331.

> *A review of the effects of information technology on macroeconomic structures. The authors present an algorithm to assess informational efficiency and aid in formulating development strategies.*

Krommenacker, Raymond J. "The Impact of Information Technology on Trade Interdependence." *Journal of World Trade Law* (July-August 1986): 381-400.

> *This is an analysis of the economics of information, the current technology and its effects on trade interdependence. A reorientation of government policies is suggested for a future interdependent technology network.*

Melody, William H. "The Information Society: Implications for Economic Institutions and Market Theory." *Journal of Economic Issues* 19, no. 2 (June 1985): 523-539.

> *The author examines some of the economic implications of the burgeoning information society and finds an uneven distribution of the benefits of technology emphasizing the oligopolistic rivalry in global markets.*

Porat, Marc Uri. "Global Implications of the Information Society." *Journal of Communication* 28, no. 1 (Winter 1978): 70-80.

The international aspects of the U.S. transformation into an information society are addressed, including human rights problems, exporting issues, and foreign policy.

Schiller, Herbert I. "The World Crisis and the New Information Technologies." *Columbia Journal of World Business* (Spring 1983): 86-90.

Europe and North America regard the emerging information technology as an aid in overcoming the current economic crisis. This article points out the specific circumstances that might prevent this from occurring.

Sheehy, Therese. "Transborder Data Flow—An Issue with Global Implications." *Data Management* (November 1984): 28-29.

International electronic data transfer has led to a multitude of restrictive laws. There is little consensus among countries as to the substance of these laws, an issue that needs to be rectified for the system to reach its full potential.

Tenkhoff, Phil. "International Communications: The Changing Environment." *Telecommunications* (April 1985): 49-52.

This paper is an overview of the services available in international communication, methods of planning, and evaluating options for specific needs and problems that arise.